mathematical talent

Hyman Blumberg Symposium on Research in Early Childhood Education (3rd : 1973 : John Hopkins University)

# mathematical talent
## discovery, description, and development

PROCEEDINGS OF THE THIRD ANNUAL
HYMAN BLUMBERG SYMPOSIUM
ON RESEARCH IN EARLY CHILDHOOD EDUCATION

EXPANDED VERSION OF A SYMPOSIUM
OF THE AMERICAN ASSOCIATION FOR THE ADVANCEMENT
OF SCIENCE ENTITLED "DISCOVERING AND NURTURING
PRECOCIOUS TALENT IN
MATHEMATICS AND PHYSICAL SCIENCE"

edited by Julian C. Stanley,
Daniel P. Keating, and Lynn H. Fox

THE JOHNS HOPKINS UNIVERSITY PRESS · BALTIMORE AND LONDON

QA
11
.A1
H95
1973

Copyright © 1974 by The Johns Hopkins University Press

All rights reserved. No part of this book may be reproduced or transmitted in any form or by any means, electronic or mechanical, including photocopying, recording, xerography, or any informational storage and retrieval system, without permission in writing from the publisher.

The Johns Hopkins University Press, Baltimore, Maryland 21218
The Johns Hopkins University Press Ltd., London

Library of Congress Catalog Card Number 73-19342
ISBN 0-8018-1585-1 (cloth)
ISBN 0-8018-1592-4 (paper)

Manufactured in the United States of America

Originally published, 1974

Johns Hopkins Paperbacks edition, 1974

Library of Congress Cataloging in Publication data will be found on the last printed page of this book.

To the late Professor Lewis Madison Terman (1877–1956)
of Stanford University, author of the Stanford-Binet Intelligence Scales,
whose five *Genetic Studies of Genius* volumes (1925–1959) launched
the gifted-child movement and gave it strong justification,
we dedicate this volume.

# acknowledgments

Figures 7.1, 7.2, and C.1 through C.8 were reproduced by special permission from the California Psychological Inventory by Harrison G. Gough, Ph.D. Copyright date 1956. Published by Consulting Psychologists Press, Inc.

Figure 8.1 was reproduced by special permission from The Self-Directed Search by John L. Holland, Ph.D. Copyright date 1970. Published by Consulting Psychologists Press, Inc.

# contents

# list of contributors

*Anne Anastasi,* Professor of Psychology, Fordham University, Bronx, New York 10458, former president of the American Psychological Association

*Helen S. Astin,* Professor of Higher Education, University of California at Los Angeles, Los Angeles, California 90024

*Susanne A. Denham,* Assistant Director, Study of Mathematically and Scientifically Precocious Youth, Department of Psychology, The Johns Hopkins University, Baltimore, Maryland 21218

*Lynn H. Fox,* Postdoctoral Fellow, Study of Mathematically and Scientifically Precocious Youth, Department of Psychology, The Johns Hopkins University, Baltimore, Maryland 21218

*Richard J. Haier,* Doctoral Candidate in Psychology, Department of Psychology, The Johns Hopkins University, Baltimore, Maryland 21218

*Daniel P. Keating,* Postdoctoral Fellow, Study of Mathematically and Scientifically Precocious Youth, Department of Psychology, The Johns Hopkins University; now at the Institute of Child Development, University of Minnesota, Minneapolis, 55455

*Julian C. Stanley,* Professor of Psychology and Director of the Study of Mathematically and Scientifically Precocious Youth, Department of Psychology, The Johns Hopkins University, Baltimore, Maryland 21218; former president, American Educational Research Association

*Daniel Weiss,* Doctoral Candidate in Psychology, Department of Psychology, University of California at Berkeley, Berkeley, California 94720

*Stanley Wiegand,* Doctoral Candidate in Psychology, Department of Psychology, University of Wisconsin, Madison, 53706

# list of tables

xi

# list of figures

# preface

The Third Annual Hyman Blumberg Symposium departed somewhat from the first two in that it was co-sponsored by the American Association for the Advancement of Science (AAAS) and in that its organizing topic was not compensatory education for disadvantaged preschoolers but rather individualized education for exceptionally gifted junior high school students. As the title of the volume and the co-sponsorship of AAAS suggest, the theme of the symposium was the nature and nurture of exceptional mathematical and scientific talent. This is the first volume of *Studies of Intellectual Precocity* (Julian C. Stanley, Daniel P. Keating, and Lynn H. Fox, general editors).

The research and discussion in the nine separate papers in this volume stem directly from the Study of Mathematically and Scientifically Precocious Youth (SMSPY), a five-year project at The Johns Hopkins University funded by the Spencer Foundation of Chicago. The first editor is director of the SMSPY, and the second and third editors are associate directors.

The study began officially on 1 September 1971, but, as is shown in chapter 1, its roots extend several years prior to that date. In this time, we have had the opportunity to meet and work closely with what is perhaps the most mathematically talented large group of 12- to 14-year-olds ever assembled in one place. The papers contained herein cover many aspects of our work with them—specifically, the methods of identification, the nature of their abilities and interests, and the kinds of educational facilitation we have tried to develop for them.

The first three papers, written by the editors of the volume, provide the background of the study, both general and specific, discuss the methods and techniques of identification, examine more closely the cognitive abilities of these students, and indicate the initial results of the efforts to facilitate their educational development. An unexpected and disconcerting finding of the first general testing was an inescapable sex difference (Keating and Stanley, 1972*b*). Helen S. Astin, well known for her studies of women in scientific careers, graciously consented to examine our findings from the standpoint of sex differences and to speculate about their origins. The fourth paper of this volume reports the results of her inquiry. Anne Anastasi, a distinguished differential psychologist, agreed to discuss these first four papers and their import for discovering and developing exceptional talent. These first five papers were presented as a symposium on "Discovering and Nurturing Precocious Talent in Mathematics and Physical Science" at the annual meeting of the AAAS on December 28, 1972, which was ably chaired by Charles Leo Thomas.

Due to the time constraints of a one-day symposium, a number of important topics concerning the study of mathematical talent had to be omitted. The last four papers are attempts to correct this. Chapter 6 reports in more detail the results of a program to teach junior high and high school mathematics rapidly to a talented and interested group of beginning junior high schoolers. A preliminary report was included in Fox's AAAS paper (chapter 3 of this volume), but it was considered worthy of the fuller treatment it receives here as a separate paper.

The next two chapters, 7 and 8, examine in detail what may be referred to as the "social and emotional development of the gifted" problem. They report some interesting findings using measurements of interests, values, and personality. Chapter 9 takes the reader into a college classroom to see how these youngsters perform in that setting. Some interesting and even surprising results are contained in this last paper.

The editors of this volume would like to thank Helen S. Astin and Anne Anastasi not only for their valuable contributions to the symposium and to this volume but also for their thoughtful comments on the project as a whole. We would also like to thank those who participated in the preparation of the four papers which were added to the original five to complete this volume: Susanne A. Denham, who was assistant director; Richard J. Haier; Daniel S. Weiss; and Stanley J. Wiegand. Many individuals assisted in various ways in the data analysis, but special thanks go to Bonnie R. Roffman for help with data collection and analysis and to Joseph L. Bates for his computer expertise.

The staff of SMSPY wishes to thank Paul R. Binder and Joseph R. Wolfson for their creative teaching reported in chapter 6; the Baltimore County School System—especially Benjamin P. Ebersole, Director of Curriculum; Vincent C. Brant, Coordinator for Mathematics; and Helen E. Hale, Coordinator for Science—for its cooperation; and the Baltimore Science Fair for its participation in the first two mathematics competitions.

Virginia S. Grim and Lois S. Sandhofer were most patient in typing the various drafts of many of the manuscripts. Our thanks go to them as well as to William C. George, who assisted ably in getting the manuscript to press.

William B. Michael provided a careful critique of the next-to-last draft of the manuscript that helped us improve the volume considerably. Of course, he is not responsible for any imperfections that remain.

We also thank William D. Garvey, who invited us to organize and present the AAAS symposium.

We thank the College Entrance Examination Board and its Trial Administration Program, especially Sam A. McCandless and Michele Mayo Battermann, for much help. Without the generous cooperation of The Johns Hopkins University, especially Vice President George S. Benton and Director of Admissions John R. Riina, much of the work reported in this volume would not have been possible.

Especially, we are grateful to the Amalgamated Clothing Workers of America for the $110,000 endowment that it funded at The Johns Hopkins University in 1969. Income from it supports the Annual Hyman Blumberg Symposium, but the union has no responsibility for the contents of the symposia or the volumes resulting therefrom.

By recognizing during the summer of 1968 the unusual quantitative ability of Joseph L. Bates, Doris K. Lidtke provided the initial stimulus for SMSPY and hence for this volume.

**Julian C. Stanley**
**Daniel P. Keating**
**Lynn H. Fox**
*Department of Psychology*
*The Johns Hopkins University*

mathematical talent

# I · intellectual precocity

## JULIAN C. STANLEY

[Editors' Note: *This chapter gives the background of the Study of Mathematically and Scientifically Precocious Youth. The history of work with the gifted is reviewed, especially that of Terman, as well as the specific events which led to the current study. The reader will become acquainted through this first chapter with the philosophy and goals of the project.*]

We are interested in mathematically precocious youth. What is intellectual precocity? The *Oxford English Dictionary* (OED) defines "precocity" as "early maturity, premature development." For persons, it defines the adjective "precocious" as "prematurely developed in some faculty or proclivity." These two words, and the noun "precociousness," date back at least three hundred years, although the seventeenth century sentences illustrating them do not seem to coincide closely with the meaning we have in mind.

Use of the words "premature" and "prematurely" in defining precocity seems pejorative, but because the concept as applied to persons and their psychological qualities is somewhat figurative, this connotation may not be intended by the OED. Physical precocity of seed, plant, or animal does not necessarily connote abnormality in the sense that psychologists usually employ that word.

Authors throughout the years, and especially during the nineteenth century, seem to have had mixed feelings about precocity. The OED provides several examples of this. Thackeray inadvertently may have helped coin the familiar expression "precocious brat" when in 1855 he wrote: "Poverty and necessity force this precociousness on the poor little brat." In 1863 he wrote the following sentence about a boy: "His 'Love Lays' . . . were pronounced to be wonderfully precocious for a young gentleman then only thirteen."

Shakespeare helped further the myth that precocity is intrinsically unhealthful when in *Richard III* he said, "So wise so young, they say, do never live long." The great French writer Musset combined both points of view succinctly when he wrote, "How glorious it is—and also how painful—to be an exception." Margaret Fuller, a famous nineteenth century American writer, warned that "For precocity some great price is always demanded sooner or later in life." In 1829 Southey

1

summed up the layman's view of both natural and induced precocity: "And as natural precocity is always to be regarded with fear, so the precociousness which art produces cannot be without its dangers." Nine years earlier William Hazlitt, British critic and essayist, had noted of some English writers, "Their productions . . . bear the marks of precocity and premature decay."

Thus it is understandable that many persons, especially parents, tend to view extreme brightness or special mental talents with some foreboding. Yet early physical prowess or musical ability is often lauded. It is not considered psychologically abnormal for a boy to play baseball unusually well when quite young, but somehow it is considered unfortunate if he can readily extract the square roots of numbers when only five years old. For complex and not fully understood reasons, many citizens of the United States are strongly anti-intellectual. As we have already noted, this pessimistic or even hostile attitude toward the intellectually gifted is not new, although our compulsory lockstep age-in-grade educational system may have intensified it. High IQs are not in fashion. Before long some state legislature may try to repeal them, as one such body is alleged to have done a few decades ago for the law of gravity.

Let us not, however, be pessimistic or defensive when introducing reports about a Study of Mathematically and Scientifically Precocious Youth that has been able to identify and help a number of mathematically highly talented youth. My associates and I do not consider that boys and girls who are unusually able to reason mathematically are destined to die young, burn out intellectually, develop lopsidedly, or become mediocre adults. Fortunately, these are more than articles of faith. Intellectually gifted individuals have been studied intensively and extensively for half a century. Results show clearly that the popular stereotypes are invalid. A brief overview of some of the main investigations may help document that point.

## Galton, Binet, and Spearman

Intellectual precocity has attracted attention throughout the ages. It has been discussed by many of the great writers. Not until the latter part of the past century, however, were these speculations systematized, notably by the British founder of the study of individual differences, Sir Francis Galton. His book *Hereditary Genius: An Inquiry into Its Laws and Consequences* appeared in 1869 and was followed in 1874 by his *English Men of Science: Their Nature and Nurture.* In 1906, when Galton was 84 years old, his book in collaboration with Edgar Schuster appeared. It was entitled *Noteworthy Families (Modern Science): An Index to Kinships in Near Degrees between Persons Whose Achievements Are Honourable, and Have Been Publicly Recorded.*

It is clear that Galton emphasized hereditary transmission of intellectual ability, but in the process of attempting to further this rather aristocratic point of view he fathered the study of intelligence and aptitudes. He also helped provide some of the statistical equipment needed for this field, especially the ubiquitous coefficient of correlation that his friend and successor Karl Pearson (1896) formalized mathematically.

Galton did not begin mental *testing* in its modern form, however. That was done by the French psychologists Alfred Binet and Th. Simon (1905a, 1905b, 1905c, 1908; Binet 1911). Their scales of mental ability were radically different from the simple sensory measures of Galton, J. McKeen Cattell (1890), and others. They measured a variety of more abstract abilities such as vocabulary knowledge, memory, and reasoning. Their tests were designed to tell which children entering school had the mental ability to succeed there. As we shall see later, however, the Binet type of scale proved excellent for measuring intelligence over an astonishingly large range, from IQs of 25 or less to those over 200, while still being useful in the middle range (80–120), where most persons score.

Almost coincidentally (but the *Zeitgeist* must have been propitious), at about the time that Binet and Simon offered their first scale of intelligence the British psychologist Charles Spearman (1904) reported his theory of intelligence. He posited a general intellective factor, called *g*, independent of the many special abilities that individuals have. His theory was too simple and provoked much controversy during the years up until about the time of World War II, particularly with Louis Thurstone of the University of Chicago. It did, however, promote the search for components of intelligence to supplement the global IQ.

### The Stanford-Binet Intelligence Scales

Binet's scale languished in France, but pragmatic psychologists in the United States soon put it to work. Henry Goddard (1910a, 1910b, 1911) at The Training School for mental retardates in Vineland, New Jersey, translated the 1908 version, which was scored in months-of-mental-age units, into English. By 1910 he had administered it to 400 mentally retarded children and reported his findings in a professional journal. The next year he published results from testing 2000 normal children.

It remained, however, for the psychologist Lewis M. Terman (see Terman 1916, Terman and Merrill 1937 and 1960, and McNemar 1942) at Stanford University to revise and adapt the scale to the native white culture of the United States. His first version, modestly called the Stanford Revision, appeared in 1916. It was followed by the 1937 Stanford-Binet Intelligence Scale, for which two forms were provided. In 1960 these were consolidated into a single form and updated. Terman's scales became the method of choice for careful mental testing at all points along the IQ scale from almost the lowest to almost the highest.

Unlike Binet and Goddard, who used the scale primarily for testing mentally retarded children and average children, Terman was concerned mainly with the intellectually gifted from 1902 until his death at age 79 in 1956. Strongly influenced by both Binet and Galton, he adopted the former's enlightened empiricism and the latter's veneration for talent. Terman's first three publications—in 1904, 1905, and 1906—were contemporary with the fundamental work of Binet and Spearman. Thus the modern study of mental ability was from its inception tri-national, but French psychologists did not pursue their initial advantage.

### Terman's "Genius" Study

Terman's doctoral dissertation at Clark University appeared in 1906 in what is now the *Journal of Genetic Psychology* under the title "Genius and Stupidity: A Study of Some of the Intellectual Processes of Seven 'Bright' and Seven 'Stupid' Boys." As Terman (1925, p. 1) remarked,

However slight the positive contribution of [my first three] studies, they at least introduced their author to the literature on the psychology of genius and gave a keen realization of the fact that the field was a promising one for experimental investigation. When in 1910 it became possible for the writer to return to the problem, the progress which Binet and others had made in the field of mental testing had created an entirely new situation. . . . As one who had worked experimentally upon the diagnosis of intellectual differences in the prescale period, the present writer had perhaps more reason than most psychologists to appreciate the value of Binet's contribution. He is willing to admit that after spending four or five hours a day for several months administering an extended series of well-selected intelligence tests individually to fourteen boys, he was unable, notwithstanding the large individual differences in performance which these tests clearly revealed, to render a judgment as to the prognostic significance of the differences found. By the Binet scale it would have been possible to make a more meaningful diagnosis after a one-hour test of each child; and it would now even be possible to do so after a single hour spent in testing the fourteen boys by a group test. . . . Previous to 1908 it was impossible for any psychologist, after devoting any amount of time to intelligence tests of ten or twenty children of different ages, to make a valid comparison of the intellectual abilities found. This is now possible for even a well-trained normal school graduate.

Thus it becomes clear that although Terman's 1916 revision of the Binet scale proved a boon to psychologists in this country who worked with children of normal or dull intelligence—there were not even any group tests of intelligence available yet—for him it was mainly a tool with which to study extremely bright children. Only five years after the revision appeared, Terman launched a large investigation entitled "Genetic Studies of Genius." In retrospect the adjective "genetic" and the noun "genius" in that title may seem unfortunate. By "genetic," however, he probably meant "longitudinal" more than "Mendelian." He planned to identify exceptionally bright children early and follow them through life as long as possible to see whether or not the popular stereotypes about such children were true.

It is very likely that Terman was almost convinced from the start that high-IQ children are, on the average, superior to lower-IQ ones on nearly all socially desirable variables. He was indeed influenced by Galton's ideas concerning an aristocracy of intellectual ability, because in the first report of the study (1925) he wrote: "To explain by the environmental hypothesis the relatively much greater deviation of our group from unselected children with respect to intellectual and volitional traits appears difficult if not impossible. Our data, however, offer no convincing proof, merely numerous converging lines of evidence" (p. 634).[1]

But Terman's monumental study of high-IQ children as they grow up can be viewed without the foreshadowing of Jensenism (Jensen 1972, 1973). From it have come most of our best-documented statements concerning extreme brightness. It may be wise, therefore, to examine rather carefully the population studied. Melita Oden (1968, p. 5) describes the composition of the group succinctly:

The search for subjects was confined chiefly to the public schools of the larger and medium-sized urban areas of California. A total of 1528 subjects (857 boys and 671 girls) were selected. For children below high school age the requirement was a Stanford-Binet IQ of 140 or higher. This group, who made up 70 per cent of the total, had a mean IQ of 151, with 77 subjects testing at IQ 170 or

[1]Galton himself was a 200-IQ prodigy, Terman (1917) inferred from evidence of childhood precocity.

higher. Because of the lack of top in the 1916 Stanford-Binet, students of high
school age were given the Terman Group Test of Mental Ability. The requirement for this test was a score within the top one per cent of the general school
population on which the norms were established. Later follow-up tests indicated
that the older subjects were as highly selected for mental ability as the Binet-
tested group. The subjects averaged about 11 years of age . . . when originally
tested and ranged in age from 3 to 19 years. The range of age by year of birth,
however, is more than 20 years; this is accounted for by the inclusion of a small
number who had been tested in a preliminary study (1917–20) and a group of 58
siblings added as a result of the testing program in the 1927–28 follow-up study
of the original group. No subjects except siblings of the original group were added
after 1923, and none at all after 1928.

It is evident that, as must occur for a pioneering study in a new area,
Terman and his assistants did a great deal of cut and trying. They could
not administer the 1916 Stanford-Binet to a random sample of all
children in the United States or even in California, because this would
have been prohibitively time-consuming and expensive. They could not
even afford to secure nomination of bright children from teachers in
rural areas and small towns of California. Perhaps at least partly for
this reason, the mean IQ of the Terman group is considerably higher than
that of the above-140-IQ portion of a normal distribution of IQs. (See
Keating, in press.) Also, the children chosen and followed were probably
somewhat superior academically to those not nominated by teachers.
They may also have averaged a little younger, because besides being
asked to nominate the three most intelligent children in her class, each
teacher was asked to list the youngest one. Terman (1925, pp. 32–33)
found that "nomination as youngest yielded more [qualifying] subjects
who would otherwise have been missed than any other kind of nomination, 19.7 per cent of the total nomination group. . . . *In other words, if
one would identify the brightest child in a class of 30 to 50 pupils it is
better to consult the birth records in the class register than to ask the
teacher's opinion*" (Terman's italics).

Despite the infrequency of acceleration today and the wide availability to teachers of scores on group intelligence tests, 50 years later
we find that many of our most mathematically or scientifically precocious youth have skipped a grade or are young in grade—i.e., have birth-
days late in the calendar year. Even among the high ability boys whom
we tested in March of 1972, the youngest third in each grade tended to
score highest and the oldest third lowest. This finding held for both
mathematics and science, though only for the boys.

Terman's study was not an experiment. There was no explicit control group, nor did he and his staff use single- or double-blind methods.
The children and their parents knew that they were chosen as being ex-

tremely bright; the appellation "genius" must have conjured up visions of Plato, Michelangelo, Mozart, and Einstein in the minds of many. The influences of this perception are virtually unfathomable, probably depending on a constellation of familial variables, but at least an appreciable number of the subjects must have found their intellectual proclivities treated more respectfully at home and school.

Despite its virtually unavoidable shortcomings, Terman's study was monumental. It began with children who now average about 63 years of age and followed them carefully at periodic intervals from 1921–22 until 1960. A further follow-up is now underway. A number of the subjects have already died, of course, and many of the others are into the years where decline in certain mental abilities can be studied. Unfortunately for this, Terman leaned too heavily on the IQ and therefore did not measure many specific cognitive abilities. He was little influenced by Spearman (1927), but one should note that fifty years ago few tests of important specific mental abilities existed. (The "primary mental abilities" work of Thurstone [1938] developed too late to affect Terman's gifted-group study much.)

Particularly relevant to the present study is the Terman (1954) monograph concerning the 800 male scientists versus nonscientists in his group. "Especially significant for the purpose of counseling and guidance are the differences observable in childhood behaviors, interests, and preoccupations that are found many years later to discriminate between scientists and nonscientists" (p. 40). He also found tentative evidence that the Strong Vocational Interest Blank usefully differentiates.

Of great interest are the children and grandchildren of the Terman subjects, though their progress may have been enhanced or retarded by having at least one parent who is a certified "genius." The cumulative effects of this word deserve far more attention than they have received.

What, then, did Terman learn? From the 1960 data Oden (1968, p. 51) concluded that "Now after 40 years of careful investigation there can be no doubt that for the overwhelming majority of subjects the promise of youth has been more than fulfilled. The Terman study has shown that the great majority of gifted children do indeed live up to their abilities." Some do not, of course, and the background factors related to such lack of success are strongly socioeconomic. I suspect, too, that some of the high-IQ vocational failures lack certain cognitive abilities useful for life success. The IQ is a valuable global measure of intellect. It tells us much overall, but not enough specifically. For example, 10-year-old boys in the fifth grade who have IQs of 150 probably differ from each other at least as much in detailed cognitive ways as they do affectively. (Or is it helpful to try to separate the cognitive elements from the affective ones, i.e., abilities from interests, attitudes, and volitions? Perhaps this is an example of the "jangle fallacy," that things with different names must be different.)[2]

## The Post-Terman Era

When Terman died in 1956 (see Sears 1957), most systematic concern for the intellectually gifted died with him. Three influences about that time hastened the demise of the movement. One was the concern generated when Russia launched the first sputnik (artificial space satellite). This led to a number of special curricula in mathematics and science for use in secondary schools. Among these were the familiar School Mathematics Study Group (SMSG) mathematics, Physical Science Study Committee (PSSC) physics, and Biological Sciences Curriculum Study (BSCS) biology programs. These were attempts to "beef-up" those subjects in order to provide better bases for later study and, to a lesser extent, better fundamental understanding of mathematics and science by the layman. Substantial elements of these curricula have entered current textbooks and teaching methods. There have been reactions to what some viewed as excessive abstractness, culminating in partial return to the "fundamentals" and an occasional competing program such as Harvard's Project Physics that is meant to be more practical and interesting than the sputnik-inspired originals.

These new programs were devised for class consumption and therefore were geared not to the very ablest students, but instead to the considerably above average ones. They did not meet the needs of the most gifted well, and they helped to turn attention away from Terman's lovingly studied upper one-half of 1 percent.

Two other influences, however, seem to have been more potent. One was the 1954 Supreme Court ruling that led to the current stress on compensatory education of culturally disadvantaged minority groups such as blacks, Mexican-Americans, Puerto Ricans, and American Indians. Although this new emphasis was salutary and long overdue, it turned out to be another shove into the coffin for concern about the intellectually gifted, except as they are found in these groups. For example, at the large annual meetings of the American Educational Research Association in 1972 and 1973 there were only a few papers concerning the intellectually gifted, all authored by my associates and me, whereas there were many *sessions* devoted to the disadvantaged.

[2]The five volumes of *Genetic Studies of Genius* were authored by Terman (1925), Cox (1926), Burks, Jensen, and Terman (1930), Terman and Oden (1947), and Terman and Oden (1959). The Oden (1968) monograph is, in effect, the sixth volume. All are still in print. Quotations in this chapter are from the second edition (1926) of volume 1.

Around 1957 Congress became concerned about mental retardation and began giving what were by the standards of that time large amounts of money to study and ameliorate it. In fact, the first budget of the Cooperative Research Branch of the U.S. Office of Education consisted of two-thirds of a million dollars, all of which was earmarked for research in mental retardation.

The federal and state dearth of monies with which to help the highly gifted children continues to the present day. Although there is now a federal office for the gifted—located in the U.S. Office of Education's Bureau of the Handicapped—little money seems available yet for studying or aiding the upper 1 to 5 percent of school children more than will occur in their regular classes. Even active city or county or state school system specialists in the gifted are rather rare. Most concern, if it exists at all, is vested in the director of special education, and one has only to glance at such professional publications as *Exceptional Children* or the *Journal of Special Education* to see how much they are devoted to cultural disadvantagement and mental retardation and how little explicitly to high ability children.

Various influences, especially some of the above, have produced a wave of egalitarianism that brands as elitist most special provisions for the gifted, that eliminates or dilutes most special schools and curricula for them, and that attacks mental testing itself and urges a return to pre-Binet subjectivism. This is another example of an attempt to throw away the baby along with the dirty bath water. IQ scores have been misused a great deal. Some uninformed persons have considered them immutable, entirely based on heredity, and infalliable predictors of success in school and life. The nature versus nurture controversy rages again. Terman preached a little too much of Galton's doctrine, it seems, and thus helped plant the seeds for the neglect of the gifted.

Also, Terman did not produce disciples to continue his work well. He chose to use chiefly highly able, mature research assistants rather than unusually bright young graduate students specializing in the area of the gifted. Thus he did not insure continuity of his main efforts via successors. In our study at Johns Hopkins we are trying explicitly to avoid this error. Already, two associates (Lynn H. Fox and Daniel P. Keating) who worked with the study from its beginning have completed their Ph.D. degrees in psychology. Another has completed the first year of graduate study. These persons, and others who worked with us less closely, are helping to rejuvenate the field.

The highly able are the most "disadvantaged" group in schools, because they are almost always grossly retarded in subject-matter placement. For example, 22 of the 223 boys tested in 1972 scored higher than the average Johns Hopkins freshman on the Scholastic Aptitude Test's mathematics items. Only two of these had reached their fourteenth birthday. Four of these highest scorers were seventh graders, one of them less than 12 1/6 years old. Five of these boys who had completed only the seventh or eighth grade did excellent work for credit in college algebra and trigonometry and in analytic geometry during the summer of 1972, earning a total of eight A's and one B. Fourteen boys and one girl, some of them less remarkable than our top scorers, have taken the basic college course in computer science at The Johns Hopkins University or Towson State College, or American University, earning a total of 11 A's and four B's. Yet many of these brilliant youngsters must sit in seventh- or eighth-grade general mathematics classes all year and pretend to be learning something. Either they already know the content of the course and far more or else they can learn its new concepts and techniques almost instantaneously. Obviously, they are ready and usually eager for much more advanced material. In chapter 3 of this volume Fox discusses some ways in which such youths can be moved ahead well.

### Precocity in Mathematics and Physical Science

The history of mathematics abounds with precocious children who became eminent mathematicians, scientists, or quantitatively oriented philosophers. (See Cox 1926.) Three familiar names that span the mid-seventeenth to mid-nineteenth centuries are Blaise Pascal, Gottfried Wilhelm Leibnitz, and Carl Frederich Gauss. As boys they displayed remarkable intellectual curiosity and learning ability. Pascal was prevented by his father from seeing or hearing about any mathematics, so on his own he reconstructed many of Euclid's propositions, even without a standard vocabulary with which to name a circle, square, or triangle.

Catharine Cox (1926), a psychologist working with Terman, studied the childhood and adult precocity of famous men and estimated their IQs at these two times. Her top person was John Stuart Mill, with an estimated childhood IQ of 190 (also see Packe 1954 and Mill 1924). Close behind him were Bentham, Macaulay, Pascal, Goethe, Grotius, and Leibnitz. Of course, her estimates were dependent on the data available. Also, we now know more clearly than she did that IQ alone is not an excellent predictor of the rare thing called adult genius. High IQ may be necessary to produce an Einstein (see Clark 1971) or a Gauss, but it does not guarantee their achievement. Other qualities, both mental and personal, are essential. To a considerable extent, also, the times and circumstances must be right. For example, the initial reception of Gregor

Mendel's work was affected by his isolation from the appropriate scientific community. Charles Babbage and Blaise Pascal tried to construct computing machines before the technology needed for them was available (see Jones 1963 and Cox 1926, p. 693). To some extent "genius will out," but the rate of previous learning that we call IQ is only one component of genius and probably not the most important one.

Many books and articles have been written about precocious children. A somewhat quaint but insightful study entitled "Contributions to the Study of Precocity in Children" was based on lectures in 1907 and 1908 by an English physician named Leonard Guthrie (1921). It shows that even without the technical equipment of modern psychology, observant persons can test a number of hypotheses concerning the concomitants and consequences of precocious childhood. Accumulated observations by Terman and others, however, broaden our data base and eliminate much of the selectivity inherent in what lawyers call "fireside inductions" (Meehl 1971).

## Recent Examples of Precocity

An outstanding example of precocity during the present century was Norbert Wiener, who completed public high school at age 11, earned his baccalaureate (Phi Beta Kappa) at Tufts College at age 14, and received his Ph.D. degree in mathematical logic from Harvard University at age 18 after two false starts in others areas. Wiener matured slowly, not becoming even an assistant professor until age 30, but then he became famous as the father of cybernetics. (See his revealing autobiography [Wiener 1953]).

Some newspapers and magazines during 1971 carried the story that Charles Fefferman, an assistant professor of mathematics at the University of Chicago, was promoted to the rank of "full" professor there at the end of one year at age 22. According to those accounts, he had entered the University of Maryland full-time at age 14, received two baccalaureates at age 17, and completed the Ph.D. degree in mathematics at Princeton University at age 19 (e.g., see *Time* 1971).

Michael Grost entered Michigan State University as a full-time student at age 10 after completing the fifth grade (see Grost 1970). He earned his baccalaureate at age 15 and his master's degree in mathematics from Michigan State at age 17. From there he went to Yale University as a candidate for the Ph.D. degree in mathematics. Now he is approximately 19 years old. We have been unable to ascertain the current status of his doctoral study.

John Bardeen, who recently received his *second* Nobel Prize in physics, was reported (Young 1972) to have "jumped from third to seventh grade" and to have graduated from high school "a few weeks after he turned 15."

A young man whom I shall call David completed his master's degree at Johns Hopkins University in August of 1973 at age 17. The story of how David, and another equally remarkable boy the next year, happened to enter Hopkins is worth recounting.

### Our First "Radical Accelerate"

Although the five-year grant from the Spencer Foundation for our Study of Mathematically and Scientifically Precocious Youth began officially on 1 September 1971, considerable informal work preceded it. The project evolved from several studies that I did in the 1950s. In its present form it began in the summer of 1968, when Doris Lidtke (then of the Johns Hopkins University Computing Center) called my attention to a boy born 20 October 1955—the "David" mentioned above—who had just completed the seventh grade of a Baltimore junior high school and displayed spectacular knowledge of computers. Lidtke had studied at Michigan State University and had known of Michael Grost there.

I was too busy with other matters at the time and therefore did not see David until January of 1969. His performance on several college-level tests of mathematical, mechanical, and verbal aptitude was so remarkable then that I asked him to take the College Entrance Examination Board Scholastic Aptitude Test, Physics achievement test, and Mathematics Level I achievement test in the regular March 1969 national administration. He also took Mathematics II at the May 1969 administration, because it was not offered in March.

David's scores were as follows: SAT-Verbal, 590; SAT-Mathematical, 669; Math I, 642; Math II, 772; and Physics, 752. Clearly, his Math II (which is the more difficult level) and Physics scores exceeded those of most regular freshmen at the Johns Hopkins University. His SAT-V score was about 40 points, some four-sevenths of a standard deviation, below that of the *average* Hopkins freshman, but approximately a third of those freshmen scored below 600. Thus it seemed evident that David, though less than 13 1/2 years old in March and in only the eighth grade of a public junior high school, was intellectually equipped to do good work as a freshman at a selective college or university such as Johns Hopkins. (As his mother told me, "David has been studying physics on his own seriously since he was 3 years old. No wonder he knows more about it than boys who have been taking it casually for nine months or less!")

David, his father, his mother, and I worried for several months about what should be done educationally to accommodate David's advanced abilities and knowledge in mathematics, physics, and general science. During the eighth grade, encouraged by his remarkable mathematics teacher, Paul Binder, he had completed at night (without credit) a two-semester course in college algebra, trigonometry, analytic geometry, and some calculus at a nearby state college, so it seemed desirable that he go into the most advanced mathematics course of a senior high school in the fall of 1969 and also take both chemistry and physics then. Unfortunately, at that time there was not enough flexibility in the local public or private schools to permit this.

Entering Johns Hopkins University without bothering to attend grades nine through twelve was a possibility that occurred to David, his parents, and me, but at first we tended to reject it as patently absurd. Could David really dispense with those four high-school grades and yet do satisfactory work at Hopkins when only 13 years old? It seemed unlikely that he would work hard enough, having only eighth-grade study habits. Also, he was shy, so it appeared that socially and emotionally he would find adjusting to the college atmosphere and demands frustrating and harmful. No other suitable alternative was in sight, however, so in September of 1969—thanks to the open mind of Dean Carl Swanson— David enrolled at Hopkins as a "special" full-time student who could begin with whatever courses seemed best for him.

I decided that initially David should take only those subjects in which he was ablest and most interested. Clearly, these were mathematics, physics, and computer science. So he signed up for *honors* calculus and *sophomore* general physics, but it was felt that he needed chemistry to prepare him for later science courses. Therefore, he registered for general chemistry. His lack of background and special interest in chemistry and the long laboratory periods were too much, however, so after a month he changed to the basic computer science course. David completed the first semester ranking fourth in the large computer science class; he also made an A in physics and a high B in honors calculus. His gradepoint average on the 13 semester-hour credits (15 is the average number needed to earn a B.A. degree in eight semesters) was 3.69, where 4.00 represents all A's. David did not have to work especially hard to earn his high grades. We estimate that he did not spend as much time on homework as the average first-semester Hopkins freshman does, and many of them do not earn even a 2.00 grade point average!

David took difficult courses and was graduated in May of 1973 at age 17 7/12 with a B.A. degree in quantitative studies and a 3.4 cumulative grade-point average. By age 17 5/6 he had completed the M.S. degree specializing in computer science. David made a few C's but performed especially outstandingly in graduate-level computer science courses.

As a student from a secure, upper-middle-class home and with loving, understanding parents, David was extremely happy at Hopkins. In his own words, he "had the best of both worlds," of home community and of selective college. He shudders to recall that, but for Lidtke's alertness, he would probably be at most a college sophomore now, very likely "turned off" intellectually. Instead, he is a doctoral candidate in computer science at a major university on a university fellowship and stipend and plans to complete the Ph.D. degree by age 19 or 20.

## The Second Radical Accelerate

One successful radical accelerate, however, does not prove that skipping high school would not be disastrous for virtually all others who attempt it. Replication of David's experience was needed. By an improbable coincidence, the parents of an extremely frustrated, bored eighth grader—whom I shall call Bill—heard in the fall of 1969 about David's age and freshman standing at Hopkins. Bill's mother immediately telephoned David's mother and insisted on knowing how David had managed to enter Hopkins so early. David's mother called me. I then telephoned Bill's mother, who urged that her son be permitted to enter Hopkins in the fall of 1970 at age 13 5/6 years, after completing the eighth grade in a public junior high school.

I administered some college-level tests to Bill and confirmed his mother's statement that he was quite superior to nearly all of his agemates. Then he took several College Board tests. His aptitude scores were a little higher than David's had been, and his achievement scores were a little lower. Like David, Bill seemed intellectually ready for a selective college. But was he well enough adjusted to succeed there? Although bored in junior high school, David had been a willing, conscientious student. In contrast, by the seventh grade Bill had begun to rebel against what he correctly perceived to be, for him, unprofitable busy work. By the middle of the eighth grade he was about to drop out of the picture intellectually. Also, he was quite unpopular with most boys his age. They resented his long hair and intellectual conversation and threw rocks at him. He was thoroughly miserable, both scholastically and socially. Was his maladjustment mainly situational, mainly personal, or both?

Bill's parents became almost indignant when I questioned his readiness for a selective college. They did not want to deliberate about their son's educational future as David's parents had about his. Just let Bill attend Hopkins, they said, and we know that he will do at least as well as David is doing. I proceeded cautiously, first asking the family to see what special curricular arrangements could be made at the senior high school adjacent to the junior high school Bill attended. In February of 1970 I wrote the principal there a long letter explaining Bill's precocious abilities in mathematics and science and suggesting that in the ninth grade he be allowed to take biology, chemistry, physics, senior mathematics, honors social studies, and English. At the parents' conference with him, the principal rejected most of this program.

Finally, I offered to let Bill try Hopkins in the fall of 1970 if before that he would take a couple of relevant college summer courses and do well in them to demonstrate that he could adjust to the demands of college work. Bill took descriptive astronomy in the Hopkins summer session and earned a grade of B; he took a good theory course in mathematics at a local state college and earned an A.

Thus while still 13, and almost a month younger than even David had been, Bill enrolled at Hopkins for honors calculus, physics, and computer science, a 12-credit load. He made A's in both calculus and physics and a B in computer science. (The next semester he took the second course in computer science and made an A.) His GPA for that initial semester was 3.75. His parents had indeed been right. He was fully ready intellectually to do splendid work at a selective college.

Bill is now a 16-year-old senior. After performing brilliantly the first two years, he has encountered adjustment problems which are taking some time to solve. Fortunately he is three years accelerated, so there is no need to hurry.

Leaving junior high school for Hopkins "cured" Bill's academic and personal maladjustment for two splendid years. Few students or faculty members at Hopkins paid much attention to his long blond hair or his dirty field jacket and nobody threw rocks at him, literally or figuratively. He was keenly attuned to the Hopkins atmosphere intellectually ("Seems like a bright, highly articulate graduate student," one faculty member told me). During his first year he commuted from home (requiring some five miles of walking daily), but since that wasted so much time he moved into a dormitory on campus in October of his sophomore year. This seemed to work out well. Bill is neater now and appears to have friends on campus and also in the Sierra Club for hiking and mountain climbing. Dave, on the other hand, is an enthusiastic figure skater and attends a five-week skating camp each summer. Both boys, then, have physical recreations as well as intellectual ones. Both are splendid with computers, too, but their basic personalities are rather dissimilar. They have not associated much with each other.

Remarkably few faculty members or students in classes seemed to suspect that these two boys were only 13 years old their first semester (Dave until October, Bill until November). In fact, as a 14-year-old second-semester freshman Bill took a course in developmental psychology from a young faculty member who had spent two years post-doctorally working with Jerome Bruner at Harvard University. He knew that on the campus there were two extremely young boys. Yet, although Bill entered the class discussion a great deal and talked with the instructor after class more than any other student did, this man was startled the next fall when I told him that Bill was only 14 years old. He had never suspected that Bill was younger than the other students in the class. This is our usual finding. If a teacher is *told* that a given student is young, he will say, "Of course. That's obvious." If not told, however, the teacher is unlikely to discover this fact if the student does excellent work in the course.

## The Third Radical Accelerate

Martin came to Hopkins in the fall of 1972 from the tenth grade of a public high school. He lived at home and commuted. Despite not bothering with the eleventh and twelfth grades, he was super-ready for a highly selective college. When tested on 22 April 1972, while a 15-year-old tenth grader, he scored 780 on SAT-Verbal, 740 on SAT-Math (on a retest recently with another form he raised that to 770), 710 on English Composition, and 800 on Math II, Biology, and Chemistry. In fact, he scored 14 points above the minimum needed for an 800 in Chemistry! These scores put him in the upper few percent of Hopkins freshmen. Also, his high school record had been superb. His grade-point average for the first year was 4.00 on 40 credits. Then he transferred to Princeton University.

For further information concerning these three radical accelerates, see Jablow (1972), Jenkins (1973), Keating and Stanley (1972), Stanley, Keating, and Fox (1972), and Stanley (1973).

## Future Accelerates

It seems likely that a large percentage of the highest scorers in our study will enter college at least a year early, often with some college credits already earned. Two entered in the fall of 1973 at age 14. They had already completed 12 credits of college computer science, mathematics, and English composition. One of them made all A's the first semester. As Fox points out in chapter 3, acceleration, especially in mathematics and science, is one of the main goals of our study.

## The Study and Its Companion

In the Study of Mathematically and Scientifically Precocious Youth we identify, study, and facilitate educationally those youngsters who are especially adept at mathematical reasoning while still in the first two years of junior high school, i.e., grades seven and eight and ages 12 to 14. Three other psychology faculty members at Hopkins (Catherine Garvey, Robert Hogan, and Roger Webb) have a five-year grant to study verbally precocious youth, including those who score high on SAT-V. Also financed by the Spencer Foundation, it began in September of 1972. For our two related but independent studies we administered the SAT in January and February of 1973 to 954 upper 2 percent seventh and eighth graders from all over Maryland.[3] These contestants in our mathematical and verbal talent search received their scores by mail. The top scorers—about 6 percent of the group—were invited back to the Hopkins campus for further testing of their special abilities along the lines that you will hear about later when our supplementary testing of the earlier group on 22 April 1972 is discussed in chapter 2. From the annual testing comes suggestions for all entrants and the selection of a small group of highly able youth with whom to work intensively.

To many parents and teachers it seems ridiculous to administer to seventh and eighth graders tests designed for above-average twelfth graders or even for college undergraduates and graduate students. It would be foolish and cruel, of course, if the examinees were average or even well above average students. For the upper 1 or 2 percent of the age group, however, only by administering difficult tests can one differentiate well enough between individuals and within individuals. The typical in-grade test does not have nearly enough "ceiling" for these exceptional children.

For example, all of our 16 Saturday morning algebra students (see chapter 6 by Fox) scored at the 99th percentile of their age group on national norms for the numerical ability subtest of the Academic Promise Test. That is, all of them are among the upper 1 percent. But

---

[3] All but one of these completed both 75-minute parts, V and M; he became ill after finishing SAT-M (administered first). (On 27 January 1974, 1519 took SAT-M.)

where within that percent? The lowest scorer in the group earned 40 points, barely the 99th percentile. The highest scorer earned 58 points. The 18-point difference between 40 and 58 points is the same as the difference between 22 points (the 65th percentile) and 40 points, the 99.0th percentile. Thus within that upper 1 percent there is about as much variability in mathematical aptitude as occurs in the upper third of a typical school class. Small wonder that even within a class that seems to have been grouped strictly homogeneously some students find the work too easy and others find it too difficult, unless self-pacing study techniques are used. Keating (1973) discusses this "ceiling" problem well.

Another reason for administering difficult tests to able youths is that mental power and persistence are well tested by them. When a 12- or 13-year-old can take one difficult test after another all day and still score well, that person is likely to be able to handle the demands of a college course. If he or she wilts, it may be well to defer the rigors of college classrooms until mental stamina improves.

We are trying via descriptive, clinical, and case study techniques to explore concepts of radical acceleration in mathematics and the physical sciences. Especially, we are helping some highly precocious children to move through high school, college, and graduate school faster and better than they would do otherwise. In this endeavor, questions of articulation at the various levels occupy much of our time and thought. Subsequent authors in this book report a number of investigations based on SMSPY's precocious students.

Our study is rather local in nature, but we are developing prototypal principles and practices that can be used throughout the country. Fortunately, helping the markedly precocious is not necessarily expensive. If a school system sets up its procedures flexibly enough, it can actually save money. For example, many seventh graders who score in the upper 1 percent on a test of mathematical aptitude can master a year's algebra course in a couple of months, working mostly on their own. We have had six 13-year-old boys happily taking high school chemistry and twelfth-grade calculus. They had learned the rest of high school mathematics well part-time at college or in our special course. They have also completed a college computer science course. The opportunities are almost unlimited, as Fox shows in chapter 3.

## Conclusion

Cognitively gifted children were first studied extensively by Lewis Terman, particularly from 1922 until his death in 1956. Since then they have received little attention in most educational quarters. For example, seldom are mathematically talented seventh and eighth graders adequately stimulated in schools. In the Study of Mathematically and Scientifically Precocious Youth at The Johns Hopkins University we have shown that some 13-year-olds can do excellent full-time college work, quite a few of the top 1/2 percent of the age group can learn four or more years of high school mathematics in two hours per week during a single 13-month period, many can take college courses part-time and make excellent grades, many can skip one or more school grades to their advantage, and many can succeed in college before completing the usual kindergarten through twelfth-grade lockstep.

Two 10-year-olds in our study had no difficulty with college algebra and trigonometry. A number of accelerated ninth and tenth graders handled twelfth-grade honors advanced placement calculus well at age 13 in competition with the mathematically ablest twelfth graders. A boy completed 23 college credits in computer science, mathematics, and chemistry shortly after his fourteenth birthday, being the best student in the calculus I class at a selective college, and went on to calculus II and III. A boy earned his master's degree in computer science and while still 17 years old began work for the doctorate at a major university.

The list of examples could go on and on. It seems uncomfortably probable that much of the intellectual alienation of brilliant high school graduates is due to their having been educated at a snail's pace too many years. It is time for parents to arise and *demand* that their schools do feasible, sensible things to prevent this atrophy of intellectual motivation. Mathematics is a good place to start; in this book we report our efforts to help talented children and encourage others to do so.

In *Your Bright Child: Handbook for Parents and Teachers of Intellectually Gifted Children*, to appear in two years, Fox, Keating, and I plan to present in practical detail ways to help these grossly neglected students. We will stress procedures by which groups of parents can insist that schools make needed provisions for their especially bright children. Expensive curricular adjustments are made, quite justifiably, for slow learners. It is past time that fast learners get the much less costly "special education" they deserve.

### References

Binet, A. 1911. Nouvelles recherches sur la mesure du niveau intellectuel chez les enfants d'école. *L'année psychologique* 17: 10–201.

Binet, A., and Simon, T. 1905a. Sur la nécessité d'établir un diagnostic scientifique des états inférieurs de l'intelligence. *L'année psychologique* 11: 163–90.

_____. 1905b. Méthodes nouvelles pour le diagnostic du niveau intellectuel des anormaux. *L'année psychologique* 11: 191–244.

_____. 1905c. Application des méthodes nouvelles au diagnostic du niveau intellectuel chez des enfants normaux et anormaux d'hospice et d'école primaire. *L'année psychologique* 11: 245–336.

_____. 1908. Le développement de l'intelligence chez les enfants. *L'année psychologique* 14: 1–94.

Burks, B. S.; Jensen, D. W.; and Terman, L. M. 1930. The promise of youth: Follow-up studies of a thousand gifted children. *Genetic studies of genius*, vol. 3. Stanford, Calif.: Stanford University Press.

Cattell, J. M. 1890. Mental tests and measurements. *Mind* 15: 373–80.

Clark, R. W. 1971. *Einstein: The life and times.* New York: World.

Cox, C. M. 1926. The early mental traits of three hundred geniuses. *Genetic studies of genius*, vol. 2. Stanford, Calif.: Stanford University Press.

Galton, F. 1869. *Hereditary genius: An inquiry into its laws and consequences.* London: Macmillan.

Galton, F. 1874. *English men of science: Their nature and nurture.* London: Macmillan.

Galton, F., and Schuster, E. 1906. *Noteworthy families (modern science): An index to kinships in near degrees between persons whose achievements are honourable, and have been publicly recorded.* London: Murray.

Goddard, H. H. 1910a. A measuring scale for intelligence. *The Training School* 6: 146–55.

_____. 1910b. Four hundred feebleminded children classified by the Binet method. *Pedagogical Seminary* 17: 387–97.

_____. 1911. Two thousand normal children measured by the Binet measuring scale of intelligence. *Pedagogical Seminary* 18: 232–59.

Grost, A. 1970. *Genius in residence.* Englewood Cliffs, N.J.: Prentice-Hall. (Written about Michael Grost by his mother.)

Guthrie, L. G. 1921. *Contributions to the study of precocity in children.* London: Millar.

Jablow, M. 1972. Hopkins students who skipped high school. *Sun* [Baltimore newspaper] *Magazine*, 25 June, pp. 5, 7, 10.

Jenkins, E. 1973. Express route to learning fashioned for precocious. *New York Times*, February 28, pp. 35, 66.

Jensen, A. R. 1972. *Genetics and education.* New York: Harper and Row.

_____. 1973. *Educability and group differences.* New York: Harper and Row.

Jones, L. V. 1963. Beyond Babbage. *Psychometrika* 28: 315–31.

Keating, D. P. 1973. Discovering quantitative precocity. Unpublished paper.

_____. In press. Possible sampling bias in *Genetic Studies of Genius. Educational and Psychological Measurement.*

_____, and Stanley, J. C. 1972. Extreme measures for the exceptionally gifted in mathematics and science. *Educational Researcher* 1(9): 3–7.

McNemar, Q. 1942. *The revision of the Stanford-Binet Scale.* Boston: Houghton Mifflin.

Meehl, P. E. 1971. Law and the fireside inductions: Some reflections of a clinical psychologist. *Journal of Social Issues* 27: 65–100.

Mill, J. S. 1924. *Autobiography of John Stuart Mill.* New York: Columbia University Press.

Oden, M. H. 1968. The fulfillment of promise: 40-year follow-up of the Terman gifted group. *Genetic Psychology Monographs* 77: 3–93.

*The Oxford English Dictionary.* 1933. Oxford, England: Oxford University Press.

Packe, M. S. J. 1954. *The life of John Stuart Mill.* New York: Macmillan.

Pearson, K. 1896. Mathematical contributions to the theory of evolution: III. Regression, heredity and panmixia. *Philosophical Transactions* 187: 253–318.

Schonberg, H. C. 1970. *The lives of the great composers.* New York: Norton.

Sears, R. R. 1957. L. M. Terman, pioneer in mental measurement. *Science* 125: 978–79.

Spearman, C. 1904. "General intelligence," objectively determined and measured. *American Journal of Psychology* 15: 206–19.

———. 1927. *The abilities of man.* New York: Macmillan.

Stanley, J. C. 1973. Accelerating the educational progress of intellectually gifted youths. *Educational Psychologist* 10: 133–46.

Stanley, J. C.; Keating, D. P.; and Fox, L. H. 1972. Annual report to the Spencer Foundation on its five-year grant to The Johns Hopkins University covering the first year of the grant, 1 September 1971 through 31 August 1972, "Study of mathematically and scientifically precocious youth (SMSPY)." Mimeographed report. Baltimore, Maryland 21218: The authors, Department of Psychology.

Terman, L. M. 1904. A preliminary study in the psychology and pedagogy of leadership. *Pedagogical Seminary* 11: 413–51.

———. 1905. A study in precocity and prematuration. *American Journal of Psychology* 16: 145–63.

———. 1906. Genius and stupidity: A study of seven "bright" and seven "stupid" boys. *Pedagogical Seminary* 13: 307–73.

———. 1916. *The measurement of intelligence.* Boston: Houghton Mifflin.

———. 1917. The intelligence quotient of Francis Galton in childhood. *American Journal of Psychology* 28: 209–15.

———. 1925. Mental and physical traits of a thousand gifted children. *Genetic studies of genius*, vol. 1. Stanford, Calif.: Stanford University Press.

———. 1954. Scientists and nonscientists in a group of 800 gifted men. *Psychological Monographs* 68(7): 1–41.

Terman, L. M., and Merrill, M. A. 1937. *Measuring intelligence.* Boston: Houghton Mifflin.

———. 1960. *Stanford-Binet Intelligence Scale: Manual for the third revision,* Form L-M. Boston: Houghton Mifflin.

Terman, L. M., and Oden, M. H. 1947. The gifted child grows up. Twenty-five years' follow-up of a superior group. *Genetic studies of genius*, vol. 4. Stanford, Calif.: Stanford University Press.

———. 1959. The gifted group at mid-life. *Genetic studies of genius*, vol. 5. Stanford, Calif.: Stanford University Press.

Thurstone, L. L. 1938. Primary mental abilities. *Psychometric Monographs*, no. 1.

*Time*. 1971. Making waves. 98 (Sept. 6): 34–35.

Wiener, N. 1953. *Ex-prodigy*. New York: Simon and Schuster.

Young, P. 1972. The transistor's coinventor makes history with a super-cold superprize. *National Observer*, 11(50): 1, 22.

# II · the study of mathematically precocious youth

## DANIEL P. KEATING

---

[Editors' Note: *In this chapter the reader will find a general overview of the results of the study during the first year. It contains many topics which in later chapters are discussed in detail, and thus the general framework of what is to be reported is outlined in this chapter.*]

---

One of the enduringly refreshing aspects of the history of psychology, particularly the British and the American disciplines, has been its concern with and attention to individual differences. This interest was accurately expressed by Sir Francis Galton (1889, p. 62) in a statement about those who would ignore such differences:

> Their souls seem as dull to the charm of variety as that of the native of one of our flat English counties, whose retrospect of Switzerland was that, if its mountains could be thrown into its lakes, two nuisances would be got rid of at once.

In our Study of Mathematically and Scientifically Precocious Youth at the Johns Hopkins University, individual differences are of monumental importance. Although the group of subjects we have found thus far is narrowly defined by age and precocity in specified areas, there is considerable variability among them. Later I shall discuss this interindividual variability in more detail. Lynn Fox will also be concerned with these differences and their impact on the predictions of success in challenging courses (see chapter 3).

In general, however, several things might be pointed to as quite characteristic of the group as a whole. Without becoming enmeshed in the "nature-nurture" controversy, we may fairly say that these students' innate (i.e., genotypic) abilities, both general and specific, are well above average, and that the environment which nourished them provided the necessary interactions for at least partial phenotypic expression. These terms should be interpreted with regard to the "reaction-range concept" (Gottesman 1963). Genotypes are expressed phenotypically in a specific environment; the range of phenotypic expression for a given genotype may be large. For these students, however, aspects

23

of the total environment, particularly the school environment, are usually far from ideal, and part of the purpose of the study is to examine the ways in which they can be made to approximate the ideal more closely.

## Precocity and Later Achievement

Stanley has examined the concept and the history of precocity (see pp. 1–11, 18); thus we need not do so further here. But it should be carefully noted that when much greater than average ability flourishes in an adequate environment, the empirically observable result is often early expression of those abilities through some assessable performance.

This statement implies several caveats which should be spelled out. It does not contradict the possibility of latent talent of the sort which is ascribable to insufficient or inappropriate environmental stimulation or to the confounding effects of personality or other factors which might prevent the manifestation of such talent. Also, precocity in mathematics or science is certainly not a sufficient and possibly not even a necessary condition for eventual achievement in those areas. It is often indicative of great interest in those subjects, however, and it provides a base for the rapid and successful development of achievement in those areas. It is difficult to make a psychological argument from historical sources, but the careful and thorough research of Cox (1926) and Lehman (1953) would seem to indicate that not only is there a history of precocity in the childhood years of a large percentage of generally accepted geniuses but also that this was frequently expressed in some sort of early achievement as well.

The advantage gained by such early precocity may, however, be severely attenuated or lost altogether if it is not properly nurtured. It would seem that lack of "intellectual nourishment" in school is the rule rather than the exception for these special students when active intervention by some agency outside the school (e.g., parents) is absent. Fox (see chapter 3) discusses these issues further, as well as the methods we are learning for nurturing mathematical and scientific precocity.

Thus, we are not neglectful of these conditions of necessity and sufficiency but have attempted to concentrate our efforts on those students who *have* achieved high scores on measures we employ rather than on those who may at some other time, past or future, attain high scores. Some of the reasons for this decision have already been discussed by Stanley (see chapter 1). The result has made the pertinent analyses more complex in some ways and simpler in others. The group is easily defined by reference to specific criteria: for example, Scholastic Aptitude Test Mathematical (SAT-M) score greater than or equal to 600 while still less than 14 years old. Only 11 percent of high school seniors would score that high.

But we must be aware also for purposes of analysis that we are dealing with one extreme of the distribution of developed talent, at least the upper one-half of 1 percent of the age group.

## Finding Precocious Talent

The first problem then was to find these precocious students in some systematic fashion. Informal methods such as teacher or parent references proved insufficient, so a mathematics and science competition was organized for seventh and eighth graders. There was no official screening beforehand, but a number of would-be contestants dropped out after receiving the SAT practice booklet and working the practice test. The total number of test takers was 450, with 396 taking math, 192 taking science, and 138 taking both.

In table 2.1 are listed the mean scores on SAT-M, Mathematics Achievement Level I (M-I), and STEP II Science (1969) of all the contestants, grouped by sex, grade, and test(s) taken. Perhaps the single most important finding of our study thus far, and one which we are inclined to overlook because we have become acclimated to it, is that there is a remarkable number of almost unbelievably able and academically accomplished young students in grades seven and eight. (Accelerated ninth graders were also eligible.) The level of their ability can be inferred from table 2.1, but the picture becomes even clearer when we look at the highest scorers within this able group.

As noted above, a score of 600 on SAT-M places one at the 89th percentile of male high school seniors. In the group of 396 students who participated in the competition 53, or 13 percent, scored 600 or higher, and 23, or 6 percent, scored at or above 650, which is the 94th percentile. On M-I, which is an achievement test for high school seniors who have taken seven or more semesters of mathematics, a score of 550 is about the 41st percentile. Twenty-three (6 percent) of these students scored 550 or greater. The grouped frequency distributions on SAT-M and M-I are given in table 2.2. Clearly, whether aptitude *or* achievement tests are used to measure the ability of these students, the best of them are competitive with superior high school seniors. Although it is with

Table 2.1: *Mean scores of students on three measures: SAT-M, M-I, and Science*[a]

| Tests Taken | Test | Statistic | 7th grade | | 8th grade | | 9th grade | | All Examinees |
|---|---|---|---|---|---|---|---|---|---|
| | | | Female | Male | Female | Male | Female | Male | |
| Math Only | | N | 59 | 67 | 63 | 67 | – | 2 | 258 |
| | SAT–M | Mean | 416 | 450 | 472 | 516 | – | 620 | 466 |
| | | S.d. | 71 | 104 | 76 | 100 | – | 42 | 97 |
| | M–1 | Mean | 393 | 398 | 431 | 451 | – | 540 | 420 |
| | | S.d. | 46 | 63 | 48 | 76 | – | 28 | 65 |
| Math and Science | | N | 18 | 23 | 32 | 62 | 1 | 2 | 138 |
| | SAT–M | Mean | 448 | 487 | 427 | 531 | 510 | 760 | 492 |
| | | S.d. | 86 | 100 | 104 | 109 | – | 42 | 115 |
| | M–1 | Mean | 407 | 437 | 414 | 467 | 500 | 695 | 445 |
| | | S.d. | 58 | 86 | 52 | 86 | – | 106 | 84 |
| | Science 1A & 1B | Mean | 74 | 83 | 69 | 88 | 100 | 106 | 81 |
| | | S.d. | 13 | 19 | 16 | 21 | – | 3 | 20 |
| Science Only | | N | 7 | 13 | 4 | 29 | 1 | – | 54 |
| | Science 1A & 1B | Mean | 65 | 66 | 69 | 80 | 103 | – | 74 |
| | | S.d. | 7 | 13 | 19 | 18 | – | – | 17 |

[a]The total number of students taking the mathematics tests was 396. The total number taking the science test was 192. *Both* sets of tests were taken by 138 students.

Table 2.2: *Grouped frequency distribution by grade and sex on SAT-M and M-I of 396 students participating in mathematics contest*

| Score | 7th Grade SAT-M B[b] | 7th Grade SAT-M G[c] | 7th Grade M-I B | 7th Grade M-I G | 8th Grade SAT-M B | 8th Grade SAT-M G | 8th Grade M-I B | 8th Grade M-I G | 9th Grade[a] SAT-M B | 9th Grade[a] SAT-M G | 9th Grade[a] M-I B | 9th Grade[a] M-I G |
|---|---|---|---|---|---|---|---|---|---|---|---|---|
| 760-800 | 0 | 0 | 0 | 0 | 1 | 0 | 0 | 0 | 1 | 0 | 1 | 0 |
| 710-750 | 2 | 0 | 1 | 0 | 2 | 0 | 2 | 0 | 1 | 0 | 0 | 0 |
| 660-700 | 2 | 0 | 1 | 0 | 13 | 0 | 1 | 0 | 0 | 0 | 0 | 0 |
| 610-650 | 3 | 0 | 0 | 0 | 17 | 0 | 6 | 0 | 1 | 0 | 1 | 0 |
| 560-600 | 8 | 3 | 0 | 0 | 19 | 11 | 8 | 0 | 1 | 0 | 1 | 0 |
| 510-550 | 11 | 8 | 6 | 3 | 21 | 23 | 15 | 9 | 0 | 1 | 1 | 0 |
| 460-500 | 20 | 16 | 9 | 5 | 19 | 20 | 27 | 17 | 0 | 0 | 0 | 1 |
| 410-450 | 14 | 17 | 27 | 22 | 17 | 14 | 33 | 34 | 0 | 0 | 0 | 0 |
| 360-400 | 18 | 22 | 31 | 36 | 13 | 14 | 32 | 29 | 0 | 0 | 0 | 0 |
| 310-350 | 7 | 7 | 11 | 10 | 6 | 7 | 4 | 6 | 0 | 0 | 0 | 0 |
| 260-300 | 3 | 2 | 4 | 1 | 1 | 3 | 1 | 0 | 0 | 0 | 0 | 0 |
| 210-250 | 2 | 2 | 0 | 0 | 0 | 3 | 0 | 0 | 0 | 0 | 0 | 0 |
| N | 90 | 77 | 90 | 77 | 129 | 95 | 129 | 95 | 4 | 1 | 4 | 1 |
| Median | 457 | 420 | 394 | 388 | 534 | 470 | 442 | 421 | 690 | 510 | 590 | 500 |
| Mean | 460 | 423 | 408 | 396 | 523 | 457 | 458 | 426 | 690 | 510 | 618 | 500 |
| S.d. | 104 | 75 | 71 | 49 | 105 | 88 | 81 | 50 | 88 | - | 110 | - |

[a]Accelerated ninth graders were eligible, i.e., those not yet 14 at time of testing (March 4, 1972).

[b]Boys.

[c]Girls.

these highest scoring students we will be actively involved, since they are the truly precocious ones in this group, it is important to look at the original group of 450 students more closely.

There is clearly a difference in ability as measured by all three tests between those students who chose to compete in both the mathematics and science contests and those who chose to take only math or only science. The 138 math and science contestants were significantly better than the 258 math only contestants on both SAT-M ($.02 < p < .05$) and M-I ($.001 < p < .01$) and also significantly better than the 54 science only contestants on science ($.01 < p < .02$).

A strong "self-concept" factor, which is fairly accurate, may tentatively be inferred to be operating in the self-selection for which test(s) to take. Those students who do in fact score higher than other gifted youngsters on tests such as these would appear to perceive themselves as being knowledgeable in more than one area.

One of the striking and unexpected differences which emerged from this large screening session was the sex difference in mathematical precocity, as can be seen in tables 2.1 and 2.2. There were 43 boys with a SAT-M score of 610 or greater, whereas the three highest scoring girls earned 600. Astin's paper deals with this matter in greater detail.

Parenthetically, the science test was relatively inefficient in screening in the level of talent we are seeking; additionally, quantitative aptitude and achievement seem to be a growing necessity for scientists. Thus, we are dropping the science tests in our future large screening sessions. Those who are screened in on the basis of mathematical talent will, of course, be subsequently tested for their knowledge of general science.

Approximately six weeks after the general testing, we invited back the high scorers for some additional testing, both cognitive and noncognitive. These students were those who had ranked the highest on math and/or science. Accordingly, 35 boys were called back for further testing, and all of them came. Ten girls who ranked highest among the girls were also asked to come, and eight of them came. Since the girls' scores on the competitive measures (SAT-M, M-I, and science) were not as high as the boys', nor even as high as some boys who were not invited back for reasons of space and material, the subsequent analyses of the "high group" will refer to the 35 boys who were tested a second time.


## Concomitants of Mathematical Precocity

There is some corollary information available about the total group. With the registration materials was sent a questionnaire, which the students were requested to bring with them on the day of the testing. Of the total of 450 contestants, 416, or 92 percent, returned the questionnaire. On none of the three test measures (SAT-M, M-I, or science) was there a difference even approaching significance between those who returned questionnaires and those who did not; thus information gleaned from the returned questionnaires may be assumed to be representative of the whole group. Also on the day of the testing a rearranged checklist of occupations from Holland's (1965) Vocational Preference Inventory (VPI) was administered to all the students. In terms of the total group (i.e., not breaking down by sex or grade) and the high group, it will be fruitful to look at the VPI and at three items from the questionnaire: the students' reported liking for school; the level of education attained by the father and the mother; and the sibling position of the student.

## Liking for School

On the questionnaire, the students were asked, "How would you describe your liking for school?" There were four options listed: strong liking, fair liking, slight liking, and dislike. The responses were purposely weighted in *favor* of a positive response (three "liking" categories and only one "dislike" category) so that a negative response would have to be intentional. As can be seen in figure 2.1, the mean scores for the total groups *increase* monotonically as the degree of reported liking for school decreases for all three tests. The number of students responding in the first two categories is much larger than in the second two, which complicates the interpretation, and the picture in science is further confounded by the overlapping math and science people. But generally the trend is quite clear: gifted seventh- and eighth-grade students who were advanced enough to get the high scores on these college-level tests reported less "liking for school" than gifted students who do not do as well on such difficult tests.

If we look at the high group in comparison with all boys, the picture is even clearer. For all boys, the percentage reporting each of the four

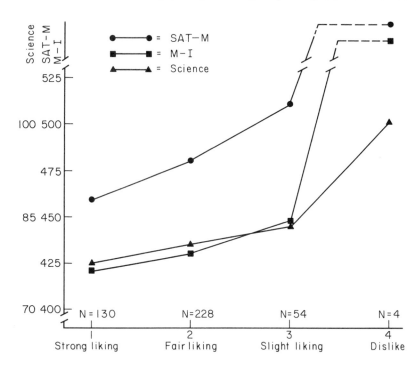

Figure 2.1: *Mean scores of all students on three measures for degrees of reported liking for school*

categories, strong liking to disliking, were: 27.9, 55.1, 15.4, and 1.6; for
the high group, the comparable figures were respectively: 17.7, 55.19,
20.6, and 5.9. Also striking is the fact that of the total of four boys who
reported dislike for school, two were in the high group, with SAT-M
scores of 780 and 740 and M-I scores of 720 and 630.

This result confirmed expectations derived from earlier informal discussions with some of the precocious students who had been identified
prior to the general testing. They reported a disillusionment with school
in particular and academic pursuits in general. The boredom and frus-
tration generated by their school situation were expressed in different
ways by different students, as might be expected, but it was frequently
present.

A completely different interpretation of these data is possible if one
were so disposed, i.e., that bright, precocious students are on the average more maladjusted than "normal" ones. In a sense, this would be
true: *situationally*, some of them do seem to be maladjusted. But this
may well be a healthy reaction to intolerable circumstances. *Personally*,
they appear to be a well-adjusted group. The California Psychological
Inventory (CPI-Gough 1964) was administered to the high group when
they were called back for retesting. Although there is considerable
variance in the sample, there is no indication that mathematically
precocious boys are especially subject to disabling inter- or intra-
personal weaknesses. Thus the "maladjustment" interpretation is im-
plausible if its meaning is anything other than situational maladjustment (see chapter 7).

In the light of the tentatively confirmed expectation of lack of enthusiasm for school, it is indeed difficult to value highly some of the frequently heard arguments against significant restructuring of these students' educations because of the potential harm to their social and
emotional development. A number of studies suggest strongly that such
a fear is unfounded (e.g., Pressey 1949; Oden 1968). But the obverse of
that concern is one voiced much less often: What is the potential harm
to the social and emotional development of these students if they are
required to remain in an unstimulating, hence frustrating, environment? It may be great, as we have suggested elsewhere in case-study
fashion (Keating and Stanley 1972) and as these data tentatively indicate.

Some of the best students, however, did report "strong liking" for
school. Being placed in an educational situation far below one's capacity
does not inevitably result in less liking for school. This is merely another
expression of the fact that even though this high group is homogeneous
on a number of variables, it is quite heterogeneous on others such as
temperament (i.e., those not used for selection). In the second large

screening session to be held soon, the questions will be rephrased slightly in an attempt to separate liking for school and liking for mathematics.

### Sibling Position

It can be anticipated that birth order will be associated with most data about individuals one might conceivably wish to collect, including aptitude and achievement (Lunneborg 1971; Breland 1972). But, just as there was an unexpected sex-difference in these data, there was an unanticipated *lack* of any differences due to sibling position in the total group. The three virtually straight lines in figure 2.2 illustrate this point well.

Standing in contrast to this flat profile is the distinct pattern within the high group, as shown in figure 2.3. On SAT-M and M-I, those in the high group born second score higher than only children, first-borns, or those born third or later (but none of these differences are statistically significant). This observation relates to a finding by McGurk and Lewis (1972), who report an effect on dependency behavior for those born second. As they suggest, it is a "phenomenon in search of an explanation." It is also a phenomenon showing up inconsistently and weakly enough in these data to militate against excessive speculation.

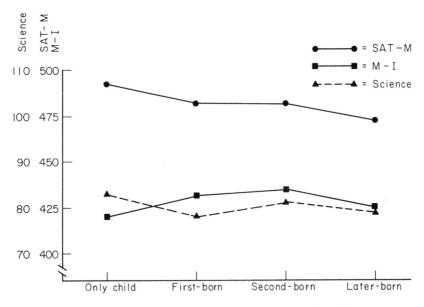

Figure 2.2: *Mean scores of all students on three measures by sibling position*

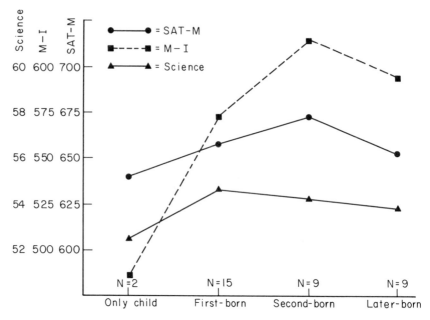

Figure 2.3: *Mean scores of the high group on three measures by sibling position*

## Parents' Education

If in our study the unexpected and the unusual has been the rule, then the association of the parents' education and children's test scores is the exception: it followed the often replicated pattern to perfection. In the total group, the higher the reported educational level of the parents, the higher was the mean test scores of their children on all three measures (SAT-M, M-I, and Science). Indeed, the relationship was monotonic for both mother's and father's education on SAT-M and nearly so on M-I and Science. Figure 2.4 depicts this relationship for father's education, and figure 2.5 for mother's education.

This result is not surprising nor, unfortunately, especially informative. Does this merely reflect the finding that bright parents tend to have bright children? Or does it say something about the relatively different types of experience to which the children with the higher test scores might have been exposed? Or both? These data offer no solution to that dilemma.

Slightly more informative are the figures for the high group. The pattern is similar within that group, with 47 percent of the fathers and

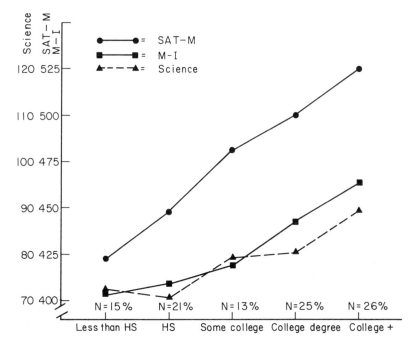

Figure 2.4:  *Mean scores of all students on three measures by level of father's education*

28 percent of the mothers having education beyond a college degree. *But*, and these are noteworthy exceptions, 29 percent of the fathers and 51 percent of the mothers had less than a college degree. Twelve percent of the fathers, in fact, were reported not to have even a high school diploma. Thus, while both the fathers and the mothers of the high group were reported to be significantly better educated than the parents of the remainder of the contestants, there was a substantial amount of this high level talent coming from homes where the parents were *not* professionals.

The contestants reported the highest educational levels attained by the father and the mother. These were coded in the following fashion: 1—less than high school diploma; 2—high school diploma; 3—some college; 4—college degree; and 5—courses beyond the college degree. Interestingly, the larger difference between the high group and the remainder group was in terms of the mother's education, with a mean of 3.56 for mothers of the high group and 2.57 for mothers of the remainder group ($p < .001$). For fathers the means were 3.91 and 3.24 respectively ($.001 < p < .01$). This is partially attributable, of course, to the

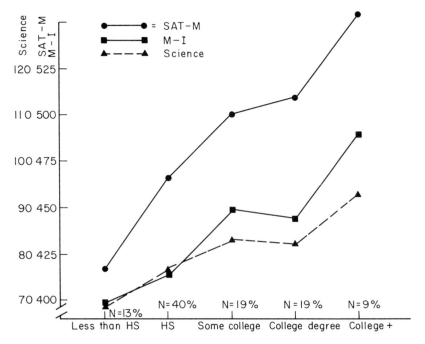

Figure 2.5:   *Mean scores of all students on three measures by level of mother's education*

relatively high correlation (r = .62, a correlation significantly different from 0 at p < .001) between the reported educational level of the fathers and mothers within the high group. In figure 2.6 the percentages of the comparison group for the highs and the total group for each educational level are shown for both mothers and fathers. There is a fairly consistent pattern in the differences between the groups for mothers and fathers.

*Vocational Interest*

All the contestants were requested to complete the checklist taken from the VPI. The resulting codes are thus somewhat more unreliable than they would presumably be if the longer (but for our purposes somewhat less appropriate) instrument were used. For these and other reasons, only the first letter of the Holland three-letter code will be discussed in this paper. (For a more detailed treatment of vocational interest, see chapter 8.)

In figure 2.7, the percentages of three groups (total, highs, and boys) having each of the six code letters as the first letter are shown. The

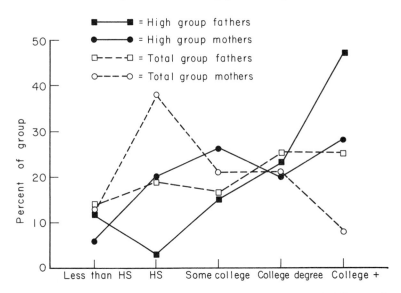

Figure 2.6:   *Percent of high group and total group parents at different educational levels*

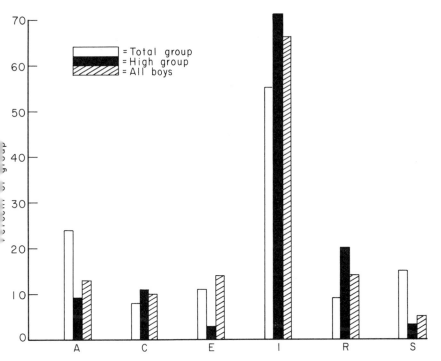

Figure 2.7:   *Percent of total group, all boys, and high group with each VPI code (1st letter)*

codes are (A)rtistic, (C)onventional, (E)nterprising, (I)nvestigative, (R)ealistic, and (S)ocial. The percentages across codes, incidentally, sum to over 100 percent, since it is possible to have more than one first letter code (i.e., a tie for first letter). Eighteen percent of all boys and 11 percent of the high group had more than one first letter.

Immediately striking is the height of the Investigative columns. Over 66 percent of the boys overall, and 71 percent of the boys in the high group had I as at least one of their first letters. This is not surprising, since all of the I occupations are science oriented, whereas only a few under the other five codes are even remotely related to science. There is a further confounding in that the status and educational level of the I occupations (exclusively professional) is unmatched by any other code.

It is, nevertheless, a result which confirms some earlier speculations about the interests of students like these. They appear above all to be interested in finding out things, discovering things, learning things. The absence of any difference in the relative percentages of the high-group boys and all boys on the first letter of the Holland code would seem to indicate that the interests are the same, but the high boys have for some reason acted upon those interests more effectively.

Interestingly enough, as figure 2.8 portrays, the mean scores for boys having the different letters as the first one of their Holland code follow a consistent pattern. Despite the large number who had I as their first letter, which would tend to depress the mean score for I toward the grand mean of the boys, its mean is highest in science and second highest in both SAT-M and M-I. Those boys having (A)rtistic and (E)nterprising as their first letter were consistently the lowest on all tests. This indicates that precocity is more than just a high level of ability, that it is a subtle blend of ability, interest, personality, and probably other factors as well. These other factors may well include evaluative attitudes, as we shall see later.

## The Psychometry of Mathematical Precocity

If the best of the students on the basis of the general competition were to be facilitated educationally, and if more was to be learned about the pattern of their abilities, it was essential that they be tested more extensively and intensively than had already been done. Accordingly, as mentioned above, 35 boys (the "high group") were invited back for further testing. These included: Scholastic Aptitude Test-Verbal (SAT-V), which was the most crucial and which all in the high group took; SAT-M for the few science only qualifiers; Science (Form A

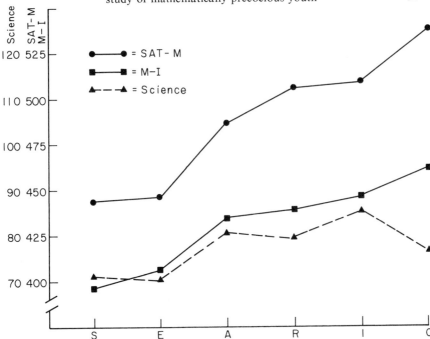

Figure 2.8:  *Scores of all boys on three measures by first letter of VPI code*

only) for those math only qualifiers; Mathematics Achievement, Level II (M-II) for nine boys who had done especially well on M-I; Raven's Progressive Matrices, a test of nonverbal reasoning ability; Terman's Concept Mastery Test of vocabulary and verbal reasoning; Bennett's Mechanical Comprehension Test; and the Revised Minnesota Paper Form Board Test. Obviously, not all the high group could take all the tests even in a day-long testing session. A second retesting has been conducted, and all the available scores and summary statistics on the tests enumerated above are listed in table 2.3.

There are a number of observations to be made concerning the means in table 2.3. The SAT-M mean of 660 was "expected" since it was the major criterion for an invitation to come to the retesting. It is actually lowered by the fact that several contestants who qualified on the basis of their science score, but who had relatively low SAT-M scores, are included.

The SAT-V mean score of 546 for this group is about 0.4 of a standard deviation lower than the mean SAT-M score, based on the national sample of male high school seniors. This again is to be understood partially in terms of the selective criteria and the expected

Table 2.3: *Scores of high scorers[a] from Science Fair Competition on various cognitive measures*

| Student Boys | Scholastic Aptitude Test | | CEEB Math Achievement | | Science[b] | | RPM[c] | | CMT[d] | | MCT[e] | | RMPFB[f] | |
|---|---|---|---|---|---|---|---|---|---|---|---|---|---|---|
| | Math | Verbal | Level I | Level II | A | B | A | II | I | II | AA | CC | MA | MB |
| 1 | 790 | 560 | 770 | 750 | 54 | 52 | 59 | 33 | 26 | 49 | – | 34 | 57 | – |
| 2 | 780 | 620 | 720 | 720 | 60 | 66 | 59 | 31 | 43 | 48 | 53 | 50 | 48 | 52 |
| 3 | 740 | 620 | 660 | 670 | 51 | – | 59 | 33 | 29 | 51 | – | – | – | – |
| 4 | 740 | 460 | 630 | 620 | 38 | – | 57 | 33 | 14 | 25 | 20 | 27 | 61 | 59 |
| 5 | 730 | 560 | 620 | 610 | 46 | 54 | 55 | 30 | 31 | 33 | 38 | 32 | – | – |
| 6 | 710 | 530 | 730 | 800 | 69 | 68 | 57 | 32 | 19 | 31 | 54 | 45 | 49 | 51 |
| 7 | 710 | 640 | 640 | 690 | 53 | 56 | 58 | 29 | 33 | 52 | 35 | 22 | 59 | 58 |
| 8 | 690 | 550 | 590 | – | 56 | – | – | – | 17 | 48 | 48 | 40 | – | – |
| 9 | 690 | 450 | 520 | – | 43 | 36 | 58 | 35 | 26 | 39 | 32 | 31 | 40 | – |
| 10 | 680 | 670 | 720 | 690 | 43 | – | 55 | 26 | 34 | 31 | – | 18 | 42 | – |
| 11 | 680 | 620 | 570 | – | 63 | 65 | 56 | 35 | 46 | 51 | 48 | 37 | – | – |
| 12 | 680 | 540 | 610 | – | 48 | – | 58 | 33 | 23 | 38 | 41 | 39 | – | – |
| 13 | 680 | 450 | 500 | – | 42 | – | 51 | 25 | 21 | 29 | 39 | 33 | – | – |
| 14 | 680 | 500 | 510 | – | 44 | – | – | – | 28 | 20 | 41 | 23 | – | – |
| 15 | 670 | 650 | 660 | 620 | 64 | 61 | 55 | 33 | 19 | 37 | 50 | 11 | 48 | 50 |
| 16 | 670 | 570 | 610 | 710 | 60 | 66 | 59 | 29 | 34 | 33 | 50 | 46 | – | – |
| 17 | 670 | 590 | 600 | – | 59 | 59 | 54 | 33 | 26 | 50 | 53 | 52 | – | – |
| 18 | 660 | 490 | 520 | – | 47 | – | – | – | 8 | 27 | 42 | 34 | – | – |
| 19 | 660 | 460 | 520 | – | 54 | – | 60 | 30 | 8 | 27 | 50 | 32 | 37 | 43 |
| 20 | 660 | 460 | 580 | – | 40 | 10 | 58 | 32 | -1 | 22 | 39 | 30 | – | – |
| 21 | 660 | 420 | 530 | – | 44 | 49 | 60 | 29 | 12 | 29 | 40 | 34 | – | – |
| 22 | 660 | 310 | 600 | – | 39 | – | 56 | 31 | 9 | 29 | 41 | 21 | – | – |
| 23 | 650 | 540 | 560 | – | 46 | – | 56 | 30 | – | – | 43 | 36 | – | – |
| 24 | 640 | 580 | 610 | – | 57 | 55 | 58 | 29 | 6 | 35 | – | – | – | – |
| 25 | 640 | 400 | 510 | – | 39 | – | – | – | 12 | 28 | 24 | 34 | – | – |
| 26 | 630 | 580 | 500 | – | 53 | 63 | 59 | 28 | 46 | 26 | 53 | 47 | 52 | – |
| 27 | 620 | 740 | 520 | – | 59 | 59 | 58 | 31 | 48 | 47 | 20 | 27 | 52 | 58 |
| 28 | 620 | 530 | 640 | – | 39 | – | 53 | 27 | 2 | 28 | 12 | 18 | – | – |
| 29 | 610 | 530 | 520 | – | 57 | 55 | 59 | 34 | 6 | 35 | 56 | 52 | – | – |
| 30 | 600 | 600 | – | – | 62 | 64 | 56 | 30 | 37 | 42 | 41 | 36 | 51 | 41 |
| 31 | 600 | 550 | 520 | – | 58 | 61 | – | – | 22 | 37 | 38 | 36 | 48 | – |
| 32 | 590 | 550 | – | – | 56 | 54 | 57 | 31 | 14 | 33 | 45 | 36 | – | – |
| 33 | 560 | 620 | 540 | – | 57 | 57 | – | – | 45 | 40 | 47 | 40 | – | – |
| 34 | 530 | 550 | 470 | – | 66 | 64 | 59 | 33 | 19 | 30 | 49 | 46 | – | – |
| 35 | 520 | 630 | 510 | – | 56 | 57 | 51 | 28 | 38 | 48 | – | – | – | – |
| N | 35 | 35 | 33 | 10 | 35 | 22 | 29 | 29 | 34 | 34 | 30 | 32 | 13 | 8 |
| Mean | 660 | 546 | 585 | 688 | 52 | 58 | 57 | 31 | 24 | 36 | 41 | 34 | 50 | 52 |
| S.d. | 60 | 86 | 77 | 61 | 9 | 8 | 2 | 3 | 14 | 9 | 11 | 10 | 7 | 7 |

[a]The 35 highest scoring competitors on math and/or science, all boys, ranked in order of
SAT-M score. Students 29 thru 35 qualified on basis of *science* score.

[b]Sequential Tests of Educational Progress, Series II (STEP II), Forms 1A and 1B. (Educational Testing Service).

[c]Raven's progressive Matrices, Sets A, B, C, D, E (listed as "A" in table) and Set II ("II" in table).

[d]Concept Mastery Test, Parts I and II (Psychological Corporation).

[e]Bennett's Mechanical Comprehension Test, Forms AA and CC (Psychological Corporation).

[f]Revised Minnesota Paper Form, Board, Forms MA and MB (Psychological Corporation).

regression toward the mean.[1] But it may also be indicative of something a bit deeper. Verbal precocity may be rather rarer than the quantitative variety. Mathematics may be, in some psychologically meaningful sense, a closed system, whereas vocabulary and perhaps verbal reasoning may be somehow "openended," more dependent on accumulated experience. This will be subject to investigation in the future, especially in the analysis of results from the second large screening competition, which included a mathematical and a verbal section.

It has been suggested to us by a number of teachers that the use of such rigorous tests for seventh and eighth graders is perhaps useless or harmful or both. What is the rationale for using these high-level tests at such an early age?

There are really three related answers to that question, one pragmatic and the other two somewhat more theoretical. As we have reported elsewhere (Keating and Stanley 1972), the two "radical accelerates" at Johns Hopkins were evaluated on the basis of the tests normally given to prospective freshmen. Their successful performance on them was in fact indicative of their ability to succeed admirably at college-level academic tasks. In simple language, the tests work. The continuing predictive success of these tests for this purpose has justified their continued use.

The second point has to do with the unbounded nature of the distribution beyond the 99th percentile. All z-scores of 2.33 or greater are included in the traditionally reported 99th percentile, beyond which age-in-grade testing simply does not make distinctions or, more characteristically, does not possess enough ceiling to make such distinctions.

[1]Whenever a group is selected on the basis of a test score criterion above or below the population mean, the mean score of the select group on a subsequent measure will be closer to the population mean than on the original measure. This statistical phenomenon is known as "regression toward the [population] mean."

The top 1 percent of seventh and eighth graders comprises a group from which those capable of such advanced and rapid learning must be identified. Although further in-grade testing is therefore unproductive, evaluation with college-level tests yields important information.

Third, these high-level tests are more appropriate than in-grade tests because the former almost necessarily tap higher-level abilities than the latter. The following example demonstrates this distinction. A student who has learned the formula for finding the area of a right triangle will apply it readily when presented with that type of problem. The ability required to solve the problem in that circumstance is of a lower order than the ability required when the same task is presented to a student who has not yet learned the formula directly and must deduce it. Similar distinctions may be drawn between the high school senior taking the SAT and the seventh or eighth grader doing so. The "stimulus" is objectively the same, but it is a quite different task in terms of the individual. This is discussed more fully elsewhere by the author (Keating 1973).

The small size of the target group is relative, not absolute. A conservative estimate of the number of junior high school students (seventh, eighth, and ninth graders) nationwide fitting into this exclusive category is 2,500 to 3,000. The principles and practices being developed in this study would presumably extend beyond even this limited group, however.

The only other test taken by all 35 boys was science, again including those who had chosen not to take it the first time around. The mean score on Form A for this high group is 52 (of a possible 75), which is the 80th percentile of college sophomores tested in the spring. Several of these students, however, demonstrated a grasp of general science knowledge better than 95 percent of the comparison group of college students.

Most of the 35 students have taken the Raven's Progressive Matrices, Sets A-B-C-D-E and Set II. Their mean score on Set II is 31 (of a possible 36) and the median is 30. These are 2.5 and 2.3 standard deviations above the mean of British university students. The British standardization may be slightly suspect (it was not an excellent sample of subjects or situations), but clearly these students excel at nonverbal reasoning ability by any standard. Two of the students (one of them a seventh grader) missed a perfect score by only one item on this extremely difficult test, and several more by but two or three items.

Terman's Concept Mastery Test, which he devised to measure the adult intellectual stature of his gifted group (Terman 1947), consists of two parts. The first is a pure vocabulary test, and the second is a test of verbal reasoning by use of incomplete analogies. Further insight into the strengths and weaknesses of these mathematically precocious youngsters is gained from comparing scores on the two parts. With only two exceptions, these students had corrected raw scores on the second part which were higher than those on the first part, even though there are 115 items on part one and only 75 on part two. Thus as a group, and as individuals, they are better at reasoning at an early age, even verbal reasoning, than at tasks requiring purely verbal aptitude.

Little in the way of general conclusions can be drawn from the tests of mechanical comprehension and spatial ability. On the average, these students score at the 36th percentile of engineering freshmen on mechanical comprehension and at the 55th percentile of a similar group on spatial relations. There is great variability in the scores, however. Several students who are good at spatial relations are almost totally lacking in mechanical comprehension. The converse may also be true, but not enough of the students took the spatial relations test for us to know.

This does, however, raise an important point which requires further elaboration: the inter- and intra-individual variability of the group mentioned earlier. Figure 2.9 depicts the latter quite vividly. The students were ranked on SAT-M and their z-scores within this group computed and plotted. It is the solid line going from top to bottom, left to right. The same procedure was followed for their SAT-V and RPM scores. The maze of criss-crossing dotted lines is the result. What the figure shows is that there is a decided lack of predictability of rank within the

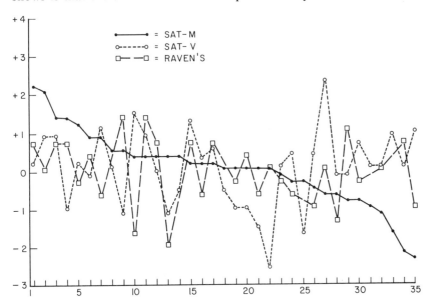

Figure 2.9:   *Z-scores on three measures for each student in high group*

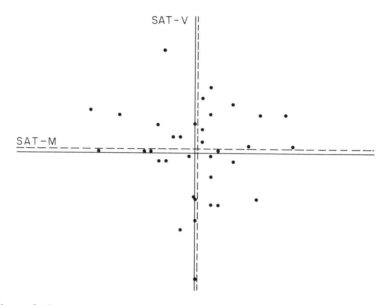

Figure 2.10:   *Scatterplot of z-scores on SAT-M and SAT-V in high group*
*(r = −.08)*

group from any of these three tests to any of the others. Some of these
students are far better than the others on some tasks and poorer on
others.

In a more conventional format, figure 2.10 shows the lack of relationship within this group between SAT-M and SAT-V. The correlation
equals −.08. The correlation between SAT-M and RPM is .20. Neither is
significantly different from zero. This admittedly borders on the re-
striction of range fallacy, i.e., within such a select group a high correlation between the criterion and other aptitude measures is not to be
anticipated. But one additional analysis lends support to the intuitive
perception of great variability. The mean absolute z-score differences
(i.e., disregarding directionality) between SAT-M and SAT-V and
between SAT-M and RPM for this group are 1.18 and .96, respectively.
Thus the average difference in both cases is approximately a standard
deviation. This also reflects the variability of the high group.

In addition to these tests, the students were also given the Allport-
Vernon-Lindzey Study of Values (AVL) and the California Psychological Inventory (CPI). The CPI results are examined in detail by Weiss,
Haier, and Keating (see chapter 7). The AVL was used to determine
whether the evaluative attitudes of these students were similar to those
of creative scientists, on the assumption that this might be a good indication of their potential for later achievement. MacKinnon (1962) re-

ported that the classic pattern of eminent *adult* scientists is Theoretical-Aesthetic. These values appear to be conflicting, but the combination seems conducive to creativity in science. A desire for knowledge and understanding for their own sake is the *sine qua non*, but this must be mediated by an appreciation of form and harmony (e.g., the "elegant" proof in mathematics).

The theoretical value is prevalent in this sample. Twenty of the thirty-five students had it as their first (highest) value (on the basis of male college population percentiles, not raw scores), and seven of the remaining fifteen had it as the second. This result, taken together with the information from the Holland checklist, confirms the common sense notion that these precocious youngsters must possess a strong intrinsic interest in learning and knowing. Thus one of the first (and perhaps major) noncognitive, personological ingredients for eventual creative achievement in the sciences seems to be present in abundance.

There is also some evidence to validate the importance of the theoretical scale. The science scores seemed to be a good indicator of independent interest in science. The raw score on the theoretical scale was correlated at $r = .55$ with the science score within the high group. It correlated more highly with the science score than any cognitive measure except SAT-V.

The aesthetic value, however, did not fare too well in this group. Only nine people had it as either their first or second highest value. Five who had theoretical as their first value had aesthetic as their second, showing the "classic" creative scientist pattern. This may indicate several possibilities. First, it may be that the theoretical-aesthetic pattern is rare in the population and that our finding represents a marked positive deviation from the base rate. Research on this specific point has not, to our knowledge, been done. Thus, the expectation should perhaps be lower, and finding even these few is significant.

Second, it may be that the adult creative scientists who were studied developed their evaluative attitudes when they were much older than these students. Perhaps very few 12- to 14-year-olds show much of an aesthetic evaluative attitude, and the theoretical-aesthetic creative scientists did not when they were that age. This suggests two further possibilities. One is that this is a maturational-developmental sequence which may emerge in any event. The other is that certain adolescent or post-adolescent experiences of the creative scientists engendered this value construct, and experiences similar to these need to be made available to these students. There is some evidence that this is true for a more diverse group. Huntley (1965) reported a significant increase on the aesthetic value for science majors over four years of college. One may be concerned to learn, however, that fathers of boys in the high group do not score much higher on the aesthetic scale than their sons do. A third point to be considered is much more speculative but also more disturbing. McCurdy (1957) reviewed the childhood patterns of 20 geniuses. One strong pattern that emerged is a long and continuous contact of the genius-to-be with adults on a nearly equal basis from a very early age. Peer-group interaction of the sort prized above all else in today's schools is conspicuously absent. It is not a simple task to construe the relationship between this and creativity, or even an aesthetic attitude, but perhaps one exists. This would constitute a historical-cultural interaction of childrearing practices and the frequency of creative individuals. It would mean that by constructing our schools as we have and by making such education universal and compulsory from age five or six onward, we may have in fact unknowingly militated against the development of creativity. To speculate further involves difficult and complex questions beyond the scope of this paper. Fox and Denham discuss this problem in more detail (see chapter 8).

### Educability of Mathematical Precocity

The screening of gifted seventh and eighth graders by means of a general test competition turned up a number of youngsters who are mathematically precocious. The analyses of the total group of contestants and the high group sought to answer important questions about the nature and development of their talent. The results suggested the possibility that "precocity" might be educable (in the root sense of "leading or drawing out from") with a highly select group of students and effective techniques.

On hand from a related study were the names and scores on the Academic Promise Tests (APT) of 392 sixth graders who had been nominated by their teachers or principals as gifted (ten students from each of forty schools). The scores were on four subscales: number (N), verbal (V), abstract reasoning (AR), and language usage (LU). On the basis of the following criteria, approximately 30 students were invited to participate in an algebra class to be conducted on Saturdays during the summer but which would rely primarily on independent study during the week. The student had to have a 99th percentile score for the sixth grade national norms on N and also a 99th percentile on either V or AR.

The class began June 1972 with 19 students, 16 of whom came from the pool of 392 students. Three special subjects were also offered the opportunity and took it, including a remarkably able boy who had just completed the third grade. Fox reports the results of this study in chapter 6.

## Conclusion

As is inevitably the case when one confronts an uncharted area of investigation, we are more aware of what we do not know than what we do know. Although that is true of our study of mathematical precocity, we have learned a great deal.

Chapanis (1971) discusses several "levels of explanation" for behavioral data. We have begun to get a good grasp on the first level, which concerns practical applications. We have developed and will be refining adequate methods for identification of mathematically precocious youth, and our armamentarium of facilitative techniques is large and growing, as the following paper will demonstrate.

At the deeper level of basic understanding, however, we are still groping. We have some leads in the correlational data we have collected and some speculations about them. Fortunately, our ability to use new methods and approaches is frequently not limited by our understanding of the rules which underlie them.

## References

Allport, G.; Vernon, P. E.; and Lindzey, G. 1970. *Manual for the study of values* (3rd ed.), Boston: Houghton Mifflin.

Breland, H. M. 1972. Birth order, family configuration, and verbal achievement. *Research Bulletin*, Educational Testing Service. RB-72-47.

Chapanis, A. 1971. The search for relevance in applied research. In W. T. Singleton, J. G. Fox, and D. Whitfield (eds.). *Measurement of man at work*. London: Taylor and Francis Ltd.

Cox, C. M. 1926. *The early mental traits of three hundred geniuses*. Vol. 2 of *Genetic studies of genius*, ed. L. M. Terman. Stanford, Calif.: Stanford University Press.

Galton, F. 1889. *Natural inheritance*. New York: The MacMillan Co.

Gottesman, I. I. 1963. Genetic aspects of intelligent behavior. In N. Ellis (ed.), *Handbook of mental deficiency: Psychological theory and research*. New York: McGraw-Hill. Pp. 253-96.

Gough, H. G. 1964. *Manual for the California Psychological Inventory*. Palo Alto, Calif.: Consulting Psychologists Press.

Holland, J. L. 1965. *The Vocational Preference Inventory*. Palo Alto, Calif.: Consulting Psychologists Press.

————. 1970. *The self directed search*. Palo Alto, Calif.: Consulting Psychologists Press.

Huntley, C. W. 1965. Changes in Study of Values scores during the four years of college. *Genetic Psychology Monographs* 71: 349–83.

Keating, D. P. 1973. Discovering quatitative precocity. Unpublished paper.

————, and Stanley, J. C. 1972. Extreme measures for the exceptionally gifted in mathematics and science. *Educational Researcher* 1(9): 3–7.

Lehman, H. C. 1953. *Age and achievement*. Princeton, N.J.: Princeton University Press.

Lunneborg, P. W. 1971. Birth order and sex of sibling effects on intellectual abilities. *Journal of Consulting and Clinical Psychology* 37(3): 445.

MacKinnon, D. W. 1962. The nature and nurture of creative talent. *American Psychologist* 17(7): 484–95.

McCurdy, H. S. 1957. Childhood pattern of genius. *Journal of the Elisha Mitchell Scientific Society* 73: 448–62.

McGurk, H., and Lewis, M. 1972. Birth order: A phenomenon in search of an explanation. *Research Bulletin*. Educational Testing Service. RB-72-20.

Pressey, S. L. 1949. *Educational Acceleration: Appraisal and Basic Problems*. The Bureau of Educational Research Monographs, no. 31. Columbus: Ohio State University Press.

Terman, L. M., and Oden, M. H. 1947. *The gifted child grows up*. Vol. 4 of *Genetic studies of genius*, ed. L. M. Terman. Stanford, Calif.: Stanford University Press.

# III · facilitating educational development of mathematically precocious youth

## LYNN H. FOX

[Editors' Note: *The education which is available for gifted children should be everyone's concern, and it is clearly the driving force behind SMSPY. In this chapter many different ways of improving the education of gifted children are reviewed and evaluated on the basis of previous research as well as evidence from the current study. The motivating concern over the education of the gifted makes this the key chapter of this volume.*]

Discovering and meeting highly precocious youth is in itself fascinating and enlightening. However, the goal of our project is not limited to the identification and study of such gifted students. We are committed to a task which is perhaps even more challenging—that of trying to facilitate the educational development of these very talented young people.

What are the educational needs of highly mathematically and scientifically precocious junior-high-age youths? Suppose we consider the case of Roger. Roger's SAT verbal aptitude score was 620 and his mathematical aptitude score was 780. His scores on the CEEB math achievement tests I and II were 720 and 720 respectively. At present he thinks he might be interested in a career in the area of systems engineering.

With such excellent test scores Roger sounds like a prospective candidate for a first-rate university. However, Roger's school did not encourage him to go to college this year. In fact, they expected him to enter the ninth grade. Absurd? Why should Roger need to take ninth-grade courses when his College Board scores are those of a superior entering college freshman? Because Roger earned those scores while he was an eighth grader.

Let us consider this example more carefully. To what extent should one's place in the educational system be determined by chronological age and to what extent should it be determined by one's demonstrated level of knowledge? Suppose we ask the following four questions:

1. How likely is it that a *high school senior* with CEEB scores like Roger's would be successful at a first rate college?
2. What justification would there be for placing a high school senior with those test scores into the ninth grade?

3. How likely is it that Roger as a 13-year-old with those test scores would be a successful student at a superior college?
4. What justification would there be for placing 13-year-old Roger in the ninth grade?

In trying to answer these four questions we realize that we have only age and test scores to base our judgments on. As scientists we might think that it is not fair to ask us to make important decisions about the academic future of these able boys on such scanty information. Yet, in everyday practice there is usually only one additional consideration for educational placement and that is the grade point average in the course work at the preceding educational level.

If we posed these four questions to a group of traditional educators, the consensus of their answers might very likely be as follows:

1. A high-school senior with those high scores would have an excellent chance of being successful at a good university. Over the past 46 years of the existence of the SAT probably no other measures have shown a more useful relationship to the criterion of college achievement (Schrader 1971).
2. There is no logical justification for placing a high-school senior with excellent SAT scores in the ninth grade, and it is a foolish question.
3. Predicting the likelihood of college success for a 13-year-old with those test scores is an almost unprecedented question.
4. The justification for placing 13-year-old Roger in the ninth grade is that it is the normal thing to do for a 13-year-old eighth grader.

Thus, the first of our four questions is a typical one which educators face annually and for which they have precedents. The second question seems trivial. The third question is one that few educators have ever seriously pondered because rarely have such able youngsters been identified at such an early age. But once the educator accepts the principle of this question, it may cause him to reconsider his pat answer to question four.

By and large, educators are aware of the wide range of individual differences which occurs within an age-grade group. As early as 1911 educators such as Edward L. Thorndike protested against the uniformity of method which prevailed in the schools and failed to recognize individual differences. Terms such as *homogeneous grouping, acceleration, the track system,* and *individualized instruction* began to fill not only the professional education journals but newspapers and parent-teacher conferences as well. While countless studies have tried to analyze the advantages and disadvantages of these various procedures, the practical implementation of truly flexible and all-encompassing educational programs has not yet been realized.

Part of the reason that no specific program exists for such precocious, able youngsters as we are finding is that there are relatively few in any given school system and quite few or none in individual schools. While many schools have special programs for the upper 10 or 15 percent of their student body in terms of ability, the students we have identified are so different and special that even very large schools and school systems may have only one or two such youngsters in any given grade. They are approximately in the upper 1/2 of 1 percent of the student population in terms of mathematics ability and often in overall ability. It is not really surprising that no specific program has been designed for them.

Thus, when we were first faced with the question of how to facilitate the educational development of precocious youth, our task was three-fold. The first phase was to consider the effectiveness of current educational policies and practices in meeting the needs of these youths and also to look for new methods which might be tried. Our aim was to formulate several alternative plans which could be adapted to meet the needs of the ablest youngsters we had identified through our testing. The second step was to consider each student in turn to decide which of the several alternatives was apt to be the most appropriate for him and to make recommendations to the student and his parents. The third phase was to work with the student, his parents, and sometimes the schools to implement our recommendations.

## Exploring Educational Alternatives for the
## Intellectually Gifted

In the first phase—that of exploring alternative methods to facilitate the development of a flexible model for educational matriculation of the exceptionally gifted—we felt that the most important criterion would be the degree to which a program or method allowed a person to proceed as rapidly as his abilities and interest dictated. Clearly, the highly precocious youth we have identified to date have progressed to their present level of achievement largely by self-paced independent study. The key input needed had been encouragement and opportunity to study on their own. With this criterion in mind, let us briefly examine some of the educational programs and policies which are presently advocated and practiced.

## Homogeneous Grouping

Homogeneous grouping (sometimes called ability grouping, segregation, streaming, or multiple track curricula system) has long been advocated and used in our educational system. It consists of assembling students for instructional purposes who are somewhat nearer together in general capacity for learning. This is sometimes done for only special subject areas such as mathematics, but more typically a child will be placed in an advanced or general or remedial track which will be the same for all his classes. Usually, the top group is comprised of the upper 10 to 20 percent of the student population based on some general composite measure of intelligence.

For our highly precocious group this method seems inappropriate for three reasons. First, there are not enough such students in a given school to form a special track for them. These students comprise the upper 1 or 1/2 percent. Second, their abilities are not so highly developed in all subject matter areas that they should be labeled as generally superior and equally advanced in every subject. Third, unfortunately the curriculums for homogeneously grouped superior classes for seventh, eighth, and ninth grade are rarely advanced enough from the general courses to be at a proper level in subjects such as mathematics and science for the type of student with whom we are dealing. Homogeneous grouping as it is practiced now would not offer the opportunity for these precocious youths to work independently at their own rate.

## Special Schools for the Gifted

Analogous to homogeneous grouping is the idea of creation of special schools for the gifted. This seems impractical. Again, there are too few of these students in geographic proximity (except perhaps in very large urban areas) to make this feasible. If the school were organized according to the traditional model it would probably prove too costly to justify for such a small number of students. The type of school which might benefit the gifted would have to be one of radically different design, perhaps patterned along the lines of a "school without walls" concept.

## Enrichment

Probably the most widely accepted method of planning for the gifted is "enrichment" of the curriculum. However, articles advocating this approach rarely give concrete suggestions for how this can be accomplished. Too often the enrichment activity is left for the classroom teacher to devise. It is little wonder that in practice it results in a student who completes class work quickly and accurately merely being assigned more of the same work at the same level. One doubts that gifted students are very much challenged by such "busy work."

Other types of enrichment often consist of allowing the best students to take extra courses in music, art, or other special interest areas. Although probably valuable in itself, this is not the type of enrichment that many of these youngsters need. Many of the students have already developed a broad range of interests. The concept of enrichment for these students should be expanded to include the idea of increasing the depth of coverage and the degree of challenge of their work.

## Acceleration

Although grade-skipping is probably less common today than it was 60 years ago, there has never been any major case made for abandoning it. Indeed, a recent report to the Congress on education of the gifted by the U.S. Office of Education concluded that acceleration by one or more grades was a viable method of enhancing the educational development of academically gifted pupils. We, too, have concluded that grade-skipping can meet the needs of some of the least advanced of our precocious group and can be used in conjunction with other alternatives for the more highly advanced students. Grade-skipping might be particularly appropriate for capable students who are old-in-grade. Grade-skipping is subject to one of the major limitations of homogeneous grouping. Students are not usually equally advanced in all subject areas. While some of our precocious seventh- and eighth-grade students may be ready for twelfth-grade calculus, they may only be ready for tenth-grade English or social studies because their verbal abilities may not be as advanced as their quantitative talents. The solution to this dilemma seems to be to combine some grade-skipping with subject matter acceleration. Thus, an able eighth-grade student might skip the ninth grade and enter the tenth grade in a high school where he can substitute twelfth-grade calculus for his tenth-grade algebra II class.

The idea of subject matter acceleration is fairly straightforward. However, this concept seems to be missing from both the educational literature and educational practice. Since the usual objection to more than one year of acceleration (although not documented as a true problem) is the idea that students' social and emotional well-being may suffer from being placed in school with students who are chronologically older, it would appear that partial acceleration might serve to facilitate the educational development of highly precocious youths in those subject areas where they most need to be accelerated and not in those areas in which they are less ready for advanced work.

## Early Admission to College

Another major type of facilitation for academically gifted students which is now gaining a great deal of support across the country is early admission to college. It is of course not reasonable to suppose that very many students are ready to enter college at the end of the eighth grade or even earlier, as were those boys who have been described in one of the previous papers, but the fact that there are some is in itself important. Certainly, the concept of entering college at the end of the tenth or eleventh grade is not new. For several years this policy was practiced quite successfully under the sponsorship of the Ford Foundation. Today, several of the colleges, universities, and community colleges in the Baltimore area have some variation of an early admission program.

Early admission is an excellent method for the facilitation of the progress of highly precocious youths. This enables the student to telescope his educational experience and to save time toward earning an advanced degree. Certainly, college campuses offer these students an opportunity to find a considerable number of intellectual equals. The more advanced nature of the courses provides the needed challenge and stimulation to the student and often makes available to him courses not offered in the high school.

Although a few of the most precocious youths might be ready to enter college at the end of the eighth grade, most of the competition winners and near-winners need some bridging mechanisms to enable them to prepare for early admission to college. Some may need to stay in school only one or two years between the eighth grade and full-time admission to college.

## New Alternatives to Education of the Intellectually Gifted

We have already mentioned acceleration of one year or more and subject matter acceleration. Both of these are excellent bridging mechanisms between junior high school and college. Some youngsters might, for example, take advantage of both methods by skipping from eighth grade in a junior high school to the tenth grade in a high school. This would then enable him to take eleventh- or twelfth-grade math or science courses in the high school which would not have been available if he had remained in the ninth grade at a junior high.

Some junior high school students are so advanced in their knowledge and understanding of mathematics and science that they can do excellent work in college courses such as algebra, trigonometry, and computer science. Since college courses are usually quite fast-paced as compared with high school courses, they often prove to be an excellent supplement to the precocious youth's high school program. There are numerous advantages to this type of bridging mechanism. Not only do the courses provide rich sources of intellectual stimulation, but they seem ideally geared to the high achieving student's already developed learning pattern. The courses usually spend about one-fourth as many classroom hours as an equivalent high school class would on the same material. The student is encouraged to work independently and often quite rapidly and to use the college instructor and class as a resource for getting help with difficult problems and occasionally for more exciting theorizing. Not only do these able students quickly become adjusted to the college course format, but they also are able to earn double credit for their time in school. They accumulate college credits at the same time that they fulfill high school subject requirements. Students who remain in high school but also attend selected college courses during the summer, in the evening, or on released time from high school are able to have the intellectual stimulation of their college teachers and classes and still participate in social and athletic events with their age peers. Although at first mention this may seem to be an extreme measure, our experiences to date, which will be elaborated on a little later, have convinced us that this is a very satisfactory approach for many of our very ablest youngsters.

Some students do not live near enough to college campuses to be able to take college course work while still in secondary school. Many of these students could benefit from taking college correspondence courses. We have written to the major universities which offer correspondence work and have found that they are quite willing to offer these courses to qualified junior and senior high school students. A great advantage of such courses is that the student is able to pace himself and adjust the course work to his schedule more easily than in part-time college enrollment. Correspondence courses in a wide variety of subject areas are offered by such excellent universities such as Wisconsin and California.

Another innovative idea at the college level which could readily be adapted to meet the needs of our precocious youth is that of earning college credit by examination such as CLEP—the College Level Entrance Program. Students attending colleges which participate in this program could shorten their undergraduate college years by demonstrating their advanced standing in selected subjects.

A final bridging mechanism which might be used with some youngsters is simply to release them from their regular mathematics class and allow them to work independently. Perhaps tutors could be used or a small self-paced class outside of the regular school program could be formed which would allow the very bright child to master materials such as basic algebra I and algebra II very rapidly and mostly on his own; he would then be ready to enter the more advanced courses.

In summary, we feel that there are two major goals for the educational facilitation of highly mathematically and scientifically precocious youths. The first is to create ways to telescope the students' time in school, particularly promoting early admission to college. Second, individualization of the students' program is necessary. Many students will simply benefit from the opportunity to study independently; others will need more structured experiences. There are several alternative methods of bridging the student's education from junior high to college. These include grade-skipping, subject-matter advanced placement, taking college courses for credit either as part-time students or by correspondence, earning college credits by examination, independent study programs, and any combination of these. The best method for any given student will depend on several considerations. Table 3.1 summarizes our conclusions about the relationship of various methods of facilitation to educational objectives for the gifted.

## Educational Counseling for the Intellectually Gifted

Having thus decided on various appropriate alternatives for articulation of educational facilitation, we needed in the second phase to consider each of the thirty-five winners and near-winners and the eight highest scoring girls from our Mathematics and Science Competition and to make recommendations to them. As noted in chapter 2, the information about each student included scores on the SAT, both verbal and quantitative, math achievement I of the CEEB, Raven's Progressive Matrices (tests of abstract reasoning, sometimes considered a culture-fair type of intelligence test), the two forms of a college science

Table 3.1:  *The effectiveness of nine alternatives for the educational facilitation of extremely gifted youth in relation to six educational goals*

| Method of Facilitation | Goals[a] | | | | | |
|---|---|---|---|---|---|---|
| | 1 | 2 | 3 | 4 | 5 | 6 |
| Homogeneous grouping | − | − | − | − | ? | − |
| Special school | ? | ? | − | ? | ? | ? |
| Enrichment | − | − | + | − | − | − |
| Grade-skipping | + | − | + | − | ? | + |
| Advanced courses | + | ? | + | + | + | + |
| Independent study of textbook | + | + | + | + | − | + |
| College courses | + | + | + | + | + | + |
| College correspondence courses | + | + | + | + | − | + |
| College credit by examination | + | + | + | + | − | + |
| Early admission to college | + | + | + | + | + | + |

[a]Goal 1:  Opportunity for learning stimulating material.
Goal 2:  Opportunity for self-paced study.
Goal 3:  Practical for small number of students.
Goal 4:  Allows for individual differences.
Goal 5:  Allows for social involvement with both age and intellectual peers.
Goal 6:  Shortens number of years toward earning college degree.

*Key*
+   Indicates that the method of facilitation is believed to be effective for attaining the goal.

−   Indicates that the method of facilitation is believed not to be effective for attaining the goal.

?   Indicates that the relationship of that method of facilitation to the goal is not known or would depend on the specific characteristics of the situation.

test, the Bennett Mechanical Comprehension Test, and the Concept Mastery Test (a difficult test of verbal ability developed by Lewis Terman to study his group of gifted children when they reached adulthood), the California Psychological Inventory, the Allport-Vernon-Lindzey Study of Values, and a checklist of occupations consisting of six categories of the Vocational Preference Inventory (VPI). Because of the untimed nature of many of the tests administered to the high scorers on April 22, not all students took all of the tests at that time.

Table 3.2 shows some of the test data for seven of our forty-three cases. Let us reconstruct for this sample the decision-making process which was used to determine the recommendations for educational facilitation for all forty-three of the winners and near-winners of our mathematics and science competition. The key for table 3.2 briefly describes each of the tests and explains the letter scores for the Holland vocational inventory and the Allport-Vernon-Lindzey Study of Values.

Table 3.2: *Test score data for seven of the high scorers on Science Fair tests*

| Student | Grade | SAT-Verbal | SAT-Math | CEEB Math Achievement Level I | Raven's II | Science | CMT | VPI | AVLSV | Type of School |
|---|---|---|---|---|---|---|---|---|---|---|
| A | 8 | 460 | 740 | 630 | 33 | 38 | 39 | I | TER | Private |
| B | 8 | 530 | 550 | 470 | 33 | 66 | 49 | I | TAS | Public |
| C | 7 | 530 | 710 | 730 | 32 | 68 | 50 | I | TER | Public |
| D | 8 | 740 | 620 | 520 | 31 | 59 | 95 | I | T SR P | Public |
| E | 7 | 450 | 690 | 520 | 35 | 43 | 65 | I | SRA | Private |
| F | 8[1] | 310 | 660 | 600 | – | 39 | 38 | R | ETR | Priavte |
| G | 9[1] | 560 | 790 | 770 | 33 | 54 | 75 | I | TEA | Public |

[1] Already accelerated one year.

Key

*SAT-Verbal:* Scholastic Aptitude Test. Highest possible score is 800. Average score for high school senior boys is 390 and for typical SAT candidate is 463. (Educational Testing Service.)

*SAT-Math:* Scholastic Aptitude Test. Highest possible score is 800. Average score for high school boys is 422 and for SAT candidates 510. (Educational Testing Service.)

*CEEB Math Achievement (Level I):* Highest possible score is 800. A score of 600 is the 59th percentile for high school seniors who have at least seven semesters of mathematics. (Educational Testing Service.)

*Raven's II:* Raven's Progressive Matrices Advanced form. Highest possible score is 36. A score of 21 is the 95th percentile of 14 year olds. (Psychological Corporation.)

*Science:* Sequential Tests of Educational Progress, Form 1A. The highest possible score is 75. A score of 61 is the 99th percentile for high school seniors (Educational Testing Service).

*CMT:* Concept Mastery Test. A score of 55 is probably typical of graduates of state colleges. (Psychological Corporation.)

*VPI:* A checklist of occupations consisting of six categories of the Vocational Preference Inventory. The letters represent the category of jobs most often checked by the student. The categories are: I—investigative, R—realistic, C—conventional, A—artistic, E—enterprising, S—social. (Consulting Psychologists Press.)

*AVLSV:* Allport-Vernon-Lindzey Study of Values. The three letter combination represents the highest, second highest, and lowest of six values: A—aesthetic, E—economic, P—political, R—religious, S—social, T—theoretical. (Houghton Mifflin Company.)

### Case A

We see that student A has an extremely high SAT-Mathematical score (99th percentile of high school seniors) but only a relatively modest SAT-Verbal score (70th percentile for high school seniors). His relatively low verbal abilities are reconfirmed by his low score on the Concept Mastery Test. His Raven's Progressive Matrices score of 33 of 36 items indicates excellent reasoning ability. The fact that his math achievement score is 110 points lower than his aptitude score (69th percentile of high school seniors who have seven semesters or more of math) reflects the fact that he has had no formal instruction in algebra or higher mathematics. The mathematics he does know he has apparently taught himself by working the math puzzles in the *Scientific American* for the past three years. His interests are theoretical and investigative.

Case A's relatively low verbal score and lack of formal instruction in mathematics made it unlikely that he was ready for a college-level mathematics course. However, his high math aptitude, reasoning ability, and theoretical interest made it indeed seem plausible that he could do well in a beginning computer science course. A's parents should try to work with the school to see if A can begin studying more advanced courses in mathematics.

### Case B

While B's scores of 530 (84th percentile for high school seniors) and 550 (81st percentile for high school seniors) on V and M are probably as good as average entering freshmen at many state colleges, we did not recommend that B take any college-level courses at this time. We did suggest that B should take as much advanced math and science as could be arranged between now and the eleventh grade. B should definitely apply for early admission to college at the end of the eleventh grade.

### Case C

C's scores of 710 and 730 (99th percentiles for high school seniors) on the SAT-M and Math Achievement are particularly remarkable since he is only a seventh grader. C has been studying independently algebra, trigonometry, and geometry with the help of his father. Although his verbal scores are not extremely high, it seemed reasonable to recommend a college mathematics course for C during the summer. It was also suggested that C's parents try to work with the schools to let him continue independent study of mathematics and release him from the regular in-grade mathematics. C's knowledge of science is quite extensive. In our competition he won prizes for both the mathematics and science tests. It is certainly likely that C will be ready for full-time college admission in two to three years.

## Case D

D entered the science competition but not the mathematics one. Although he has high theoretical and investigative scores, he is not interested in mathematics. His verbal scores of 740 and 95 on the SAT-V and CMT are certainly spectacular for a 13-year-old eighth grader. We suggested that D will probably be ready for college in a year or two. We offered D the opportunity to take a college course in the summer in either computer science or astronomy.

## Case E

E is also a seventh grader, but he has not been doing the type of independent study in mathematics that C has done. Although E's scores are impressive for a seventh grader, he needs more basic mathematics such as algebra I. We suggested that E skip a grade and take advanced mathematics and science if possible. E will be eligible for our competition again this year. We will watch closely to see to what degree he can improve his scores.

## Case F

F's mathematics scores are excellent, but his verbal scores are disappointingly low. However, it should be realized that F has already skipped one year of school. His school (which is a private junior-senior combination) is already making special arrangements for him to take advanced mathematics and science. His parents already plan to have F apply for admission to college at the end of the eleventh grade. Therefore, the only recommendations we needed to make were suggestions for improving his verbal scores.

## Case G

G had already been accelerated one year and is in an advanced ninth-grade program at a local high school. G has learned most of his mathematics from independent study while in the seventh grade. G was referred to us prior to our science fair testing, and he was already taking a computer science course at Johns Hopkins that semester. His high SAT-M and Math Achievement scores confirmed what we already knew about him. We recommended that G take some college mathematics and science courses during the summer and plan on entering college in the fall or in the following year.

As you can see, we had no arbitrary cut-off score on which to base our decisions. We simply had to try to piece together a picture of the whole person and make an educated guess as to which of the alternative bridging mechanisms would be most appropriate. There is no real precedent for these types of decisions.

Of the 35 winners and near-winners (all boys) and eight girls tested on 22 April 1972, 24 were considered to have excellent enough profiles on the various test measures to suggest that they could do well in a college course during the summer. The very highest scorers were offered the chance to take a college algebra and trigonometry course at either Towson State College or The Johns Hopkins University. Others were offered the chance to take a computer science course or a science course at either Johns Hopkins or Towson State. Ten of these students decided to take courses. (It should be noted that some of the Mathematics and Science Competition winners were already known to us before the test, and two of these boys were enrolled at Johns Hopkins for a computer science course that spring semester.) The remaining 14 students declined the opportunity for various reasons: living too far away, vacation and camp plans already made for the summer, or simply not interested. We have been fortunate to date in finding financial help for students whose families cannot afford the tuition.

For the 19 students to whom no courses were offered, suggestions were made to parents to try to get their son or daughter into more advanced course work in math and science, to skip a grade if the students were old-in-grade, and in all cases to consider early admission to college at the end of the eleventh grade or even earlier.

Table 3.3 shows the means on the various tests broken down by the three groups: courses taken in the summer of 1972, courses offered but not taken, and courses not offered. Table 3.4 shows some other characteristics of the group, such as birth order, type of school attended, and education and professional backgrounds of parents. We see that the

Table 3.3: *Number and mean score for 43 winners and near-winners of mathematics competition*

| Test* Taken | Group Taking College Courses | | | | Group Offered but Declining College Courses | | | | Group Not Offered College Courses | | | |
|---|---|---|---|---|---|---|---|---|---|---|---|---|
| | Male | | Female | | Male | | Female | | Male | | Female | |
| | No. | Mean | No. | Mean | No. | Mean | No. | Mean | No. | Mean | No. | Mean |
| SAT-Verbal | 9 | 570 | 1 | 610 | 12 | 590 | 2 | 530 | 14 | 492 | 5 | 468 |
| SAT-Math | 9 | 701 | 1 | 600 | 12 | 671 | 2 | 555 | 14 | 626 | 4 | 558 |
| CEEB Math Achievement Level I | 9 | 630 | – | – | 11 | 609 | 2 | 510 | 13 | 525 | 3 | 477 |
| Science | 9 | 56 | 1 | 53 | 12 | 52 | 2 | 43 | 14 | 49 | 5 | 41 |
| CMT | 9 | 64 | 1 | 61 | 11 | 70 | 2 | 54 | 14 | 52 | 1 | 48 |
| Raven's ABCDE | 9 | 58 | 1 | 55 | 11 | 56 | 2 | 57 | 10 | 57 | 5 | 51 |
| Raven's II | 9 | 31 | 1 | 23 | 11 | 30 | 2 | 29 | 10 | 31 | 4 | 26 |
| MCT, AA | 8 | 46 | 1 | 35 | 10 | 38 | – | – | 13 | 41 | 4 | 29 |
| MCT, CC | 8 | 39 | 1 | 20 | 11 | 33 | – | – | 13 | 35 | 3 | 28 |

*Key

SAT-Verbal: Scholastic Aptitude Test-Verbal. Highest possible score is 800. Average scores for high school senior boys and girls are 390 and 393 respectively. Typical SAT candidates score 463 and 464 respectively. (Educational Testing Service.)

SAT-Math: Scholastic Aptitude Test-Mathematics. Highest possible score is 800. Average scores for high school senior boys and girls are 422 and 382 respectively. SAT candidates score 510 and 466 respectively. (Educational Testing Service.)

CEEB Mathematics Achievement (Level I): Highest possible score is 800. A score of 600 is the 59th percentile of high school seniors who have taken at least seven semesters of mathematics. (Educational Testing Service.)

Science: Sequential Tests of Educational Progress, Form 1A. The highest possible score is 75. A score of 61 is the 99th percentile for high school seniors tested in the spring. (Educational Testing Service.)

CMT: Concept Mastery Test. Few norms exist for this test. However, from Dr. Stanley's experience with the CMT, it seems likely that the average graduate of a state college would earn a total score of not more than 55 on it. (Psychological Corporation.)

Raven's ABCDE: Raven's Progressive Matrices Test. A test of nonverbal reasoning. The maximum score is 60. A score of 53 is the 95th percentile for 14 year olds. (Psychological Corporation.)

Raven's II: Raven's Progressive Matrices, the advanced adult form. The highest possible score is 36. A score of 21 is the 95th percentile for 14-year-olds. (Psychological Corporation.)

MCT, AA: Bennett's Mechanical Comprehension Test, Form AA. Highest possible score is 60. A score of 40 is the 20th percentile for engineering freshmen. (Psychological Corporation.)

MCT, CC: Bennett's Mechanical Comprehension Test, Form CC. Highest possible score is 60. A score of 37 is the 25th percentile for Princeton freshmen. (Psychological Corporation.)

61

Table 3.4: *Selected characteristics of the 43 winners and near-winners of the mathematics and science competitions*

| Groups of Students | No. | Father's Occupation | | College Education | | Birth Position | | Attending Public School |
|---|---|---|---|---|---|---|---|---|
| | | Professional | Business or Other | Both Parents | At Least One Parent | First Born or Only Child | Not First Born | |
| Total | 43 | 21 | 22 | 17 | 32 | 23 | 20 | 33 |
| College courses taken | 10 | 7 | 3 | 3 | 8 | 5 | 5 | 9 |
| College courses offered but declined | 14 | 8 | 6 | 9 | 11 | 9 | 5 | 10 |
| College courses not offered | 19 | 6 | 13 | 5 | 13 | 9 | 10 | 14 |

mean score is slightly higher for the group that took college courses than for the other two groups on the tests of quantitative ability, science knowledge, abstract reasoning, and mechanical comprehension. The Raven's is the one test which is not directly related to educational experience. We see that about three-fourths of the group had at least one parent who had graduated from college, and about four-tenths of the group had parents who both had graduated from college. About half of the group had fathers whose occupations would be considered professional. About three-fourths attended public school, and about half are first-born or only children.

## Implementing the New Alternatives

The third phase of our facilitation project was to aid parents and students in carrying out our recommendations. For those students for whom no course was recommended, we encouraged parents to take the various letters we had written to the students, reporting their test scores, to the school principal or guidance counselor. The school was told that they could contact us for further consultation if they desired. Meanwhile, the Baltimore County school system contacted us, and we have conducted a series of meetings with them. We have supplied them with the names of the various students in their school systems and our recommendations. They are making an effort to help us plan for these able youngsters. Most principals are delighted to learn of the talent that exists in their schools and are usually most anxious to cooperate with the parents. We suspect that there is a substantial relationship between the skill of the parents in dealing with the schools and the degree of cooperation they gain from school officials. Many parents were already aware of their child's great talent and had already established a good working relationship with someone at their child's school.

Since the most extreme measure we tried was to enroll students in college courses, let us examine the results of that effort. Table 3.5 summarizes the courses taken and grades earned for 14 students.

Three students who were referred to us prior to the test competition took the Introduction to Computer Science course at The Johns Hopkins University in the spring of 1972. All earned A's. Student 1 entered college as a full-time freshman the following fall. Student 2 is continuing in secondary school but supplements his program with college courses in mathematics. Student 3 was allowed to skip to the eleventh grade in his high school.

Ten of the winners and near-winners of the mathematics and science competition took courses during the summer. We were fairly confident

Table 3.5: *Educational progress report for students taking college courses during the 1972 calendar year*

| Student No. | Age at Time of Course | School | Course Taken | Semester | | | Grade Earned | Other Notes |
|---|---|---|---|---|---|---|---|---|
| | | | | Spring | Summer | Fall | | |
| 1 | 16 | JHU | Intro. to Computer Science | X | | | A | |
| | | JHU | Entered full-time | | | X | | |
| 2 | 13 | JHU | Intro. to Computer Science | X | | | A | Accelerated one year in school. Now in 9th grade. |
| | | JHU | College Algebra & Trig | | X | | B | |
| | | Goucher | Mathematical Analysis I | | | X | A | |
| 3 | 14 | JHU | Intro. to Computer Science | X | | | A | Accelerated two years. Now in 11th grade. |
| 4 | 15 | JHU | Intro. to Computer Science | | X | | A | Lives out of state during school year. Now in 10th grade. |
| | | Towson | Math I | | X | | A | |
| 5 | 14 | Towson | Math I | | X | | A | Accelerated to 10th grade. |
| | | Towson | Math II | | X | | B | |
| 6 | 13 | Towson | Math I ⎫ Taken concurrently | | X | | A | Accelerated to 9th grade. Now studying calculus. |
| | | Towson | Math II ⎭ | | X | | A | |

64

| | | | | | | |
|---|---|---|---|:-:|:-:|---|
| 7 | 14 | JHU | Intro. to Computer Science | X | | B | |
| 8 | 12 | JHU | Chemistry | X | | B | Accelerated to 9th grade. |
| 9 | 13 | JHU | Intro. to Computer Science | X | | A | |
| 10 | 14 | JHU | Intro. to Computer Science | X | | B | Accelerated. Now in 10th grade. |
| 11 | 14 | JHU | Intro. to Computer Science | X | | B | Accelerated to 10th grade. Participates in Sat. math class. |
| 12 | 16 | Towson | Math I | X | | B | |
| 13 | 14 | Towson | Math I | X | | A | Plans to enter JHU in the fall. |
| | | Towson | Math II | X | | A | |
| | | Towson | Computer Science | | X | A | |
| 14 | 14 | Towson | Math I | X | | A | Skipped to 10th grade. Plans to enter JHU in the fall. |
| | | Towson | Math II | X | | A | |
| | | JHU | Intro. to Computer Science | | X | B | |

that the students who took the computer science course would do very well. However, we were curious how well the four boys at Towson State College would do in college math. To gain an "unobtrusive measure" (Webb, Campbell, Schwartz, and Secherest 1966) we enrolled an undergraduate auditor in the course; he reported to us daily. A full report of this class is in chapter 9. Three of the four boys were eighth graders and of size and appearance as to make them not particularly noticeable. We did wonder if the teacher would notice and challenge the seventh grader, who we felt did look his age. In fact, the teacher did notice the young seventh grader quickly the first day of class, but it was not entirely because of his youthful appearance. His participation in class the first few days apparently so impressed her that she suggested that he should be in her more advanced class that met immediately afterward. Since he had not earned the necessary prerequisite credit for that course, it was decided that he should take the two courses simultaneously. He of course earned A's in both and was the most outstanding student in either class.

  We feel that we can safely conclude from our spring and summer experience that the high SAT scores earned by these bright junior-high-age students do indeed indicate that they are ready for college-level courses in mathematics and science. We see no reason why their age should keep them from having the challenging experiences of the college classroom, the opportunity for earning college credits while still in secondary school, or the chance to meet with other young people who are their intellectual peers.

  We are particularly delighted with the success of this method of facilitation. It is certainly a model for working with the highly gifted which could easily be adopted nationwide without requiring large costs or major changes to the educational system per se. It simply requires that these students be recognized while they are in the secondary schools and be allowed to combine a class schedule of high school and college courses.

  People often ask what effect taking college courses or entering college early has on the social and emotional development of these youngsters. We find no evidence that this experience is in any way harmful to these children. In fact, it seems to have definitely positive effects. We have taken this issue very seriously and do keep in close touch with the student and his parents. The reports we get from them are most encouraging. Students who previously have been unhappy in school because of the lack of challenge and have had vague feelings of uneasiness because they perceive themselves as somehow different from their peers now find that they are different in a positive way. They have increased enthusiasm for school and learning and life in general. Many of them are able to enjoy the best of both worlds by having friends who are intellectually their peers as well as friends who are age-mates for out-of-school activities.

## Individualizing Education

In conclusion, it is not enough for us to be simply awed by and appreciative of the amazing amount of precocity in mathematics and science which exists. We must ponder the question how to change our traditional educational system to accommodate these bright and able youth. Today our elementary and secondary schools do not provide the freedom necessary to exercise such exceptional individual talents. We must consider how to create a more flexible educational system in which individuals would be provided with the opportunities and encouragements needed for them to perform at their highest level and at their own rate.

At present we are strongly advocating only relatively small changes in the present educational system per se in order to accommodate these highly precocious youths. We recommend early admission to college, an idea which has been adopted in the past two years by a number of colleges in the Maryland area and throughout the United States. For some students we advocate advanced placement in selected courses within the high schools. While this is perhaps a new idea, it is not one to cause any real disruption to the ongoing system. It is simply a matter of scheduling. We advocate grade-skipping and opportunities for independent study, both of which are old-time terms in education but rarely practiced. And last, we recommend that able youngsters begin taking college courses for credit on a part-time basis whenever they are ready for them.

In order for a school system, either statewide or local, to have a flexible program for the gifted such as we have outlined, the minimum requirement would be a full-time educational psychologist who could properly identify the course of action best suited to the individual and make the necessary recommendations to parents and school personnel. This is really a small requirement for such great potential benefits to the individuals and the school system involved. It is probably the first educational program that has been suggested in a long time that would actually save the school system and the parents money. The school system is likely to save money because the children who are able to finish their high school program in fewer years will cost less money to educate. If the school spends $800 per pupil per year and a student cuts two years from his secondary schooling, the system saves $1600. If he finishes school at an early age and becomes self-supporting two years earlier, his parents actually save two years of his support. It seems almost too good to be true.

However, as long-term goals for a more flexible educational system, it is possible to conceive of major changes which would not only adjust for individual differences of the highly precocious but also better accommodate educational needs of all students. At a time when testing is coming under attack from several groups, we dare to take the unpopular side of the issue and support *more* testing, not less. What we abhor is not the testing itself but the current failure to use testing as a direct means to benefit most test-takers. What many students need is more testing and the necessary counseling services to help them interpret their test scores in terms of their educational needs and eventual career plans. Unfortunately, today few if any elementary or secondary schools have the necessary staff to conduct intensive testing and counseling programs which would aid students in understanding themselves and the relationships of their interests, personalities, and abilities. We hope that schools will eventually institute large-scale evaluation and counseling services along with flexible curricula which include many possible points of entry and types of instruction. Some attempts are being made to research the possibilities of "modular" organizations of curricula which would allow students to proceed through subject areas at their own speed and to skip certain sequences or acquire the prerequisites on their own. We applaud such exploratory research but caution that such radical changes to our educational system must be accompanied by adequate assessment and counseling services such as we have outlined.

The individualization of instruction is by no means a new idea for education, but it is far from being implemented in today's schools. We hope that we will soon see the rapid growth of awareness at all our educational levels of the need for dynamic educational processes which capitalize upon the uniqueness of individuals and their varying potentials for achievement instead of penalizing them for their inability to conform to some uniform standard of "normal" development.

# References

Keating, D. P., and Stanley, J. C. 1972. Extreme measures for the exceptionally gifted in mathematics and science. *Educational Researcher* 1(9): 3–7.

Marland, S. P., Jr. 1971. *Education of the gifted and talented.* Vol. 1: *Report to the Congress of the United States by the U.S. Commissioner of Education.* Washington, D.C.: U.S. Department of Health, Education, and Welfare.

Schrader, W. B. 1971. The predictive validity of College Board admissions tests. In W. H. Angoff (ed.), *The College Board admissions testing program: A technical report on research and development activities relating to the Scholastic Aptitude Test and Achievement Tests.* New York: College Entrance Examination Board.

Thorndike, E. L. 1911. *Individuality.* Cambridge, Mass.: The Riverside Press.

Webb, E. J.; Campbell, D. T.; Schwartz, R. D.; and Sechrest, L. 1966. *Unobtrusive measures: Nonreactive research in the social sciences.* Chicago: Rand McNally.

# IV · sex differences in mathematical and scientific precocity

## HELEN S. ASTIN

[Editors' Note: *The sex differences in mathematical and scientific precocity which were found in the first year of the study were both unexpected and disconcerting. Helen Astin, well known for her studies of women in science, was invited to look at our data from this perspective. She examines two samples: first, the junior high school students who have been discussed in chapters 2 and 3; second, a group of sixth graders in a special mathematics program which Fox examines in detail in chapter 6.*]

In the three previous chapters, Stanley, Keating, and Fox described the characteristics of the students in the sample of mathematically and scientifically precocious youth. Their aptitudes, values, occupational interests, likes and dislikes regarding school experiences, and some characteristics of their parents were examined and discussed. This paper deals specifically with sex differences in samples of exceptional sixth graders and junior high school students.

This study of sex differences dates back to findings from earlier studies of determinants of career choice and development of women (Astin 1968, Astin and Myint 1971). In those studies, the recurring and most intriguing finding was that career-oriented girls scored significantly higher in mathematical aptitude than girls with less interest in careers. These findings raised a number of interesting questions that required further inquiry. Are these girls somewhat "deviant," in that unlike their cohorts they score very high on math and, again unlike their female contemporaries, subsequently develop a strong career interest in professional and scientific occupations? Do they happen to be more independent, more autonomous, and thus more interested in problem-solving activities, which, in turn, facilitate their exceptional development in mathematical aptitude and achievement? What kinds of home and school experiences do these young girls have that contribute to their exceptional development in math?

The two studies on girls' career choices and development used two different age cohorts. The first study examined the career interests and the determinants of such interests of a group of girls between the ninth and twelfth grades. The second study looked at the determinants of career choice between the twelfth grade and five years after high school.

70

In both studies, high mathematical aptitude was the best predictor of career plans in the sciences, professions, and teaching as opposed to plans to be a homemaker or do office work. Therefore, one of the purposes of the present examination of sex differences in mathematical and scientific precocity is to provide information that could ultimately assist in the understanding of career choice and development of the subjects and of women in general.

A critical review of the research literature of the 1960s prepared and delivered by Eleanor Maccoby (Maccoby and Jacklin 1972) at the Invitational Conference of the Educational Testing Service in the fall of 1972 highlighted the following findings regarding sex differences on cognitive functioning:

1. Boys and girls do not differ systematically on measures of total or composite abilities—that is, IQ measures.
2. Girls tend to be superior on verbal abilities; boys, on spatial and math aptitudes.
3. These differences in aptitudes do not become significantly apparent until adolescence.
4. Studies of children's aptitudes prior to adolescence do not provide consistent results and do not demonstrate significant differences between sexes.
5. The only significant differences in aptitudes among younger children appear to exist in children of disadvantaged backgrounds. Studies with disadvantaged youngsters show the girls to excel on verbal as well as on mathematical aptitudes even prior to adolescence.
6. In general, of all three aptitudes (math, verbal, spatial), spatial relations emerge as one of the most consistent and strongly differentiating aptitudes between the sexes.
7. There is no difference in variability within sex up to age 11. However, after that age, the standard deviation for boys tends to be between 5 and 6 percent higher than that for girls.
8. Studies that have examined genetic components, hormonal influences, or differential brain development as possible determinants of differential cognitive functioning between the sexes are as yet inconclusive.
9. There are no definitive studies as yet that can demonstrate the relationship(s) between social pressures or aspects of socialization and specific patterns of abilities.

Nevertheless, a number of investigators adhere to the theory that the cognitive differences between the sexes are the result of differential cultural reinforcement over time, since the differential increases with age (Aiken 1970).

Elton and Rose (1967) reported that a masculine orientation appears to be related to high aptitude in math. In another study, differences in problem-solving aptitudes were found to be influenced by role identification: the more feminine men achieved lower scores in problem solving, whereas the more masculine women achieved higher scores than the more feminine women. Thus the investigator in this study concluded that the more an individual identifies with a masculine sex role the greater will be his or her problem-solving skill (Milton 1957).

A number of studies have also attempted to measure the influence of interests and attitudes toward mathematics on performance of problem-solving tasks. Carey (1958) reported a positive relationship existing between scores on the Attitude Scale of math interest that she devised and actual problem-solving behavior. Moreover, she found that men scored significantly higher on the Attitude Scale than women. However, when the women were exposed to discussions about their attitudes toward math, improvement in their subsequent problem-solving performance occurred.

Haven (1972) examined differences in the attitudes and interests of senior high school girls who were taking advanced math courses and those who were not. She also differentiated among those in the math courses who were planning to continue taking such courses and pursue mathematical and/or scientific careers. Haven reported that girls in advanced math courses take such courses because of their liking for math and their past success with it and because they see these courses as instrumental to their future educational and career plans.

In a longitudinal study of sex differences in mathematics achievement, Hilton and Berglund (1971) observed that significant differences appeared at the seventh-grade level and not at any of the earlier age levels. Moreover, these differences increased with each subsequent grade level, with variability within sex also increasing with age. Interest in math, a view about the usefulness of learning math, and related activities outside the classroom were important correlates of high achievement in math. Invariably, boys reported reading books on science and math and feeling that math would be useful in helping them to earn a living more frequently than did the girls. Boys also reported having an interest in math, whereas girls reported that math courses were boring. These findings prompted Hilton and Berglund to conclude that sex differences in mathematical achievement result primarily from sex-typed interest.

A number of factorial studies of mathematical ability (Blackwell 1940, Very 1967) have concluded that a different factorial structure exists for males and females. These studies indicate that math abilities in boys are more specific and more clearly outlined than they are in girls and that certain factors involved in the mathematical functioning of boys are different from those involved in the mathematical functioning of girls.

In brief, the research literature to date suggests the following: differences grow greater with age; there are different factorial configurations for boys and girls with respect to mathematical aptitudes; interests, values, and attitudes affect mathematical development and achievement; there appears to be some biological basis for these differences, not as yet clearly identified or understood; and the evidence appears to be more convincing in the direction of a cultural reinforcement of differences because of the relationship of these differences to age and sex-role identification.

## Results and Discussion

The data on sex differences in the present study were drawn from two sample populations. The reader should keep in mind that the present analysis depends on data collected for the purpose of identifying precocious youth and providing educational programs and experiences to enhance the development of specialized talent. Therefore, there are some limitations in the assessment of differences and in the identification of possible determinants of these differences. The first sample consists of seventh-, eighth-, and ninth-grade boys and girls who participated in a math and/or science contest during the March 4, 1972, assessment (396 students took math, 192 took science, and 138 of these took both math and science). The second sample draws data from a population of sixth-grade students. The proportions of seventh-, eighth-, and ninth-grade girls who took the various tests are presented in table 4.1.

The table presents the distribution of girls by grade and test taken for only seventh and eighth grade since there were very few students from the ninth grade who met the criterion of age for entering the competition—that is, not yet 14 years of age. There were only two ninth-grade boys who took math only, two who took math and science, and none who took science only. There was one girl who took math and science and one girl who took science only.

From the distribution of students from different grade levels who registered and took the tests for the contest, it appears that more students from the eighth grade than from the seventh registered to take either math or science or both. However, fewer eighth-grade girls registered to take the science test only. Girls appear either to lose interest in

mathematical talent

Table 4.1:   *Proportion of girls by grade and test taken*

|  | Seventh Grade | | Eighth Grade | |
| --- | --- | --- | --- | --- |
| Test Taken | Total N | % Girls | Total N | % Girls |
| Math only | 126 | 47 | 130 | 48 |
| Science only | 20 | 35 | 33 | 12 |
| Math and science | 41 | 44 | 94 | 34 |

science over time or to feel less confident about their ability in science. By the eighth grade only 12 percent of those who had taken science only were girls, compared with 35 percent in the seventh grade. Similarly, 34 percent of eighth-grade students in the science and math competition were girls, compared with 44 percent in the seventh grade. Table 4.2 lists the means and standard deviations of boys and girls on the different tests.

An inspection of table 4.2 indicates that there are significant differences in math aptitude between the sexes. Both seventh- and eighth-grade boys performed significantly better than girls on SAT-Math. This was not true, however, with respect to achievement scores on Math I among those who took math only. On the other hand, boys—whether seventh or eighth grade—who registered and took both math and science scored significantly higher than girls on SAT-Math, Math I, and science test scores.

In general, boys and girls who chose to take both science and math scored higher on math and on science than those who chose to take either math or science only. This outcome appears to indicate that students who decided to compete in both areas have in general more superior aptitudes than those who chose to compete in only one area.

It is interesting to note that boys in the eighth grade who took both tests achieved higher scores than did the seventh-grade boys who also took both tests. However, the pattern for girls was somewhat reversed. That is, eighth-grade girls who volunteered to take both math and science performed less well on the SAT-Math and science tests than did the seventh-grade girls. This was not the case for the eighth-grade girls who took either math or science. However, in both instances they did better than seventh-grade girls. Why did the older girls—who might see themselves as superior performers since they volunteered to take both tests—perform less well than expected? It is possible that, with age, girls become more anxious about competing. The work of Matina Horner (1972) on the achievement-related conflicts in women suggests that when girls have to perform and to achieve in the presence of boys

Table 4.2:   *Mean differences of boys and girls on mathematics and science aptitude tests*

| Test Taken | Test | Statistic | Seventh Grade | | Eighth Grade | |
|---|---|---|---|---|---|---|
| | | | Girls | Boys | Girls | Boys |
| Math only | SAT-M | N | 59 | 67 | 63 | 67 |
| | | Mean | 416 | 450* | 472 | 516* |
| | | S.D. | 71 | 104 | 76 | 100 |
| | M–I | Mean | 393 | 398 | 431 | 451* |
| | | S.D. | 46 | 63 | 48 | 76 |
| Math and science | SAT-M | N | 18 | 23 | 32 | 62 |
| | | Mean | 448 | 487* | 427 | 531* |
| | | S.D. | 86 | 100 | 104 | 109 |
| | M–I | Mean | 407 | 437* | 414 | 467* |
| | | S.D. | 58 | 86 | 52 | 86 |
| | Science 1A | Mean | 74 | 83* | 69 | 88* |
| | and 1B | S.D. | 13 | 19 | 16 | 21 |
| Science only | Science 1A | N | 7 | 13 | 4 | 29 |
| | and 1B | Mean | 65 | 66 | 69 | 80 |
| | | S.D. | 7 | 13 | 19 | 18 |

Note: The means and standard deviations for ninth graders are not reported because of the very small N's.

Means with asterisks (*) are significant at p<.05 level. The differences are calculated between boys and girls within grade levels.

they become more inhibited and thus do less well than one would expect on the basis of their past performance.

Not only do boys appear to achieve significantly higher scores than girls in both grades, but the mean discrepancies between boys and girls also increase with each higher grade. For example, the boys' mean on SAT-Math between the seventh and eighth grades increased by 66 points, while the girls' mean increased by 56 points. Boys' mean on Math I in the eighth grade was 53 points higher than the mean in the seventh grade, while the girls' difference between the two grades was 38 points. The girls' science mean increased by 4 points and that of the boys by 14 points.

Comparing the individual test scores of boys and girls, we find that of the 223 boys who took the SAT-Math, 50 (22 percent) scored at 600 or more; of the 173 girls who took the same test, only three (2 percent) achieved a score of 600. (A score of 600 represents the 89th percentile of high school seniors.) No girl scored above 600, whereas 19 percent of the boys scored over 600, with a top score of 790.

Of the 130 boys who took the science test, 23 (18 percent) scored 100 points or more on the total (Science 1A and 1B); and of the 62 girls, two (3 percent) scored similarly (100 and 103 points). That is, 13 percent of the high-scoring boys achieved scores higher than the two high-scoring girls. A score of 61 in one of the subsets is at the 99th percentile of high school seniors. There were only five girls among the top 64 performers. High-scoring girls tended to be older than high-scoring boys. Among the high-scoring girls, there were no seventh graders, and two of the girls were in the ninth grade. Among the high-scoring boys, nine were in the seventh grade.

Stanley and associates (Keating and Stanley 1972; also see chapters 1, 2, and 3) attribute the exceptionally high scores of these junior high school students to a great deal of outside-the-classroom learning, which they equate with precocity in these areas. That such outside-the-classroom learning activities in math and science do not characterize girls was reported earlier in the review of the research literature. And it was also mentioned that girls tend to do less well on competitive assignments, especially in the presence of boys. Moreover, the self-selection procedure used in identifying the sample of boys and girls might have contributed to some extent to the aptitude differentials obtained with this sample. Maccoby and Jacklin (1972) reported that "girls tend to underestimate their own intellectual abilities more than boys do." Thus, a sex bias may exist in self-selected groups. Even though this may explain, in part, the difference in the proportion of boys and girls with high math and science aptitude, it does not explain the magnitude of the score differences between the sexes.

## Differences in Occupational Interests and
## Background Characteristics

The 43 top-scoring boys and girls (35 boys and eight girls) on the math and science tests were retested with some other aptitude measures to ascertain general profiles of ability. Table 4.3, which lists the scores on SAT verbal and on Raven's Progressive Matrices—a testing of abstract thinking—indicates that differences between the sexes continue to emerge even when other types of aptitude measures are employed.

In addition to examining differences between sexes on aptitudes, the tests supplied information on occupational plans, liking for school, and family background to contribute to an understanding of how precocious children differ by sex in terms of their aspirations, school experiences, and family characteristics.

As was indicated previously (chapter 2), Holland's (1965) checklist was used. It affords information on each of the following six categories:

1. Realistic (airplane mechanic, electrician, etc.)

Table 4.3: *Mean differences on SAT Verbal and on Raven's Progressive Matrices for high-scoring boys and girls*

| Item | N | Mean | S.D. |
|---|---|---|---|
| SAT–Math | | | |
| Boys | 35 | 660 | 60 |
| Girls | 7 | 563 | 59 |
| SAT–Verbal | | | |
| Boys | 35 | 546 | 86 |
| Girls | 7 | 501 | 76 |
| Raven's Progressive Matrices | | | |
| Form A | | | |
| Boys | 22 | 58 | 2 |
| Girls | 8 | 53 | 4 |
| Form II | | | |
| Boys | 22 | 31 | 3 |
| Girls | 7 | 26 | 3 |

2. Investigative (chemist, scientific research worker, etc.)
3. Enterprising (buyer, real estate salesman, television producer, etc.).
4. Artistic (poet, cartoonist, etc.)
5. Social (social science teacher, vocational counselor, etc.)
6. Conventional (bookkeeper, bank teller, financial analyst, etc.)

Table 4.4 indicates the distribution of boys and girls by type of occupational interest for the different grade levels. Girls tended to choose artistic, investigative, and social types of occupations, whereas the boys tended to choose investigative, enterprising, and realistic occupations. The investigative interests were the ones expected for the total sample independent of sex, since these young people were self-selected on the basis of high math and science interests and aptitudes. The other two categories differentiate the sexes in expected sex-typed directions, i.e., artistic and social for girls, and enterprising and realistic for boys.

The student's first occupational preference was examined together with his or her score on the SAT-Math (see table 4.5), giving the following results: eighth- and ninth-grade boys with realistic and conventional interests had the highest means on SAT-Math; for eighth- and ninth-grade girls, the mean for those with conventional career interests was, like the boys, the highest one.

Since some earlier studies (Folger, Astin, and Bayer 1970; Astin 1968) suggest that brighter boys and girls shift from less demanding career plans into more challenging ones over time, it would be worthwhile to follow up these students to ascertain whether this finding holds true with them, as it has in the past with youngsters in general.

Table 4.4:  *First choice occupational interests of boys and girls by grade level*

(in percentages)

| Occupational Types | Seventh Grade | | Eighth and Ninth Grades | | Total Group | |
|---|---|---|---|---|---|---|
|  | Boys | Girls | Boys | Girls | Boys | Girls |
| Artistic | 12 | 38 | 10 | 28 | 10 | 32 |
| Conventional | 5 | 5 | 10 | 5 | 8 | 5 |
| Enterprising | 10 | 4 | 12 | 8 | 11 | 6 |
| Investigative | 55 | 30 | 53 | 35 | 54 | 33 |
| Realistic | 13 | 0 | 11 | 1 | 12 | 0 |
| Social | 5 | 22 | 4 | 24 | 4 | 23 |
| Total N | (121) | (94) | (203) | (130) | (324) | (224) |

## Liking for School

One of the questions on a short questionnaire administered to the subjects asked them to indicate their liking for school on a scale from very strong liking to positive dislike. Table 4.6 shows the distribution of boys and girls by grade level on this item. Not one girl admitted she disliked school, and more girls than boys admitted they liked school. Over time the proportion of boys who admitted a strong liking for school decreased, whereas a higher proportion of eighth- and ninth-grade girls indicated a stronger liking than did girls at the seventh-grade level.

One wonders whether girls become more passive and conforming over time, whereas boys, as they enter adolescence, become more disenchanted with school and even find the experience boring. Some other reasons may account for the changes and great discrepancies that are observed between boys and girls regarding liking of school as well.

Table 4.5:  *Occupational preferences by mean SAT-M scores*

| Occupational Types | Seventh Grade | | Eighth and Ninth Grades | | Total | |
|---|---|---|---|---|---|---|
|  | Boys | Girls | Boys | Girls | Boys | Girls |
| Artistic | 459 | 421 | 510 | 451 | 486 | 436 |
| Conventional | 522 | 394 | 544 | 483 | 538 | 443 |
| Enterprising | 400 | 367 | 470 | 450 | 447 | 426 |
| Investigative | 469 | 431 | 533 | 469 | 508 | 455 |
| Realistic | 446 | – | 557 | – | 505 | – |
| Social | 407 | 410 | 462 | 454 | 444 | 437 |

Table 4.6:   *Liking for school*

(in percentages)

| Item | Seventh Grade | | Eighth and Ninth Grades | |
|---|---|---|---|---|
| | Boys | Girls | Boys | Girls |
| Strong Liking | 31 | 34 | 26 | 38 |
| Fair Liking | 54 | 58 | 56 | 52 |
| Slight Liking | 14 | 9 | 16 | 10 |
| Dislike | 1 | 0 | 2 | 0 |
| Total N | (97) | (80) | (150) | (89) |

To assess how precocity might relate to liking for school, we examined the relationship between liking for school and performance on SAT-Math. Table 4.7 lists the means on SAT-Math for students by degree of liking for school. Dislike for school is positively related to the students' SAT means on mathematics, independent of sex. That is, the more precocious boys and girls are less pleased with their school experience. Since many schools are geared for the average learner, with minimum effort and time allowed for individualized learning experiences, it is not surprising that these extremely capable students find themselves less pleased with their schooling. Nevertheless, it should be remembered that, overall, about one-third of the seventh-grade boys and girls, over one-third of the eighth- and ninth-grade girls, and one-fourth of the eighth- and ninth-grade boys indicated a strong liking for school.

## Mothers' Working

In a study of the effects of childrearing practices on the development of cognitive abilities, Bing (1963) concluded that a marked pattern of

Table 4.7:   *Liking for school in relation to SAT-M*

| Item | Seventh Grade | | Eighth and Ninth Grades | | Total | |
|---|---|---|---|---|---|---|
| | Boys | Girls | Boys | Girls | Boys | Girls |
| Strong liking | 452 | 413 | 507 | 449 | 483 | 433 |
| Fair liking | 450 | 437 | 526 | 479 | 496 | 459 |
| Slight liking | 506 | 443 | 551 | 476 | 534 | 461 |
| Dislike | – | – | 707 | – | 707 | – |

help-seeking and help-giving, which characterizes a close relationship of the highly verbal child and mother, interferes with the development of the independence and self-reliance required for nonverbal abilities. Thus one might hypothesize that, if there is any relationship between autonomy and high aptitude in math or science, then the girls of working mothers, who have been left alone more and thus allowed to explore their environment more, might have developed greater autonomy. However, when this proposition was tested with the study sample, the SAT-M means were about the same for the girls with working and nonworking mothers. The proportions of working mothers were about equal in the two samples (male and female—38 and 36 percent, respectively). Some unanswered questions remain; for example, does a relationship exist between whether a mother does or does not work and the degree of math aptitude for girls in the general population, where there would be a much greater overall variability in math aptitude?

### Parental Education and Children's Aptitude

There is a direct relationship between parents' education and mean aptitude score on SAT-Math for both boys and girls in the sample. Mean SAT-Math for girls whose fathers have less than a high school education was 396; whereas for girls whose fathers have more than a college education, it was 484. Similarly, boys with fathers who have less than a high school education achieved a mean score of 447; but boys with college-plus educated fathers achieved a mean score of 547. The same relationships held true for mother's education and student's mean SAT-Math scores. The greater the education of the mother, the higher the mean score of the child, whether boy or girl.

Both parents of the boys were somewhat better educated than were the parents of the girls in this particular sample. For example, 51 percent of the boys' fathers and 29 percent of the mothers have at least a college degree; on the other hand, 46 percent of the girls' fathers and 23 percent of the girls' mothers have similar educations. Nevertheless, in general, the education of both parents in this group is much higher than that of the parents of a typical junior high school student.

### Personal and Family Characteristics of Exceptional
### Sixth-Grade Boys and Girls

This last section presents and discusses some additional sex similarities and differences of high aptitude sixth-grade boys and girls as observed and reported by their parents. As mentioned previously (chapter 2), 392 of 400 sixth-grade students (10 students recommended as highest in achievement from each of 40 Baltimore county elementary schools) were tested with the Academic Promise Test in the fall of 1971. Thirty of the students who scored at the 99th percentile on numerical ability and at the 99th percentile on abstract reasoning *or* verbal ability were invited to participate in a summer mathematics program. Nineteen accepted the invitation. The present analysis and discussion is based on information on 17[1] of these sixth-grade students, 11 boys and 6 girls. The parents of these children were asked to complete a set of rather extensive information sheets: one for the child in the study; one each for the child's siblings; one for each parent; and last, an inventory of honors and awards received by any blood relative. The questionnaire concerning the child included the following items:

1. Age of such activities as walking, talking, reading, etc.
2. Progress and interest in school.
3. Study habits and leisure time activities and interests.
4. Further educational and career expectations.
5. Rating(s) on various characteristics such as perserverance, intelligence, sympathy, tenderness, popularity, etc.

The information on siblings included similar items for comparison with the child in the study. Parental information included items on educational background, occupation(s), religion, and a checklist of factors seen as important to success in life.

The families of these exceptional youngsters could be described as typically middle-class American families. None of the 17 children were *only* children. Six of the boys were first-borns, but none of the girls. Boys tended to be among the oldest in relatively small families, whereas girls tended to be among the youngest in relatively large families. No girls came from two-child families, but four of the boys belonged to such families.

Regarding the age of different activities, such as talking, etc., the majority of both boys and girls walked at around 11 1/2 months and talked at around 13 1/2 to 14 months. The average reading age for both sexes was reported at about 5 1/2 years.

Regarding interest in math and science, parents reported only two of the six girls showed an interest and, compared with boys, the interest appeared at a somewhat later age. The two girls with strong interest in math showed it at ages 9 and 11, and the two girls with interest in science demonstrated it at 9 and 10 years.

Nine of the 11 boys showed an early and strong interest in math, with ages of onset ranging from 2 to 9. Similarly, early and strong interest in

---

[1]One of these students could not attend often enough and did not remain in the summer program, and information on one girl was not provided by the parents.

science was observed in 7 of the 11 boys, ranging from 2 to 10 years when the interest was first noticed by parents.

These children were described as healthy. The only frequently mentioned health problem was allergic conditions. Such allergies were reported for four of the 10 boys and three of the girls.

Four of the 11 boys and three of the girls were accelerated in school: one boy skipped the seventh grade; another boy attended the first grade for a month only and was moved to the second grade; a third boy skipped the third grade; the fourth boy was allowed to find his own pace and do independent work. All three girls did advanced work, although they remained in grade.

Most of the parents in describing their children's attitudes toward school said that they were enthusiastic and interested in school. However, the parents of two boys described them as being bored with school, and one of the girls was described as not being challenged in school.

The majority were described as beginning their homework enthusiastically and immediately after school; about one-half to two-thirds of the parents said that these youngsters tended to study lying down on the floor and listening to music. One wonders whether this is the typical style for doing schoolwork with most sixth graders, or whether this style is more characteristic of exceptional children—an ability to do two things at once—study and listen to music. I might add that, as we were reviewing the characteristics of these youngsters, the feeling of a need became greater for more data and information of the same kind on a random sample of sixth graders.

For both boys and girls the most frequent leisure activity was either reading or watching television. The boys were more likely to have scientific and mathematically related hobbies. In addition, the parents of boys tended to provide them with telescopes, microscopes, scientific kits, and so forth. Parents also indicated that both boys and girls had an interest in music.

Both boys and girls were rated by their parents as above average on all characteristics listed in the information sheet. Girls were rated in general somewhat higher on all traits than were boys, except for general intelligence, on which both sexes were rated similarly and very high.

Both boys and girls were also rated relatively high on conscientiousness, common sense, desire to know, originality, and desire to excel. Characteristics such as health, perserverance, and prudence were about average for this group. Leadership, popularity, and fondness for large groups were seen as their least likely traits.

There were some interesting differences between the boys and girls on these ratings. Girls were rated very high on sympathy and tenderness, whereas most boys were rated relatively low on these traits. More girls than boys were rated as conscientious and somewhat more social. However, parents tended to describe even the girls as more shy than their siblings.

In general, the parents perceive these children in positive terms. They are seen as reasonable and easier to get along with than some of their siblings. It is important to underline and completely recognize the fact that these children, although very exceptional with respect to aptitudes, are perceived and described by their parents as very pleasant, likable, and easy children. They usually enjoy school, and they have the study habits, leisure activities, and interests similar to those of the typical sixth grader. However, one ought to examine this proposition more systematically; my comments are prompted by mere observation, perhaps selective at times.

The majority of fathers of both boys and girls are college graduates. On the other hand, 50 percent of the mothers are only high school graduates. The boys' fathers are more likely to be professionals, whereas half of the girls' fathers are either in sales work or nonprofessional occupations. Three of the boys' mothers are teachers, but none of the girls' mothers. Both parents of both sexes indicated considerable interest of their own in math and science; and the youngsters' siblings were also described as having strong interests in math and science. In general, the educational and occupational backgrounds of these children's parents do not appear to be particularly unusual, except that there is considerable interest among parents as well as siblings in mathematics and scientific matters. This might account in part for this group's exceptional interests and talents in these areas.

Although the interest the parents showed in their children's school activities and progress, as reflected in visits with teachers and principals, is rather low, their encouragement and appreciation of their children's talents are quite apparent. However, in general the boys tend to be encouraged more often than the girls. Parents say that they provide more activities and stimuli for the boys—books, reference materials, puzzles, science kits—than for the girls. This might be accounted for in part by the somewhat lower occupational status achieved by the girls' fathers. When parents were asked to report what further educational plans were foreseen for their children, 10 of the boys' parents reported definite college plans for their children, but the parents of only one girl were certain of such plans.

The occupations that girls were likely to discuss with their parents were typically feminine—nurse, teacher, singer. On the other hand, boys talked of the sciences, engineering, research, and other prestige professions such as law and medicine. The interesting thing is that these parents, even though they perceive their girls as exceptionally bright and talented, do not seem either to have for their daughters or instill in them high educational and career aspirations. They accept the daughter's rather low aspiration, as compared with her aptitude, with little concern or discomfort.

On the basis of the ratings of factors that appear to account for success in life, the mothers of girls are somewhat more achievement-oriented than the fathers. However, both the mothers and fathers of the boys tend to be more achievement-oriented than the mothers of the girls. So it appears that the differences in values that exist among the parents of girls in the sample, as compared with the parents of the boys, might account for the fact that the parents of girls have lower expectations for them than do the parents of the boys.

In general, this group of 17 exceptional sixth-grade students appears to have been rather typical with respect to developmental tasks such as age of walking, talking, and reading. In general they like school, do their homework, and are easy to get along with. As one reads their parents' description of them, the only outstanding characteristic is the parents' overall superior rating of their children on personal qualities and characteristics. Their mothers tend to be, in general, more ambitious than their fathers. However, when these parents describe their interests and aspirations for their children, they do not appear to be particularly aggressive or to demand and expect extraordinary performance from them. The only distressing trend was the finding that the parents of girls have rather average or low expectations for their daughters, considering the fact that these girls are exceptional with respect to mathematical aptitudes.

### Summary and Implications

- Boys scored significantly higher than girls on tests of mathematical and scientific aptitude, and the discrepancies between boys and girls increased with age. Moreover, among all high scorers, girls were the oldest.
- Eighth-grade girls who took both science and math performed at a lower level than did the seventh-grade girls who took both tests. In addition, fewer eighth-grade girls than seventh-grade girls competed in science. Both findings suggest that girls may lose interest over time and also become somewhat uncomfortable about competing.
- Both boys and girls indicated interests in investigative careers. However, girls also tended to choose artistic and social types of

occupations, whereas boys more often indicated interests in enterprising and realistic kinds of occupations.

- More girls than boys indicated that they liked school. More older girls showed a liking for school, whereas fewer of the older boys indicated a liking for school.
- Both boys' and girls' parents represent middle- and upper middle-class backgrounds. However, the parents of the girls have somewhat less education than the parents of the boys.
- Precocious sixth-grade boys and girls tend to come from typical middle-class families in which the mother tends to be more ambitious and achievement-oriented than the father.
- Boys in the sample tend to be among the oldest children in their families and to come from smaller families, whereas the girls tend to be the youngest in large families.
- The boys are described as having shown interest and precocity in math and/or science at a much earlier age than the girls. However, parents of boys admit that they encouraged the boys more by giving them science kits, telescopes, microscopes, or other science-related gifts.
- Parents describe both boys and girls as very likable children. Girls tend to be rated higher on tenderness and sympathy. Girls are also rated higher than boys on conscientiousness and sociability.

## Some Research Questions and Directions

The above highlights of findings from our examination of sex differences suggest a further inquiry regarding the discrepancies in math and science performance between boys and girls. Do girls become less interested and place less value on such subjects as they get older? To what extent do increased heterosexual interests in adolescence interfere with the girls' interest and performance in math and science? Does anxiety and fear of success increase with age?

The size of family, sex of siblings, and birth order remain important variables in a study of mathematical and scientific interests and performance among girls. Do the younger girls in larger families show up as precocious; and if so, are they reared differently from the older girls in smaller families? To what extent does an ambitious mother influence her children's achievement, and does she expect and reinforce performance differently for her sons than for her daughters? How do personal autonomy and independence affect the development of mathematical aptitude and, in turn, the educational and career development of women?

These are just a few of the areas of inquiry that need to be further explored in order to assess the differential cognitive development and performance of boys and girls.

## References

Aiken, L. R. 1970. Attitudes toward mathematics. *Review of Educational Research* 40(4): 551–96.

Astin, H. S. 1968. Career development of girls during the high school years. *Journal of Counseling Psychology* 15(6): 536–40.

————. 1968. Stability and change in the career plans of ninth grade girls. *Personnel and Guidance Journal* 46(10): 961–66.

————, and Myint, T. 1971. Career development and stability of young women during the post high school years. *Journal of Counseling Psychology* 19(4): 369–94.

Bing, E. 1963. Effects of child rearing practices on development of differential cognitive abilities. *Child Development* 34: 631–48.

Blackwell, A. M. 1940. A comparative investigation into the factors involved in mathematical ability of boys and girls. *British Journal of Educational Psychology* 10: 143–53.

Carey, G. L. 1958. Sex differences in problem-solving performance as a function of attitude differences. *Journal of Abnormal and Social Psychology* 56: 256–60.

Elton, C. F., and Rose, H. A. 1967. Traditional sex attitudes and discrepant ability measures in college women. *Journal of Counseling Psychology* 14: 538–43.

Folger, J. K., Astin, H. S., Bayer, A. E. 1970. *Human Resources and Higher Education*. New York: Russell Sage Foundation.

Haven, E. W. 1972. *Factors Associated with the Selection of Advanced Academic Mathematics Courses by Girls in High School*. Research Bulletin 72-12. Princeton, N.J.: Educational Testing Service.

Hilton, T. L., and Berglund, G. W. 1971. *Sex Differences in Mathematics Achievement—a Longitudinal Study*. Research Bulletin 71-54. Princeton, N.J.: Educational Testing Service.

Holland, J. L. 1965. *The Vocational Preference Inventory*. Palo Alto, Calif.: Consulting Psychologists Press.

Horner, M. 1972. Toward an understanding of achievement-related conflicts in women. *The Journal of Social Issues* 28(2): 157–75.

Keating, D. P., and Stanley, J. C. 1972. Extreme measures for the exceptionally gifted in mathematics and science. *Educational Researcher* 1(9): 3–7.

Maccoby, E. E., and Jacklin, C. N. 1972. Sex differences in intellectual functioning. Paper presented at the ETS Invitational Conference on Testing Problems. New York City. Fall 1972.

Milton, G. A. 1957. The effects of sex-role identification upon problem-solving skill. *Journal of Abnormal and Social Psychology* 55: 208–12.

Very, P. S. 1967. Differential factor structures in mathematical ability. *Genetic Psychology Monographs* 75: 169–207.

# V · commentary on the precocity project

## ANNE ANASTASI

[Editors' Note: *Anne Anastasi, a distinguished differential psychologist, evaluates and synthesizes the contributions made by chapters 1 through 4. Her comments were delivered at the summation of the AAAS-Blumberg Symposium.*]

First I should like to underscore a point made by Stanley in his paper. The social value of any efforts to identify and cultivate outstanding talent should need no justification. Yet in the present humanitarian surge of interest in the mentally retarded, the brain-damaged, and the physically disabled, we may lose sight of society's continuing need for the talented. Remember that it is discoveries by talented researchers in biochemistry, neurology, psychology, and other sciences that underlie current improvements in the condition and functioning level of the handicapped. Good intentions without the requisite knowledge base are not enough. Society needs the maximum cultivation and utilization of human talent—wherever found and in all fields of human endeavor—in order to improve the quality of life for all of us.

## The Project in Historical Perspective

Research on precocious and gifted children has waxed and waned over the past fifty years. The twenties and early thirties ushered in the case studies of conspicuously precocious children by Leta Hollingworth (1926, 1942), as well as Terman's continuing longitudinal study of California school children with Stanford-Binet IQs of 140 or higher (Terman 1925; Terman and Oden 1959). On a somewhat smaller scale, Paul Witty (1930, 1940; Witty and Coomer 1955) contributed both group surveys and case studies. In this connection, we should also note the study of Negro children with Stanford-Binet IQs between 125 and 200 conducted by Witty and his doctoral student, Martin Jenkins, who later became president of Morgan State College (Witty and Jenkins 1936). These investigators, particularly Leta Hollingworth, also stimulated the establishment of special classes and even special schools for gifted children. Such educational experiments flourished for a couple of decades and then dwindled almost to the zero point. Their decline is attributable to a variety of reasons, some intrinsically sound and some irrelevant.

## The Criterion of Precocity

The present project differs from early research in at least two major ways that reflect intervening developments in psychology. First, the criterion for identifying the subjects has been modified in line with the accumulated findings of factor-analytic research on the organization of human abilities. Accordingly, the global "IQ" was replaced by indices of outstanding performance in particular areas of developed ability. These areas, moreover, correspond to some of the principal broad group factors identified by factor analysis, namely, mathematical ability in the present study and verbal ability in a parallel study begun by another group of Johns Hopkins psychologists.

The decision to apply these more clearly defined criteria is one that I heartily applaud. Any efforts to check the widespread misuse of the loose concept of "IQ" will advance psychometrics and benefit society. And here I am not referring to the IQ as a type of score. Especially in its modern version, i.e., the deviation IQ, it can be a perfectly respectable score on a specified test. After all, such an IQ is only a standard score— and what could be psychometrically more respectable than that! Nor am I referring to the use of such so-called intelligence tests as the Stanford-Binet and the Wechsler scales. In the hands of a trained clinician, these tests are useful instruments. What I object to is the use of the term "IQ" as though it referred to a property of the organism, as illustrated in the all-too-frequent question, "What is this child's IQ?" In this context, the IQ becomes dissociated from both a type of score and any particular test. It is this disembodied spook that I should like to see permanently exorcised. And I want to congratulate the investigators of the present project for moving us closer to that goal.

## Environmental Intervention

The second major innovation in the present project is its focus on intervention. To be sure, earlier investigators were also concerned with the educational implications of their research on gifted children, and several proceeded to recommend appropriate educational changes. But in the present project, the intervention program is an integral part of the study. To me, this shift in emphasis from mere identification and description of the precocious child to the cultivation of talent through environmental manipulation reflects the growing understanding of the operation of heredity and environment in behavioral development. It is now recognized that abilities as such do not lurk in genes, awaiting an opportunity to be released. Nor do abilities develop by maturation, according to which they would emerge as soon as the requisite stage of neurological or other physical development was reached.

### Some Needed Clarifications

In this connection, I should like to urge careful scrutiny of any statements pertaining to heredity and environment made in reporting the project, especially to the general public. Because the English language—like all natural human languages—carries a heavy load of ancient traditions and outworn concepts, it is difficult to avoid making statements that may be inconsistent with one's theoretical orientation. I stress this point because it is just these statements that are often quoted and create a misleading impression of what the investigator meant. The whole thrust of a study could thereby be distorted.

Let me give a few examples from the otherwise excellent papers in this volume. In Keating's paper, for instance, I find this statement: "Without becoming enmeshed in the 'nature-nurture' controversy, we may fairly say that these students' innate (i.e., genotypic) abilities, both general and specific, are well above average, and that the environment which nourished them provided the necessary interactions for their phenotypic expression (p. 23)." Conceptually, I do not know what is meant by an innate or genotypic ability. And empirically, I maintain we know nothing about the genotypic (or biochemical or neurological) basis of the behavioral characteristics we call abilities. Nor does the present project contribute any information about genotypes. A little further on we are told that the orientation of this study "does not contradict the possibility of latent talent of the sort which is ascribable to insufficient or inappropriate environmental stimulation, or to the confounding effects of personality or other factors which might prevent the manifestation of such talent (p. 24)." What is "latent talent"? Is it perhaps a biochemical characteristic that affects glandular development, which in turn affects attitudinal and motivational development, which in certain experiential contexts leads to the early development of a specified cognitive skill? If we use such terms and leave them undefined, the reader may project his own grotesque definitions into them.

In a different connection, I noted the statement, "Clearly, whether the aptitude *or* achievement tests are used to measure the ability of these students, the best of them are competitive with superior high school seniors" (p. 25). This refers to the fact that two different tests of developed mathematical ability were administered. I trust there is no intention to perpetuate the mythical distinction between aptitude and achievement tests—a distinction that not only is conceptually indefensible but also has been empirically disproved by many correlational studies.

## Characteristics of the Talented Subjects

### Ability Patterns

Turning now to the data collected thus far in the project, I should like to comment on a few of the reported characteristics of the talented subjects. The intraindividual variability from trait to trait found in the top group of 35 cases is noteworthy. There are two aspects to the profiles of these top-ranking students. First, on all the cognitive tests, covering numerical, verbal, spatial, mechanical, and perceptual functions, the selected subgroup of 35 cases averaged well above the norms for their age or school grade. Within this highly selected group, however, there was considerable differentiation of abilities; intercorrelations among the tests appear to be generally quite low. Such independence of functions is to be expected on the basis of the accumulated research on the organization of human abilities. These findings lend further support to the selection of subjects in terms of specific areas of excellence rather than in terms of a composite measure cutting across several traits.

The special role of verbal ability deserves further attention. There are several indications in the data that the high level of mathematical development identified in this study requires a certain minimum level of superiority in verbal ability. One suggested explanation is that mathematical precocity presupposes extensive self-instruction and that superior verbal ability facilitates such self-instruction. It should be noted, however, that verbal ability is also required for the ordinary formal classroom instruction in all subjects, including mathematics. Because verbal language—both oral and written—is our principal means of communication and cultural transmission, verbal aptitude tests have generally proved to be the best predictors of performance in most academic courses. This is probably one of the reasons why verbal aptitude plays such a large part in tests of so-called general intelligence. High-level achievement in almost any area, including even art and music, presupposes a minimum level of verbal development. In human civilizations, verbal ability is the key that opens many doors.

At the other extreme, mathematical talent in the absence of normal or superior verbal development presents the picture of the typical idiot savant. Such a person may perform spectacular feats of mathematical computation, but within a narrowly limited context and with little reference to either practical or theoretical implications. He lacks breadth even within his own sphere of competence. And not surprisingly, his mathematical talents may be accompanied by a Stanford-Binet IQ of 50 or 60—a score reflecting largely his deficient verbal development.

From another angle, Keating's paper raises some interesting questions about the verbal scores found in the intensive study of the top 35 subjects (pp. 38–44). These subjects, selected principally on the basis of their performance on SAT-M, obtained a mean score of 660 on this test; on SAT-V, their mean was 546, amounting to about .4 of a standard deviation lower in terms of national norms. As Keating explained, at least part of this difference is attributable to regression toward the mean. Such regression will of course occur on any test that is not perfectly correlated with the selection instrument. Parenthetically, I might add that it would be helpful to have an estimate, on the basis of the available data, of the amount of expected regression. We would thus have a better idea of the magnitude of residual difference that would have to be explained in other ways.

With regard to other hypotheses, Keating's suggestion that mathematics may be psychologically a "closed system" while verbal learning is more nearly "open-ended" is very appealing. Mathematical concepts and procedures can certainly be developed, without any necessary external reference, by building upon prior, more elementary learning. Verbal learning, on the other hand, has a clearly external reference. Much of verbal learning concerns information about external reality. The words themselves, of course, are arbitrary in any one language and usually cannot be deduced by the individual. Some amount of social interaction seems essential, although much of it can occur vicariously through books.

Even more to the point, however, is the nature of most verbal tests, such as vocabulary, opposites, and analogies. While testing word knowledge and, in some cases, verbal reasoning, these tests often sample a good deal of general information. The Miller Analogies Test, for example, uses the analogies format to test the students' familiarity with the content of basic college courses cutting across many fields. To a large extent, this is also true of other high-level verbal tests, such as the Concept Mastery Test. On this basis, it is quite understandable that precocious development may be considerably slower in the verbal than in the mathematical sphere. Verbal abilities, as commonly defined and measured, cover a broader and more varied territory than do mathematical abilities; and their development requires more external contacts than does the development of mathematical ability. The fact that nearly all the highly talented students scored higher on the analogies than on the vocabulary subtest of the Concept Mastery Test seems to fit in with the proposed explanation. On the analogies test, the ability to reason clearly and effectively from the given data would be an asset. In the vocabulary test, on the other hand, sheer range of general information plays a predominant role. It will be interesting to check some of these speculations against the findings of the new study on verbal precocity.

### Difficulty Level of Test Items

An observation made on one of the radical accelerates raises an intriguing question about the relative difficulty of test items (Keating and Stanley 1972, pp. 4–6). This student, who was admitted to college after completing the eighth grade, had obviously engaged in an unusual amount of independent study in both mathematics and physics. The curious observation regarding his test performance was a tendency to score better on the more difficult than on the easier forms of the tests. This is illustrated by a score of 772 on Level II of the CEEB mathematics achievement test and a score of 642 on the more elementary Level I. Similarly, he performed better on the more difficult form of the Bennett Mechanical Comprehension Test (Form CC) than on the easier form (BB). Also relevant is his performance on the quantitative section of the Graduate Record Examination, taken before and after a college course in advanced calculus. On this test his performance dropped from 800 to 720 from the first to the second administration.

Taken together, these findings suggest the possibility of efficient, individual work methods or cognitive strategies that this student may have developed during his years of independent study. The atypical and idiosyncratic preparation may have appreciably altered the relative difficulty of test items for him. This is the same phenomenon observed in studies which showed differences in difficulty level of Stanford-Binet items as determined from urban and rural samples (Jones, Conrad, and Blanchard 1932; Shimberg 1929). Similarly, the first time this student took the GRE, he may have been using efficient problem-solving techniques of his own devising; the second time he may have relied more on standard and more cumbersome procedures learned in class.

The difficulty level of test items does not reside in the items but in the subject's responses to the items; and such responses are likely to be influenced by the individual's experiential background. It would be interesting to carry out item analyses of standardized mathematics tests with groups of highly precocious students. Possible differences in problem-solving techniques could then be explored in the case of items having very deviant difficulty values for such a group.

### Attitude toward School

The responses to the question about liking for school, obtained from the entire sample of contest participants, also suggest some interesting hypotheses. The results show quite clearly that mean scores on all three screening tests (SAT-M, Math I, and Science) increase as liking for school decreases. Thus within this self-selected, moderately superior sample, the most highly talented were more likely to report a dislike for school. This finding is not at all surprising. It is, in fact, in line with the early observations of Leta Hollingworth, who proposed that, under prevailing educational and social conditions, IQs between 130 and 150 represent the optimum range for personal adjustment, leadership, and acceptance by one's associates, with the rewards and privileges that such acceptance entails. It should be noted that Leta Hollingworth was the author of a book of case studies entitled *Children above 180 IQ* (1942). She was thoroughly familiar with the variety of emotional difficulties developed by extreme deviates in average environments.

### Further Research

The staff of this project has access to a group of unusual individuals not readily available for psychological research. Because of the counseling and educational services provided to the subjects, moreover, the investigators can anticipate better rapport, more cooperation, and more ready contact with both children and parents than is the case in most projects. I would urge, therefore, that these investigators utilize their opportunities as fully as possible to learn all they can about the origins and development of superior mathematical talent and about its concomitant variables.

The published research on the California Psychological Inventory (CPI), for example, suggests several hypotheses that could be tested with this population. How do these students perform on such CPI scales as achievement-via-conformance and achievement-via-independence? What about their scores on self-acceptance? Harrison Gough (1964*a*, 1964*b*) provides regression equations for predicting high school and college grades from selected CPI scales. How do the mathematically talented subjects fare in such predictions?

Other tests could also be administered to round out the picture. The Adjective Check List (Gough and Heilbrun 1965), for instance, can easily be administered to high school students, takes little time to complete, and is machine scorable. Yet it yields scores in several traits that appear relevant to the present study. In an investigation recently completed at Fordham University with creative high school students in art, writing, and science, we found a number of highly significant differences between creative and matched control groups on ACL scales (Anastasi 1970*a*; Schaefer 1969). Among the scales that seem to be especially germane to the present project are those designated as measures of autonomy, self-confidence, and lability. The last-named scale is described in the test manual as pertaining to spontaneity, flexibility, need for change, rejection of convention, and assertive individuality. If time and available facilities permit, it might also be desirable to employ more elaborate, clinically oriented instruments, such as the Loevinger and Wessler (1970) sentence completion test to measure ego development. I would expect, for example, that the highly talented subjects would often have advanced beyond the conformity stage of ego development typical of school-age children and would be characterized by more reliance on inner standards of achievement and by acceptance of their own individuality.

Still another approach I should like to see pursued further is the intensive investigation of childrearing practices, psychological climate of the home, and critical antecedent experiences. Pertinent data could be gathered not only through biographical inventories but also, if possible, through home visits and intensive interviews with the subjects and their parents. Some suggestive data are cited by Astin from a questionnaire administered to a small sample of sixth-grade boys and girls participating in the summer program at Johns Hopkins (pp. 80–84). These data afford several tantalizing glimpses into conditions that may have contributed to the development of talent. For instance, there is the frequently reported interest in mathematics and science on the part of parents and siblings, the awards and honors for distinguished achievement received by relatives, and the parents' recognition and encouragement of their child's talent. Similarly, Fox (p. 101) cites several instances in which teachers played a key role in encouraging independent study by the pupil. It would be most enlightening to have more extensive and systematic information on such questions. Also relevant would be data on broader aspects of parent-child relations. To what extent do the parents encourage independence in the child? How much opportunity does the child have to pursue his own interests? How much privacy and freedom from intrusiveness is he permitted? To what extent is the household characterized by flexibility or rigidity? These and many other questions suggested by personality theory provide hypotheses about the origins and development of talent that could profitably be investigated in the present sample.

Many of these hypotheses could be tested by within-group comparison, either by correlating the particular variable with degree of talent or by comparing extreme deviates with the rest of the group, as has already been done in some of the data analyses. For greater clarity of interpretation, however, the use of a control group of more nearly normative individuals of the same age would be highly desirable.

## Sex Differences

### Exploration of Etiology

The types of inquiries I have proposed regarding childrearing practices and antecedent experiences are even more appropriate for the analysis of sex differences in the incidence of superior mathematical talent. The general finding that girls averaged lower than boys on the mathematics and science tests or that fewer girls than boys scored in the upper reaches of the total range is not at all surprising. It is certainly consistent with the published research accumulated over many decades. The important question is why such a sex difference occurs. There is certainly suggestive evidence in the present project, as in earlier studies, that parents and teachers do not encourage girls to study mathematics or science as much as they do boys; nor do they motivate girls to excel in such mathematics or science courses as they do take; and even less do they encourage them to pursue the independent study in such subjects required for the precocity identified in the present project. One concrete example from the present project, reported by Astin, is that parents give boys such gifts as microscopes, telescopes, science kits, and reference books more often than they give such presents to girls. Systematic comparative data on boys and girls with regard to childrearing practices and parental attitudes would throw much-needed light on the origins of sex differences in particular talents.

The attitudes, motivations, and expectancies that the subjects themselves internalize at an early age provide another rich source of hypotheses regarding the development of abilities. There is evidence in the published research that girls tend to avoid mathematics courses partly because they do not perceive such training as relevant to their anticipated vocational activities, thereby in turn reflecting the expectations inculcated by parents and other significant adults. Conversely, Astin, in some of her own earlier research, found high mathematical aptitude to be the best predictor of career plans in science, teaching, or other professions. Perhaps a full-scale investigation of what makes individual girls excel in mathematics may hold the key to understanding the dynamics of female psychological development in our culture. At least, such a study would represent a promising avenue of research into sex differences.

In addition to the exploration of environmental forces acting differentially upon the two sexes, further research is needed on the possible influence of attitudinal and motivational traits on the development of cognitive styles and problem-solving approaches, and indirectly on aptitude in such a field as mathematics. Astin has referred to some of the suggestive published findings on these relations. I hope additional data can be obtained on this developmental mechanism in the present project. It would be enlightening to know the correlation, among both boys and girls, between mathematical aptitude and such characteristics as sex-role identification and masculinity of interests. The femininity score on the CPI could be used for this purpose, among other indices. Other traits that could profitably be investigated in relation to mathematics aptitude within each sex include conformity, conventionality, and interest in abstract intellectual pursuits as opposed to practical, useful activities.

It should be noted that the present project, with its focus on mathematical precocity requiring independent study, augments the contribution of such typically masculine characteristics as independence, nonconformity, and unconventionality. In this connection, Astin found that liking for school was higher among the sixth-grade girls than among the sixth-grade boys in the project. It should be remembered, too, that the most talented boys in the principal group reported more *dislike* for school than did the rest of the contestants. These two findings taken together support the hypothesis of greater conformity among girls, who would consequently be less likely to engage in the independent study required for developmental acceleration.

## Organization of Abilities

Before leaving the topic of sex differences, let me comment on the factor-analytic research. Astin refers to such research as indicating, first, that mathematical abilities are more specific and more clearly outlined in boys than in girls and, second, that different factors may be involved in the performance of the same mathematical tasks by boys and girls (p. 73). Both of these points should be examined against the perspective of more general findings about the organization of abilities, of which sex differences represent only a special case.

It has been widely demonstrated that the higher the performance level in a given cognitive area, the greater the degree of factorial differentiation in that area (Anastasi 1970b). Such differentiation is manifested, first, by the emergence of a broad group factor such as verbal, numerical, spatial, or perceptual aptitude, which is clearly separated from any general factor such as Spearman's g. A second type of development is the formation of narrower group factors into which, for example, spatial or verbal aptitude may become further differentiated.

Studies of sex differences in particular have found greater differentiation of those abilities in which each sex typically excels. Thus girls excel on verbal tests and also show higher intercorrelations among verbal tests and lower correlations between verbal and other types of tests than do boys. In numerical and spatial tests, on the other hand, boys excel in mean scores and also exhibit more evidence of trait differentiation. Some investigations provide evidence of further differentiation within these areas. In a study of primary school children, two verbal factors were required to account for the test performance of girls, while a single verbal factor was sufficient for the boys (Lindsey 1966). Similarly, an investigation of high school students identified three spatial visualization factors among boys and only one among girls (Very 1967).

The important point to note is that the same tendency toward greater differentiation with increase in performance level has been found in relation to several variables other than sex. These include: age, from early childhood to adolescence; educational level; different educational programs with varying emphasis on abstract academic instruction and practical, mechanical, or spatial training; and socioeconomic level. Investigators who have classified their subjects more directly on the basis of level of test performance find the same relationship with degree of trait differentiation (Anastasi 1970b). There is even a psychopharmacological experiment showing that the lowering of performance level by such agents as LSD or alcohol was accompanied by a dedifferentiation of the factor structure (Lienert 1964).

The same kind of generality characterizes Astin's second point, namely, that the factorial composition of the same test may be different for boys and girls. Such a difference is probably associated with differences in work methods, problem-solving styles, and cognitive strategies. In general, individuals tend to utilize their best developed abilities in performing a task. Hence the same problem may be solved in verbal terms by one person and in mathematical terms by another. Or one person may carry out a given task by applying verbal rules, another by relying on his spatial orientation. We could speculate in this connection that the individual who relies chiefly on what has been taught through formal instruction is more likely to utilize verbal solutions. This too has implications for sex differences. Whatever the reason for these differences, however, there is some highly suggestive evidence that the factorial composition of tests reflects cognitive strategies and other stylistic variables (French 1965; Frederiksen 1969).

## The Intervention Program

In closing, let me add some random thoughts about the project's intervention program. With regard to the time-worn argument about acceleration versus enrichment, I should just like to comment that enrichment is a state of mind, a set of interrelated attitudes, a network of behavior tendencies that should be established early but which should continue throughout life. You cannot properly enrich a person's education while he is in school because much of the knowledge he will need as an intellectually enriched adult has not yet been generated. Culture is advancing too fast and knowledge is being developed too rapidly to permit the formal education of children and adolescents to "produce" well-educated adults.

One feature of the intervention program that I vigorously applaud is its deliberate and explicit recognition of individual differences among the highly talented pupils. Unlike most previous efforts at special education for the gifted, there is no recommendation for the establishment of special classes, special schools, or even special programs for the telescoping of high school, college, and graduate education. Instead, the educational counseling and the implementation programs are individually tailored to each pupil in terms of his unique ability pattern, past history, interests, emotional maturity, motivation, and even his geographical circumstances—a picture that should truly gladden the heart of any differential psychologist!

Finally, may I describe my perception of the basic design of the project. As I see it, a major goal of the program is to "test the limits" of effective developmental acceleration of mathematical ability. This objective is exemplified both in the selection procedures and in the intervention program. For instance, several specific procedures can be expected to increase the student's motivation to advance in mathematics, further stimulate his interests in this area, and promote an esprit de corps and sense of identification with the talented group. The project newsletter is an example of such a technique. The close personal contacts with the project staff are another. The awarding of prizes and commendations is still another. Parenthetically, I might note that in our comparative study at Fordham of creative high school students and control subjects, one of the most highly differentiating biographical items was the record of earlier prizes and awards. Psychologically, this makes good sense: positive reinforcement is a well-established principle of operant conditioning.

It might be argued that these relatively subtle influences brought to bear upon the project sample introduce a Hawthorne effect and a self-fulfilling prophecy. If the purpose were simply to evaluate the relative effectiveness of specific educational programs in facilitating mathematical development, such a criticism would be germane. But as I perceive the program, it represents a global effort to see how much can be accomplished by carefully planned, individualized programs designed by imaginative and dedicated researchers.

### References

Anastasi, A. 1970a. Correlates of creativity in children from two socioeconomic levels. Final Report, Center for Urban Education Subcontract No. 2 (Contract OEC-1-7-062868-3060).

_____. 1970b. On the formation of psychological traits. *American Psychologist* 25: 899–910.

Frederiksen, C. H. 1969. Abilities, transfer, and information retrieval in verbal learning. *Multivariate Behavioral Research Monographs.* No. 69–2.

French, J. W. 1965. The relationship of problem-solving styles to the factor composition of tests. *Educational and Psychological Measurement* 25: 9–28.

Gough, H. G. 1964a. Academic achievement in high school as predicted from the California Psychological Inventory. *Journal of Educational Psychology* 55: 174–180.

────. 1964*b*. Achievement in the first course in psychology as predicted from the California Psychological Inventory. *Journal of Psychology* 57: 419–30.

────, and Heilbrun, A. B., Jr. 1965. *The Adjective Check List manual.* Palo Alto, Calif.: Consulting Psychologists Press.

Hollingworth, L. S. 1926. *Gifted children: their nature and nurture.* New York: Macmillan.

────. 1942. *Children above 180 IQ.* New York: World Book Co.

Jones, H. E.; Conrad, H. S.; and Blanchard, M. B. 1932. Environmental handicap in mental test performance. *University of California Publications in Psychology* 5(3): 63–99.

Keating, D. P., and Stanley, J. C. 1972. From eighth grade to selective college in one jump: Case studies in radical acceleration. Paper presented at the meeting of the American Educational Research Association, Chicago, April 1972.

Lienert, G. A. 1964. *Belastung und Regression: Versuch einer Theorie der systematischen Beeinträchtigung der intellektuellen Leistungsfähigkeit.* Meisenheim am Glan: Hain.

Lindsey, J. M. 1966. The factorial organization of intelligence in children as related to the variables of age, sex, and subculture. Doctoral dissertation, University of Georgia. Ann Arbor, Mich.: University Microfilms. No. 67–3567.

Loevinger, J., and Wessler, R. 1970. *Measuring ego development.* 2 vols. San Francisco: Jossey-Bass.

Schaefer, C. E. 1969. The self-concept of creative adolescents. *Journal of Psychology* 72: 233–42.

Shimberg, M. E. 1929. An investigation into the validity of norms with special reference to urban and rural groups. *Archives of Psychology* No. 104.

Terman, L. M., 1925. *Mental and physical traits of a thousand gifted children.* Stanford, Calif.: Stanford University Press.

────, and Oden, M. H. 1959. *The gifted group at mid-life.* Stanford, Calif.: Stanford University Press.

Very, P. S. 1967. Differential factor structures in mathematical ability. *Genetic Psychology Monographs* 75: 169–207.

Witty, P. 1930. A study of one hundred gifted children. *Kansas State Teachers College Studies in Education.* 1(13).

────. 1940. A genetic study of fifty gifted children. *Thirty-Ninth Yearbook, National Society for the Study of Education.* Part II. Pp. 401–09.

────, and Coomer, A. 1955. A case study of gifted twin boys. *Exceptional Children* 22: 104–108, 124–25.

────, and Jenkins, M. D. 1936. Intra-race testing and Negro intelligence. *Journal of Psychology* 1: 179–92.

# VI · a mathematics program for fostering precocious achievement

## LYNN H. FOX

[Editors' Note: *This chapter is the first of four written especially for this volume. It reports the results of the first program directly run by the Study for Mathematically Precocious Youth. Some of the material was originally included in chapter 3, but the editors decided that the results were significant enough for a more complete reporting in a separate chapter.*]

One of the interesting findings of our study of the high scorers on the 1972 mathematics competition was that many of these students had learned a great deal of mathematics at a rapid rate by diligent independent study. Indeed, several of the winners and the first radical accelerate student at Johns Hopkins University had at one time attended the same city junior high school and studied under the same mathematics teacher, who had allowed them as seventh graders—in fact, motivated them—to work as rapidly as they could through algebra I, algebra II, geometry, and trigonometry books on their own. The teacher provided encouragement but no formal instruction except when the student approached him for help with a difficult concept or problem. In other words, the teacher created a self-paced, independent study program for the ablest members of the class. Students who had the right combination of aptitude and interest were able to make extremely fast progress through the textbooks. Some of our contest winners who had not attended that particular school gave reports of similar encouragement from either parents or teachers.

Thus, to foster precocious achievement in mathematics, it would seem desirable to take students with high mathematical aptitude and place them in a situation where they are encouraged simply to study mathematics as fast as their ability and interest allow. The optimal situation would provide encouragement plus opportunity. It also seems likely that the ideal time for the opportunity and encouragement to be provided would be at the end of the sixth grade or during the seventh grade when students change from the elementary school setting to junior high school and before they have had much formal instruction in mathematics beyond arithmetic. It is at about this age level that students (particularly very bright ones) are presumed to be capable of more abstract thought and moving into what Piaget terms the "stage of formal operations" (Inhelder and Piaget 1958).

Since the formula for precocious achievement in mathematics (i.e., aptitude plus encouragement plus opportunity) seemed simple and straightforward, we decided to see how well it could work. We decided to conduct a pilot study to explore the question of how much mathematics able junior high students could learn well at a high level in just one year. Our plan was to test the possibility of fostering high-level achievement in mathematics by creating a special accelerated mathematics program for able students in Baltimore County, most of whom had just completed the sixth grade.

## The Nature of the Program

Our first step was to decide upon the nature of the program. We met with Paul Binder, the outstanding Baltimore City junior high school mathematics teacher who had taught the first radical accelerate and several of our contest winners (see chapter 1), to plan a strategy for the creation of the situation of encouragement plus opportunity. Binder enthusiastically volunteered his services and that of a friend, Joseph Wolfson, to conduct the special program for two hours each week on Saturday mornings for the period from 24 June 1972 to 28 July 1973. It was planned that algebra I would be studied during the summer. Those students who made excellent progress in algebra I would then continue in the program during the school year to study algebra II, trigonometry, and plane and analytic geometry. We received a great deal of cooperation from Baltimore County Public School System officials.[1] They agreed to give the students credit for the mathematics they studied in our program and to release them from their regular mathematics classes.

Thus, our criterion for precocious achievement was the learning of algebra I, algebra II, trigonometry, and plane and analytic geometry in one year with standardized achievement test scores in these subjects well above the median for the appropriate national norm groups. The first goal was to be the learning of algebra I in 12 weeks or less by attending Saturday morning classes for two hours each week.

## The Selection of Students for the Program

The next step was to identify sixth-grade students who had high mathematics aptitude and would be likely to benefit from the program.

[1]Especially Benjamin Ebersole, director of curriculum and instruction, Vincent Brant, mathematics supervisor, and Helen Hale, science supervisor.

Three able students who had just completed the sixth grade, one former third-grade boy,[2] and one former eighth-grade boy had been referred to us earlier in the year by teachers or parents who had heard about our work with junior high school students. Therefore, we already knew the names of five students who were likely to benefit from such a program. In addition, we had the results of the testing of 392 sixth-grade students who had been nominated as "gifted." The nominations were made by principals and/or teachers in each of 40 elementary schools in Baltimore County. It was suggested to those making the nominations that scores on standardized tests the students had already taken be used in making the selections; however, they were free to use any method of selection they wished. These students were tested in groups of ten at each of the 40 schools. The test used was the Academic Promise Test (APT),[3] which consists of four subtests: verbal, number (arithmetic), abstract (nonverbal) reasoning, and language usage. The first three of the four subtests seemed relevant for setting the criterion for high mathematics aptitude. Thus, students were selected who scored at the 99th percentile of sixth-grade norms on number and either one of the other two subtests—abstract reasoning or verbal.

### The Summer Study of Algebra I

We invited those 30 students (boys and girls) who met the test-score requirements to participate in the program. No other criteria were used. We knew nothing about their interest in mathematics, parents' education, or grades earned in school. The initial invitation specified only the participation in a 12-week summer class to study algebra I. The letter clearly stated that a great deal of independent study would be required and that the subject matter would probably be more difficult than the enrollee's previous school work.

Fourteen boys and seven girls accepted the challenge and enrolled for the course. Most of the students missed some of the class sessions because of vacations and summer camp. Two boys dropped the course in the first few weeks because they were unable to attend often enough to keep up with the class. Those who remained in the program attended between 10 and 18 hours of class instruction during the first nine weeks.

---

[2]Though only 9 years old, this boy is extremely bright (IQ near 200) and interested in mathematics; so we invited him to join the class.
[3]Published by The Psychological Corporation, New York, New York.

## Evaluating the Students' Progress in Algebra I

At the end of the first nine weeks Form A of the algebra I test from the Cooperative Achievement Tests,[4] Mathematics series was administered to 19 students in the class. The 15 students who scored well on the algebra test were invited to continue in the Saturday morning program during the coming 1972–73 school year to study algebra II, trigonometry, plane geometry, and analytic geometry. The four students who were considered not to have mastered the algebra I material were not invited to continue the course and were encouraged to enroll in algebra I in the seventh grade. One girl who was doing fairly satisfactory work decided not to continue with the program, probably because her best friend scored relatively low and did not continue in the class, and one of the lower scoring boys dropped out. Thus the class size was reduced to 13 of the 19 students who had taken the algebra I test after the first nine weeks.

Ten students who had not participated in the first nine weeks of the algebra class were then tested on their knowledge of algebra I. Three of these students (two former seventh graders and a former sixth grader) joined the class to begin the study of algebra II. This increased the class size to 16.

Table 6.1 shows scores on the standardized algebra test for the 19 students who participated in the algebra I class and the three students who later joined the class for algebra II. Included in the table are the students' scores on the three subtests of the APT which were used for selection. Table 6.1 also shows the students' scores on a college-level test, School and College Ability Test (SCAT),[5] Form 1C, of verbal and mathematical aptitude.

Of the nineteen students who attended between five and nine two-hour algebra classes on Saturday mornings, 13 learned algebra so well that they scored at or above the 79th percentile of national norms for ninth graders on the standardized algebra I test. Of the three late entrants to the class, two (who had completed the seventh grade) scored high on the test, 38 and 31. One former sixth grader scored lower (18) but was judged to have the ability and motivation needed to succeed in the special class.

Those who remained in the class to study algebra II were retested on another form of the same algebra I test in the fall. All scored above the 75th percentile for ninth graders nationally, and all but four scored above the 75th percentile for eighth graders. (Students who take algebra in the eighth grade usually comprise a very highly selected group, and

[4]Published by Educational Testing Service, Princeton, New Jersey.
[5]Ibid.

Table 6.1:  *Scores on a test of algebra, three subtests of the APT, and a college level test, SCAT, for students in the Saturday mathematics class*

| Student | Algebra I, Form A | | Academic Promise Test | | | SCAT | |
| | Score | Percentile 9th grade norms | Verbal | Numerical | Abstract Reasoning | Verbal | Quanti-tative |
|---|---|---|---|---|---|---|---|
| 1[a,b] | 38 | 99 | – | – | – | 43 | 42 |
| 2[a,c] | 37 | 99 | – | – | – | 44 | 45 |
| 3 | 35 | 97 | 43 | 56 | 47 | 30 | 42 |
| 4[d] | 35 | 97 | 42 | 45 | 51 | 29 | 36 |
| 5[a] | 34 | 96 | 56 | 43 | 45 | 49 | 33 |
| 6[a] | 33 | 96 | 53 | 58 | 46 | 35 | 38 |
| 7[a] | 32 | 93 | 45 | 51 | 55 | 20 | 32 |
| 8[e,a] | 32 | 93 | 41 | 34 | 51 | 13 | 26 |
| 9[a,b,d] | 31 | 89 | – | – | – | 25 | 38 |
| 10[d] | 31 | 89 | 52 | 42 | 52 | 30 | 31 |
| 11[d] | 30 | 89 | 52 | 47 | 51 | 36 | 36 |
| 12 | 30 | 89 | 45 | 50 | 49 | 23 | 37 |
| 13[d] | 29 | 87 | 45 | 45 | 50 | 25 | 32 |
| 14[f,d] | 27 | 79 | 45 | 51 | 55 | 31 | 33 |
| 15[d] | 27 | 79 | 42 | 40 | 52 | 28 | 31 |
| 16 | 24 | 60 | 43 | 44 | 50 | 22 | 36 |
| 17[f] | 23 | 60 | 44 | 47 | 49 | 16 | 31 |
| 18[f] | 20 | 42 | 36 | 45 | 51 | 9 | 38 |
| 19[f] | 19 | 36 | 38 | 46 | 51 | 16 | 28 |
| 20[f] | 18 | 27 | 48 | 58 | 55 | 30 | 47 |
| 21[b,d] | 18 | 27 | 46 | 44 | 42 | 34 | 24 |
| 22[f,d] | 15 | 15 | 34 | 41 | 51 | 15 | 31 |

[a]Math competition winner in 1972 or special referral.
[b]Late entrants to whom test administered before entering class.
[c]Had studied algebra I in school the previous year as an eighth grader.
[d]Females in the class.
[e]Nine-year-old boy.
[f]Dropped the course.

therefore the eighth grade norms are stricter.) Table 6.2 shows the scores on both forms of the algebra test and the scores on the verbal subtests of the APT and SCAT.

## The Study of Algebra II

Sixteen students remained in the program to study algebra II during the school year. There were one tenth-grade boy who had skipped the

Table 6.2: *Scores on algebra tests and verbal subtests of APT and SCAT for students in the Saturday mathematics class*

| | Algebra I | | | | APT | SCAT |
|---|---|---|---|---|---|---|
| | Form A | | Form B | | | |
| Student | Score | Percentile, 9th grade norms | Score | Percentile, 8th grade norms | Verbal | Verbal |
| 1[a,b] | 38 | 99 | 39 | 99.6 | – | 43 |
| 2[a,c] | 37 | 99 | 39 | 99.6 | – | 44 |
| 3 | 35 | 97 | 39 | 99.6 | 43 | 30 |
| 4[d] | 35 | 97 | 36 | 98 | 42 | 29 |
| 5[a] | 34 | 96 | 32 | 95 | 56 | 49 |
| 6[a] | 33 | 96 | 40 | 99.9+ | 53 | 35 |
| 7[a] | 32 | 93 | 40 | 99.9+ | 45 | 20 |
| 8[e,a] | 32 | 93 | 38 | 99.6 | 41 | 13 |
| 9[a,b,d] | 31 | 89 | 38 | 99.6 | – | 25 |
| 10[d] | 31 | 89 | 37 | 99 | 52 | 30 |
| 11[d] | 30 | 89 | 29 | 91 | 52 | 36 |
| 12 | 30 | 89 | 37 | 99 | 45 | 23 |
| 13[d] | 29 | 87 | 31 | 93 | 45 | 25 |
| 14[f,d] | 27 | 79 | – | – | 45 | 31 |
| 15[d] | 27 | 79 | 31 | 93 | 42 | 28 |
| 16 | 24 | 60 | 25 | 75 | 43 | 22 |
| 17[f] | 23 | 60 | – | – | 44 | 16 |
| 18[f] | 20 | 42 | – | – | 36 | 9 |
| 19[f] | 19 | 36 | – | – | 38 | 16 |
| 20[f] | 18 | 27 | – | – | 48 | 30 |
| 21[b,d] | 18 | 27 | 32 | 95 | 46 | 34 |
| 22[f,d] | 15 | 15 | – | – | 34 | 15 |

[a]Math competition winner in 1972 or special referral.
[b]Late entrants to whom test administered before entering class.
[c]Had studied algebra I in school the previous year as an eighth grader.
[d]Females in the class.
[e]Nine-year-old boy.
[f]Dropped the course.

ninth grade, three eighth-grade boys (two of whom had skipped the seventh grade), one eighth-grade girl, four seventh-grade boys, six seventh-grade girls, and one fourth-grade boy. They continued to meet only on Saturday mornings for two hours with the instructors. Students were not required to take any additional mathematics in their regular school program and were given a daily study period at school to work on their mathematics from the Saturday class.

One seventh-grade girl who had not been in the summer program was tutored in a self-pacing fashion by a female college student during the Saturday session. Three other seventh-grade girls who were having difficulty keeping pace with the class for algebra II soon left the regular class and were also tutored by the same college student. (Two of these girls were considering dropping out of the program but were persuaded to try the slower pace of the tutoring sessions.) Two seventh-grade boys later joined this group. The goal for these six students was to master algebra II by 9 June 1973, when this group ended.

The ten students who remained in Wolfson's class completed algebra II in the early spring and went on to study trigonometry, college algebra, some analytic geometry, and plane geometry until 28 July 1973, at which time they disbanded.

### Evaluating the Students' Progress in Algebra II

Form B of a standardized algebra II test was administered to all 16 students in March of 1973. The scores and percentile ranks are shown in table 6.3. Ten of the 11 students in the Wolfson class at that time scored at or above the 98th percentile on national norms. The eleventh, whose attendance and motivation had declined, scored at the 85th percentile and was shifted to the self-pacing group. Of the six students who left the class to be tutored, the highest scores were at the 79th and 85th percentiles. Three of these six students scored below the 50th percentile. The six tutored students continued to study algebra II through June 9, when they were tested on a different form of the algebra II test. The retest scores are also shown in table 6.3. On Form A of the algebra II test all six students showed some improvement. Only one student scored below the 50th percentile on national high school norms.

### Evaluating the Students' Progress beyond Algebra II

Ten students have now completed the study of some college algebra, trigonometry, and plane geometry. Their scores and percentile ranks on tests in these areas are shown in table 6.4.

All but two students scored at or above the 50th percentile on national high school norms for algebra III. All but two of the students scored at or above the 72nd percentile on national high school norms for trigonometry. The scores of all but three of the 10 who have gone beyond

Table 6.3:    *Scores on tests of algebra II for students in the Saturday mathematics class*

|  | Algebra II | | | |
|---|---|---|---|---|
|  | Form B | | Form A | |
| Student | Score | Percentile, national high school norms | Score | Percentile, national high school norms |
| 1 | 39 | 99.7 | – | – |
| 2 | 40 | 99.9+ | – | – |
| 3 | 40 | 99.9+ | – | – |
| 4[a,b] | 26 | 79 | 33 | 95 |
| 5[a] | 28 | 85 | 29 | 85 |
| 6 | 39 | 99.7 | – | – |
| 7 | 38 | 99.7 | – | – |
| 8[c] | 38 | 99.7 | – | – |
| 9[b] | 38 | 99.7 | – | – |
| 10[b] | 37 | 99.2 | – | – |
| 11[a,b] | 19 | 43 | 23 | 59 |
| 12 | 36 | 98 | – | – |
| 13[a,b] | 21 | 48 | 29 | 85 |
| 15[b] | 37 | 99.2 | – | – |
| 16[a] | 17 | 38 | 19 | 43 |
| 21[a,b] | 26 | 79 | 33 | 95 |

[a] In the self-pacing group.
[b] Females in the class.
[c] Nine-year-old boy.

algebra II exceeded those of 86 percent of all high school students who had completed a course in trigonometry. The mathematical achievements of these 10 students in one year's time, two hours per week, is very impressive.

## Where Do They Go from Here?

Planning the educational progress in mathematics for the sixteen students for the following year was a difficult task. Since they did not all attend the same school, special plans had to be made for each student. Two of the original sixth graders and one former eighth grader had skipped a grade in the fall of 1972. These two original sixth graders will be skipped an additional year and will enter the tenth grade next year. They are both taking college mathematics courses this summer and will be ready for honors advanced-placement calculus, a twelfth-grade sub-

Table 6.4:    *Scores on tests of algebra III, trigonometry, and analytic geometry for 10 students in the Saturday mathematics class*

| | Algebra III, Form B | | Trigonometry | | Analytic Geometry | |
|---|---|---|---|---|---|---|
| Student | Score | Percentile, national high school norms | Score | Percentile, national high school norms | Score | Percentile, national high school norms |
| 1 | 35 | 96 | 34 | 98 | 26 | 90 |
| 2 | 32 | 92 | 34 | 98 | 30 | 95 |
| 3 | 28 | 73 | 22 | 86 | 24 | 74 |
| 6 | 33 | 95 | 32 | 98 | 29 | 95 |
| 7 | 29 | 79 | 18 | 72 | 22 | 64 |
| 8[a] | 27 | 73 | 23 | 86 | 16 | 32 |
| 9[b] | 32 | 92 | 33 | 98 | – | – |
| 10[b] | 24 | 54 | 15 | 48 | 21 | 57 |
| 12 | 23 | 40 | 23 | 86 | 19 | 46 |
| 15[b] | 23 | 40 | 15 | 48 | 16 | 32 |

[a] Nine-year-old boy.
[b] Female.

ject, next year. The eleventh grader will also take the honors advanced placement calculus. The 9-year-old boy is taking a college mathematics course this summer. His grade placement for next year is still uncertain. Three of the other boys will skip one year and go into ninth grade at a high school where they can take calculus.

Thus seven of the nine boys, but none of the seven girls, will skip at least one grade. Six of the girls will take geometry next year, and one will complete the algebra II work by independent study and then begin geometry.

Table 6.5 summarizes the educational progress of students who participated in the Saturday class during the 1972–73 school year. Three of the boys have taken a college computer science course (two earned A's, one a B). One boy will take that course in the summer of 1974. Three boys are currently taking college mathematics courses.

## Preliminary Conclusions

Our experience with the Saturday mathematics class has led us to conclude that able students, at the beginning of seventh grade, can master algebra to a high degree of proficiency in a very short time through guided independent study. This indicates that for many students

Table 6.5: *Educational progress of students in the Saturday mathematics class, 1972-73*

| Student | School grade completed before entering program | Year in school during the program | School grade to be entered in fall of 1973 |
|---|---|---|---|
| 1[a,b] | 7 | 8 | 9[c] |
| 2[a,b] | 8 | 10 | 11[c] |
| 3[b] | 6 | 7 | 9[c] |
| 4[d,e] | 6 | 7 | 8 |
| 5[c] | 6 | 7 | 9[c] |
| 6[a,b] | 6 | 8 | 10[c] |
| 7[a,b] | 6 | 8 | 10[c] |
| 8[a,b] | 3 | 4 | |
| 9[b,e] | 7 | 8 | 9 |
| 10[b,e] | 6 | 7 | 8 |
| 11[d,e] | 6 | 7 | 8 |
| 12[b] | 6 | 7 | 9 |
| 13[c,e] | 6 | 7 | 8 |
| 15[b,e] | 6 | 7 | 8 |
| 16[f] | 6 | 7 | 8 |
| 21[c,e] | 6 | 7 | 8 |

[a] Had taken college course before September 1973.
[b] Taking calculus next year at a high school.
[c] Senior high school.
[d] Taking geometry next year at a high school.
[e] Females.
[f] Finishing algebra II, then taking geometry.

the pace of a typical eighth- or ninth-grade algebra class is far too slow and comes later than is necessary. The fact that most of these young students were so successful leaves a question about the most realistic time for highly able boys and girls to begin the study of algebra. Apparently, the abler they are the earlier they should begin and the faster they should proceed.

One case of special interest is student 8, who was only 9 years old and scored rather well on all of the tests. His interest and achievement in mathematics are greatly facilitated by his home situation. Interestingly, although he is far younger than any other boy in the class, he is not the smallest. His physical appearance is such that he is not usually recognized by uninformed observers as the youngest in the group.

Many parents have expressed very positive feelings about their child's participation in this project. Many feel that their child always knew that he or she was somehow different from his or her classmates but now is learning that the difference is a positive one. Yet, participating in a class where the other students are also unusually bright and where there is a great spirit of competition has kept the students from becoming egotistical about their mathematical abilities.

In order to understand how one could determine the readiness of a student to benefit from an accelerated mathematics program and to learn which factors seem to contribute to success, let us examine more closely the abilities, interests, and backgrounds of some of the students. We will want to consider some of the cognitive abilities, interests and motivation, and background variables which seem to be related to the success of these students.

## Cognitive Abilities

Table 6.6 shows the mean scores for boys and girls in the program on several different cognitive measures. The key to table 6.6 explains the nature of each test.

### Abstract Reasoning

Students in the accelerated mathematics program have excellent non-verbal reasoning abilities. A score of 53 on the Raven's Progressive Matrices test,[6] Form ABCDE, is listed in the manual as being the 95th percentile for 14-year-olds. Boys in the math program averaged 54 and girls 53. On the more difficult advanced form a score of 21 is the 95th percentile for 14-year-olds. All of the students in the accelerated math program who took the test scored 21 or above. One boy scored 31 out of the 36 items. However, it should be remembered that abstract reasoning was one of the subtests of the APT initially used for selection.

A score of 49 or above was at the 99th percentile of national sixth-grade norms on the abstract reasoning subtest of the APT. Only five students of the original 19 scored below 49 on the abstract reasoning subtest. Student 3, who scored only 47 on the APT subtest, had the highest score of the class (31) on the advanced form of the Raven's Progressive Matrices test.[7]

---

[6]Published by The Psychological Corporation, New York, New York.

[7]It is interesting to note that, strictly speaking, he had not met the minimum criteria for admission to the class. His APT-V score of 43 was two points below the 99th percentile, as was his APT-AR score of 47. He had scored higher on APT-N, however (56, where 40 is the 99th percentile), than any other of the 392 students tested in our Baltimore county sixth-grade talent search, and so we made an exception for him. This proved to be wise because he performed better in class than any of the other seventh graders. In view of his excellent performance on Raven's II, the "low" APT-AR score may have contained a sizable negative error of measurement.

Table 6.6:    *Mean scores for boys and girls in the Saturday mathematics class on various cognitive tests*

| | All students who participated in the class for whom data are available | | | | Students who have remained in the class for algebra II | | | |
|---|---|---|---|---|---|---|---|---|
| | Boys | | Girls | | Boys | | Girls | |
| Test taken* | Number | Mean | Number | Mean | Number | Mean | Number | Mean |
| Raven's ABCDE | 9 | 54 | 7 | 53 | 9 | 54 | 7 | 53 |
| Raven's II | 7 | 27 | 4 | 26 | 7 | 27 | 4 | 26 |
| Space Relations | 13 | 46 | 8 | 52 | 9 | 46 | 7 | 52 |
| Science Knowledge | 9 | 40 | 7 | 39 | 9 | 40 | 7 | 39 |
| SCAT-Verbal | 13 | 27 | 9 | 28 | 9 | 33 | 7 | 30 |
| SAT-Verbal | 10 | 466 | 8 | 460 | 8 | 503 | 6 | 482 |
| SCAT-Quantitative | 13 | 36 | 9 | 33 | 9 | 36 | 7 | 33 |
| SAT-Math | 10 | 610 | 8 | 534 | 8 | 635 | 6 | 567 |

*Key:

*Raven's ABCDE:* Raven's Progressive Matrices Test. An untimed test of nonverbal reasoning. The maximum score is 60. A score of 53 is the 95th percentile for 14-year-olds. (The Psychological Corporation.)

*Raven's II:* Raven's Progressive Matrices, the advanced adult form. The highest possible score is 36. A score of 21 is the 95th percentile for 20-year-olds. (The Psychological Corporation.)

*Space Relations:* Revised Minnesota Paper Form Board Test, Form MA. Twenty minutes, 64 items. A 46 is the 60th percentile of 12th-grade boys, and a 52 is the 85th percentile for 12th-grade girls. (The Psychological Corporation.)

*Science:* Sequential Tests of Educational Progress, Form 1A. One hour. The highest possible score is 75. A score of 61 is the 99th percentile for high school seniors tested in the spring. (Educational Testing Service.)

*SCAT-Verbal:* School and College Ability Test, Verbal, Level 1 (college), Form C. Sixty items, 25 minutes. A score of 49 would be the 93rd-96th percentile band for college freshmen in the fall. A score of 31 would be the 43rd-66th percentile band. (Educational Testing Service.)

*SAT-Verbal:* Scholastic Aptitude Test, Verbal. Ninety items, 75 minutes. Highest reported score is 800. Average scores for high school senior boys and girls are 390 and 393, respectively. Typical SAT-takers average 463 and 464, respectively. (College Entrance Board.)

*SCAT-Quantitative:* School and College Ability Test, Quantitative, Level 1 (college), Form C. Fifty items, 45 minutes. A score of 47 would be the 99th-99.7th percentile band for college freshmen tested in the fall. A score of 31 would be the 54th-75th percentile band. (Educational Testing Service.)

*SAT-Math:* Scholastic Aptitude Test, Mathematics. Sixty items, 75 minutes. Highest reported score is 800. Average scores for high school senior boys and girls are 422 and 382, respectively. SAT-takers average 510 and 466, respectively. (College Entrance Examination Board.)

## Spatial Relations

Typically, differences between the sexes on tests of spatial relationships favor the boys (Anastasi 1958). However, the girls in our accelerated mathematics program seem to be superior to the boys in this ability, as measured by the highly speeded test we used. The highest score earned on the Revised Minnesota Paper Form Board Test,[8] form MA, by a member of the class (61 out of a possible 64) was earned by a girl. Five boys scored below the lowest-scoring girls, one of them receiving only 32 points. There was a six-point mean difference favoring the girls. According to the manual for this test, an average score for twelfth-grade males in New England is 44.8 and for twelfth-grade females 42.9. The mean for the boys in the accelerated mathematics program (46.8) was close to the mean for twelfth-grade boys, while the mean for the girls in the program (51.5) was almost nine points higher than the mean for twelfth-grade girls. This difference in spatial abilities is difficult to evaluate because of the small number of girls in the program. Perhaps girls who show high spatial abilities are more willing to seek out special stimulation in mathematics. Other speculations could be made. It will be interesting to investigate this more fully in the future.

## Science Knowledge

Students in the accelerated mathematics program show an excellent knowledge of science for their age. On a difficult college-level test of science knowledge, STEP science test,[9] form 1A, the boys in the class scored between 30 and 54 points out of 75. The score of 30 was earned by the third-grade boy, and that is at the 24th percentile for college freshmen tested in the spring. A score of 54 is at the 91st percentile. The boys in the class averaged 40 points, which is at the 59th percentile for college freshmen. (However, this is not so high as the average score of 52, earned by the 35 high scorers in the mathematics and science competition, which is at the 89th percentile of college freshmen. See chapter 2.) The girls in the class scored between 35 (the 42nd percentile of college freshmen) and 44 (the 71st percentile), with an average of 39 (the 55th percentile of college freshmen). Although the students in the special program exhibit an excellent knowledge of science for their age, only one of the students has expressed a strong interest in science. Only six listed "scientist" as an occupational preference on a questionnaire given them, and only one listed it as first

[8]Published by University of Minnesota Press.
[9]Published by Educational Testing Service, Princeton, New Jersey.

preference, although eight listed careers in medicine or engineering. Eight students indicated a strong liking for reading about science on the questionnaire.

*Verbal Ability*

Aiken (1971) notes that a positive relationship exists between verbal ability and achievement in mathematics, and that the correlation between scores on reading tests and mathematics is not due simply to overlap between these tests and measures of general intelligence. Certainly, for those in our accelerated mathematics program we see evidence of a relationship between verbal ability and success in the program. In table 6.2 we see that there was little spread among the verbal scores on the APT but that there was a great deal of spread among the verbal scores on a college level test, SCAT. Of the four boys and two girls who dropped the course, three of the boys and one of the girls did so because of difficulty in keeping pace with the class. It is interesting to note that of the 19 students in the original algebra I class who took the APT, the three lowest ranking students on the verbal subtest of the APT (scores of 34, 36, and 38) were among the six students who dropped the course. Of the five lowest scorers on the verbal subtest of the college-level test, SCAT (9, 13, 15, 16, and 16 points), four were students who dropped the course and one was the 9-year-old boy. The other two dropouts were not low on verbal ability (30 and 31 on SCAT-V); one of these was a girl who could have continued in the program but chose to drop out because her friend was not asked to continue in the program, and the other was a boy who was very bright but not interested in the class from the beginning. He attended infrequently and did little homework.

In table 6.6 we see that the mean score on the verbal subtest of the SCAT for boys who remained in the program for algebra II (33) was higher than the mean for all boys (27). The mean for girls who stayed in the program (30) was slightly higher than for all the girls (28). On the verbal section of the Scholastic Aptitude Test (SAT),[10] the mean score for boys who remained in the program (503) is higher than for all the boys (466), and the same relationship holds for the girls, with means of 482 and 460, respectively. It is interesting to note that the mean score for the girls is lower than that for the boys when the total group is considered and when only the group who remained in algebra II is considered. Since sex differences in verbal abilities typically favor girls

[10]Published by Educational Testing Service, Princeton, New Jersey.

(Anastasi 1958), this result is curious, but the number of girls is so small as to make firm conclusions impossible.

In table 6.7 the scores on the SAT are shown with the scores on both algebra I tests. The three highest scores on the verbal section of the SAT (630, 610, 580) were earned by boys who continued with the program into algebra II. The two lowest verbal scores (310, 330) were both earned by boys who were dropouts of the class.

Table 6.7:   *Scores on algebra I tests and the Scholastic Aptitude Test for students in the Saturday mathematics class*

| | Algebra I | | | | SAT | |
| | Form A | | Form B | | | |
| Student | Score | Percentile, 9th grade norms | Score | Percentile 8th grade norms | Mathe-matical | Verbal |
|---|---|---|---|---|---|---|
| 1[a,b] | 38 | 99 | 39 | 99.6 | 660 | 580 |
| 2[a,c] | 37 | 99 | 39 | 99.6 | 630 | 580 |
| 3 | 35 | 97 | 39 | 99.6 | 590 | 430 |
| 4[d] | 35 | 97 | 36 | 98 | – | – |
| 5[a] | 34 | 96 | 32 | 95 | 670 | 630 |
| 6[a] | 33 | 96 | 40 | 99.9+ | 750 | 610 |
| 7[a] | 32 | 93 | 40 | 99.9+ | 600 | 440 |
| 8[e,a] | 32 | 93 | 38 | 99.6 | 630 | 380 |
| 9[a,b,d] | 31 | 89 | 38 | 99.6 | 630 | 460 |
| 10[d] | 31 | 89 | 37 | 99 | 600 | 480 |
| 11[d] | 30 | 89 | 29 | 91 | 550 | 530 |
| 12 | 30 | 89 | 37 | 99 | 550 | 370 |
| 13[d] | 29 | 87 | 31 | 93 | 460 | 480 |
| 14[f,d] | 27 | 79 | – | – | 440 | 400 |
| 15[d] | 27 | 79 | 31 | 93 | 590 | 480 |
| 16 | 24 | 60 | 25 | 75 | – | – |
| 17[f] | 23 | 60 | – | – | – | – |
| 18[f] | 20 | 42 | – | – | – | – |
| 19[f] | 19 | 36 | – | – | 490 | 310 |
| 20[f] | 18 | 27 | – | – | 530 | 330 |
| 21[b,d] | 18 | 27 | 32 | 95 | 570 | 460 |
| 22[f,d] | 15 | 15 | – | – | 430 | 390 |

[a]Nine-year-old boy.
[b]Dropped the course.
[c]Math competition winner in 1972 or special referral.
[d]Late entrants to whom test administered before entering class.
[e]Females in the class.
[f]Had studied algebra I in school the previous year as an eighth grader.

Thus, it seems that, when students have mathematical aptitude, their success in learning advanced mathematics such as algebra at a rapid rate and scoring well on timed standardized tests is related to their verbal ability. The data suggest that the greater the verbal ability, when mathematical aptitude and interest are present, the more easily one can master algebra quickly by independent study. In other words, the greater one's verbal ability, the more likely it is that one can read a mathematical textbook with rapid comprehension or complete a 40-item algebra I test well in 40 minutes. The APT-number and SCAT-quantitative scores seem to indicate aptitude *level*, whereas the APT-verbal and SCAT-verbal scores seem (when adjusted for age) to indicate learning *rate*. Independent support of this hypothesis was provided by some observations offered us by one of the teachers of the class. He commented on what a difference he noted among four of the top boys in the class. Two, he said, never needed to be told something twice, but the other two seemed to need to spend a great deal more time learning a new concept, although after repetition and diligent practice they really learned it well. Sure enough, the two "fast learners" were the boys with the highest scores on the SAT verbal subtest and the two "slower learners" had much lower verbal scores (although their scores were high relative to their age-grade group).

But, as in most studies of human beings in natural contexts, there are exceptions. For instance, student 5, a seventh grader with a phenomenal SAT-V score of 630 and very high SAT-M score of 670 (higher on each than the *average* freshman at Johns Hopkins), started out well but seemed to lack sufficient interest in mathematics per se. His hobby is World War II history, about which he knows much. He is active in his church and the scouts. Apparently, he got far less stimulation from the upper 1 percent group and superb teacher than did all but one—far less able—of the other boys. High IQ does not guarantee success in a course like this.

Another student (no. 4), an able girl, did not like the competitive atmosphere of the Wolfson class and had to be moved to a self-pacing plan, where she did rather well.

### Mathematical Ability

All the students selected for the original class scored at the 99th percentile on the number subtest of the APT except the brilliant 9-year-old boy, who at that time knew very little arithmetic. (See table 6.1; a score of 40 or above is at the 99th percentile.) On a difficult 50-item college-level test, SCAT, there was a range of mathematical ability with scores between 24 and 47 and a mean of 36 for the boys and 33 for the girls. A score of 24 is slightly below the median for college freshmen tested in the fall, and a score of 47 is at the 99th percentile. Scores of 36 and 33 are in the upper quarter for college freshmen. Thus, the group which appeared homogeneous in mathematics aptitude on a grade level test actually ranged from average to superior when compared with college freshmen.

On the mathematics section of the SAT the scores ranged from 430 to 740. (This includes scores for four of the six dropouts but does not include scores for three students who continued in the class for whom scores were not available.) All students who remained in the class and took the test scored above 460. (A score of 460 is at the 66th percentile for eleventh grade males.) Two of the dropouts scored above 460. Seven of the students in the class scored above 600 (see table 6.7). This is rather remarkable since all but one of them were in grades seven or eight and had completed only the study of algebra I and some algebra II at that time. In table 6.3 we can see that the mean scores for boys and girls who stayed in the program for algebra II were 635 and 567, respectively. A score of 630 is at the 93rd percentile for eleventh-grade males, and a score of 560 is at the 86th percentile.

## Interests and Values

Students were asked several questions about their interest in mathematics, liking for school, and eagerness to participate in our program. All students indicated that they were either very eager or somewhat eager to participate. Eleven students indicated strong interest in being in the program. When asked to rate the importance of several factors in their decision to come into the program, all students responded that they came because mathematics is "fun to do" and because they would like to try something more difficult than their regular school work.

Although all but one also indicated that parents' interest was a factor, all but two indicated that a desire to try working on their own was important. Only six students indicated that their parents' interest was so strong that they had no choice but to come and participate. However, for most of the students their parents' interest in the program was rated as only moderately compelling. Seven students indicated that their parents' interest in the program was completely unrelated to their decision to come. The social attractiveness of the situation was apparently not perceived as being particularly strong—only one student indicated that her desire to come was motivated by the fact that a friend was coming and only one boy indicated that he was strongly motivated by the opportunity to meet other students who also like mathematics.

Students were asked about their liking for school and for mathematics. Ten students expressed a strong liking for school. Only one boy expressed a weak liking for school. (He dropped the course because of lack of motivation.) No student rated his or her liking of arithmetic and mathematics as less than average, and 13 rated their liking of math as strong. So it appears that for these students mathematics is better liked than school in general. This relates to the fact that all of them see themselves as highly successful in their mathematics class. They all indicated that they were better than all but one or two of their classmates in their sixth-grade mathematics class. Ten students even rated themselves as the best students in their junior high school classes. Fourteen of the students indicated that they were so good in their classes that they were encouraged by the teacher to do some independent work in mathematics. Three worked on extra assignments in the regular class book, four worked on mathematics puzzles, and seven worked in a different textbook either alone or tutored by the teacher.

All but three students indicated that they thought mathematics would be very important to them in the jobs they would someday have. Two boys said it would be fairly important, and one boy said it would not be at all important (his occupational preferences were singer, astronaut, and baseball player).

Most of these students already perceive themselves as abler than their classmates in mathematics and are not intimidated by the challenge to perform at a higher level; indeed, they are generally eager for the opportunity. It is interesting to relate this to their rating of desires to be best among their peers in several different areas of competency. Students were asked to rank their preferences for being the tallest and strongest, the best-looking, the smartest, the most popular, the best at school work, and the best-behaved in their classes. None of the students ranked tallest and strongest or best-looking first. However, seven wished first to be most popular, five to be the smartest, two to be the best at school work, and one to be the best-behaved. The average rank order of the six categories for the boys, from most desired to least desired, was as follows: smartest, most popular, best at school work, best-looking, best-behaved, and tallest and strongest. The rank order for girls was as follows: most popular, smartest, best at school work, best-looking, best-behaved, and tallest and strongest. (The last item was not particularly appropriate for the girls, but the boys did not favor it, either.) The only difference between the boys and girls was in the ordering of the first two categories, smartest and most popular. The girls preferred being the most popular to being the smartest in the class.

The occupational interests and expectations of the students were assessed by a short form of the Vocational Preference Inventory (VPI) developed by Holland (1965).[11] On this one-page occupational checklist, students were asked to indicate their interest for various occupations that cluster under six major categories:

1. Realistic (R)—electrician, mechanic, etc.
2. Investigative (I)—scientist, mathematician, etc.
3. Enterprising (E)—real estate salesman, buyer, etc.
4. Artistic (A)—actor, writer, etc.
5. Social (S)—teacher, housewife, etc.
6. Conventional (C)—bookkeeper, secretary, etc.

Each student (except the 9-year-old boy) received a one-letter code from the checklist, as shown in table 6.8. The VPI categories were also used to classify the occupations listed as first choice on the questionnaire, as shown in table 6.8. All but four of the students preferred occupations in the investigative category on the checklist. On their questionnaires, 13 of the 21 students listed an investigative occupation such as scientist, mathematician, etc., for their first choice occupation.

Of the four boys and two girls dropped from the program at the end of algebra I, only two (33 percent of the dropouts) had investigative preferences for both the checklist and their first-choice occupation. All but one student who continued in the program beyond algebra I had chosen investigative for either the checklist or the first-choice occupation.

Ten students have gone beyond algebra II to complete trigonometry, plane and analytic geometry, and college algebra. One of these is the 9-year-old boy. Seven of the nine other students preferred investigative occupations on both measures.

Having interests in scientific pursuits is certainly not enough to guarantee success in a rapidly paced mathematics program, but a lack of such interests may contribute to poorer performance than one's abilities might predict. The more interest a student has in pursuing careers which require a great deal of mathematics and an investigative outlook, the more likely that he will be willing to meet the demands in time and effort which are required to learn so much mathematics quickly and by independent study. This dedication to the study of mathematics is probably too much to ask of even very able young students if they have little interest in careers and activities of an investigative nature.

Table 6.8 also shows the students' highest, second highest, and lowest values as ascertained from the Allport-Vernon-Lindzey "Study of Values."[12] The six values are as follows:

[11]Published by Consulting Psychologists Press, Palo Alto, California.
[12]Published by Houghton Mifflin Company, Boston.

mathematical talent

Table 6.8: *Occupational interests and Allport-Vernon-Lindzey "Study of Values" scores for students in the Saturday mathematics class*

| | VPI Code[1] | | AVL-SV[2] |
| --- | --- | --- | --- |
| Student | Checklist | First-choice occupation on questionnaire | Two highest, one lowest, on six values |
| 1[a,b] | I | I | PS,A |
| 2[a,c] | I | I | AE,P |
| 3 | I | I | TP,A |
| 4[d] | I | S | PS,E=A |
| 5[a] | I | E | TR,A |
| 6[a] | I | E | PT,R |
| 7[a] | I | I | T=P,S |
| 8[e,a] | – | – | – |
| 9[a,b,d] | I | I | TP,A |
| 10[d] | I | S | AS,E |
| 11[d] | A=S | I | SA,E |
| 12 | I | I | TE,R |
| 13[d] | I | I | TP,R |
| 14[f,d] | I | S | SR,T |
| 15[d] | I | I | AT,R |
| 16 | C | S | ET,S |
| 17[f] | I | I | TR,A |
| 18[f] | I | S | TP,A |
| 19[f] | I | I | TP,A |
| 20[f] | E=C | A | P=E,R |
| 21[b,d] | I | I | TR,P |
| 22[f,d] | S | I | S,T=R,A |

[a]Math competition winner in 1972 or special referral.
[b]Late entrant to whom test administered before entering class.
[c]Had studied algebra I in school the previous year as an eighth grader.
[d]Females in the class.
[e]Nine-year-old boy.
[f]Dropped the course.
[1]The VPI codes are for the following six occupational categories: I, investigative; A, artistic; S, social; E, enterprising; C, conventional; R, realistic.
[2]The AVL-SV codes are for the following six values: P, political; S, social; A, aesthetic; E, economic; T, theoretical; R, religious.

Theoretical (T)—corresponds to the investigative category of the VPI codes
Economic (E)—does not correspond directly to any single category of the VPI codes
Aesthetic (A)—corresponds to the artistic category of the VPI codes
Political (P)—does not correspond directly to any single category of the VPI codes

Social (S)—corresponds to the social category of the VPI codes
Religious (R)—does not correspond directly to any single category of the VPI
code

Of the six dropouts, two (33 percent) did not have theoretical interests as one of their highest values. They were both students who
dropped out because of poor motivation rather than low ability. (One
was the girl who dropped out because her friend was not asked to continue in the program.) Of those who remained in the course for algebra
II, five (33 percent) did not have theoretical interests as one of their
two highest values.

The theoretical value was the highest or second highest value for the
majority of students (67 percent) who participated in the mathematics
program (14 of the 21 tested). The proportion of students who valued
theoretical highest was the same (67 percent) for the six dropouts
(four of six) as it was for the 15 (10 of 15) who completed algebra II
and for the nine (six of nine) who went beyond algebra II.

Thus, for this particular group, knowledge of investigative interests
would seem to be a better predictor of success in the program than
knowledge of theoretical interests. If we had predicted that every
student who had expressed investigative preferences on at least one
measure of vocational interest would be successful in the program and
continue beyond algebra I and every student who did not score highest
on investigative interests for at least one of the two measures would
drop out, we would have been correct for 15 of 21 students. Had we
based our predictions on the theoretical value as indicated on the AVL,
we would have been correct only for 12 of the 21 students.

The values and interests of the students are perhaps more useful in
understanding failures in individual cases (such as why a student with
high abilities but low investigative and theoretical interests and values
might want to drop out of the program even though he or she was doing
well) than they are in predicting success or failure in advance for specific students.

## Home Environment

All of the students come from middle-class homes where education is
valued. Some selected background characteristics are shown in table 6.9.
More than half of them have fathers who are in professions such as
medicine, law, teaching, or engineering. About three-fourths of the
students have at least one parent who has a college degree (89 percent

Table 6.9: *Selected background characteristics of students in the Saturday mathematics class*

| | | Parents' Occupations | | | | Parents' College Education | | | | Birth Position | | | |
| | | Father Professional | | Mother Professional | | Both parents | | At least one parent | | First-born or only child | | Not first-born | |
| | Number | Number | % | Number | % | Number | % | Number | % | Number | % | Number | % |
|---|---|---|---|---|---|---|---|---|---|---|---|---|---|---|
| Boys | 13 | 8 | 54 | 1 | 8 | 4 | 31 | 9 | 69 | 9 | 69 | 4 | 31 |
| Girls | 9 | 5 | 56 | 2 | 22 | 5 | 56 | 8 | 89 | 1 | 11 | 8 | 89 |

of the girls and 69 percent of the boys), and six students have parents who have advanced degrees. Only four students, two boys and two girls, have mothers who work outside the home. A larger proportion of the boys (69 percent) are first-born or only children, whereas all but one of the girls are not.

Students were asked to rate their parents' eagerness for them to participate in the program. Eleven rated their fathers as very eager and 13 rated their mothers as very eager. Only one parent, the mother of a boy, was rated as less than very or somewhat eager for her child to participate. Only one child said that his parents' interest in the program was not a factor in his decision to come.

We are beginning to suspect from observation and from informal discussion with students and their parents that there is a very important factor underlying the failure of some students with high ability and theoretical and investigative interests and the success of other students with somewhat lower ability or with values and interests other than theoretical and investigative. This underlying factor is good study habits, which includes regular class attendance, regular study hours, and completion of written homework assignments. Although we have never systematically tried to study this, repeated conversations with parents of highly successful students and less successful ones lends strong support to this hypothesis. In many of the homes of the 10 most successful students, parents carefully supervise their children's study habits and require or lovingly encourage the students to complete their assignments well in advance of each class meeting. In some of the homes of the less successful students, there seems to be less parental emphasis on study habits, regular attendance, and completion of homework assignments. Indeed, some parents said that they almost avoided discussing their child's academic assignments or progress with him or her, believing that a child should never be "forced" to study.

Apparently, the commitment of the parents to the special mathematics program was a very potent influence in some cases. Just how potent it really was is difficult to say. In table 6.9 we have shown that in the majority of cases (69 percent for boys, 89 percent for girls) at least one parent had a college education. But if we re-analyze this in terms of the 10 most successful students versus the six dropouts, we see some interesting facts which may be related to parents' interest in their child's study habits. The fathers of all 10 of the most successful students completed at least four years of college, and six have advanced degrees. Of the six dropouts, three had fathers who had completed college, and one had a father with an advanced degree. (Of the six students who successfully completed algebra II but went no further, four of their fathers had completed college, and none had advanced degrees.) Of the 10 most successful boys, six had mothers who had completed four years of college. Only one mother of a dropout had a college degree. (Two mothers of the remaining six students had college degrees.)

Closely related to level of educational attainment is the level and type of employment. Typically, occupations which require advanced degrees are classified as professional. Most such occupations are classified on the VPI as investigative, social, or enterprising (Viernstein 1972). Thus it is not surprising that if one compares the occupations of the fathers with the VPI codes one finds that eight of the 22 fathers have jobs classified as investigative, and 11 have jobs classified as enterprising; one occupation is social, and only two are classified as realistic. What is interesting is that of the 10 most precocious students, 50 percent have fathers in investigative occupations, while only 27 percent of the remaining 11 students have fathers in investigative occupations.

## Conclusion

Our experience with the students in this program leads us to suspect that the formula for precocious achievement needs to be expanded. It appears that what motivates able youngsters to attend a difficult, accelerated summer program of mathematics instruction is their great enjoyment of mathematics and their desire for a challenging experience together with encouragement from their parents. Not only do they wish to study material which will be more difficult than their usual school work, but they also are eager to try studying it on their own. This was not taken into account explicitly in selecting students for the special program. Further, verbal ability (which seems rather closely related to IQ and hence to rate of learning) plays an important role in the students' ability to work fast and well in mathematics. Therefore, the selection of students for this type of accelerated program should include specific emphasis on verbal aptitude and motivation as well as high mathematical aptitude. In addition, the commitment of the parents to the program and their attitude toward the child's "homework" should be more carefully studied to assess the possible impact upon the child's success. An added emphasis on interest in mathematics might help to eliminate the differences between the sexes; however, it is conceivable that for girls, although the formula for selection may remain the same, the set of conditions for encouragement plus opportunity may need to be different from those appropriate for the boys.

The extent to which participation in this special mathematics program has lasting effects upon these students in terms of their later educational experiences and careers remains to be seen. It will be interesting to see which of these students, if any, major in mathematics or closely allied subjects in college and someday become high-level professionals.

We believe that the major achievement of our work with these students lies in the immediate effects that it has had upon their knowledge of mathematics and their advancement in school. As noted earlier, four of the nine boys in the class have skipped one school grade after entering the Saturday morning program, and three boys have skipped two grades. None had previously skipped a grade. Moreover, several of the 16 students will probably enter college before completing high school or finish four years of high school in three. We estimate that the majority of the 16 will earn PH.D. or M.D. degrees at unusually young ages.

This project has clearly demonstrated that our present educational system greatly underestimates the level at which most of the ablest youngsters can operate. While few seventh-grade students can be expected to learn the greater part of high school mathematics in one year, some individuals can and should be encouraged to do so. Individual differences in learning rates have too long been ignored by traditional lockstep, age-grade approaches to instruction. We anticipate that in the not too distant future most school systems will begin to provide the type of opportunities necessary to encourage students, especially the highly able ones, to learn at their own pace—whatever that pace may be.

## References

Aiken, L. R. 1971. Intellective variables and mathematics achievement: Directions for research. *Journal of School Psychology* 9(2): 201–12.

Anastasi, A. 1958. *Differential Psychology: Individual and Group Differences in Behavior.* New York: Macmillan.

Holland, J. L. 1965. *The Vocational Preference Inventory.* Palo Alto, Calif.: Consulting Psychologists Press.

Inhelder, B., and Piaget, J. 1958. *The Growth of Logical Thinking from Childhood to Adolescence.* New York: Basic Books.

Viernstein, M. C. 1972. The extension of Holland's occupational classifications to all occupations in the Dictionary of Occupational Titles. *Journal of Vocational Behavior* 2: 107–21.

# VII · personality characteristics of mathematically precocious boys

## DANIEL WEISS, RICHARD J. HAIER,

## and DANIEL P. KEATING[1]

[Editors' Note: *Perhaps the most serious and longest-lived concern over the effects of educational programs for gifted students like those carried out by our study is for what is known as "social and emotional development." The authors of this paper look critically at the traditional assumptions and sources of concern about this problem from a perspective of personality assessment.*]

The Study of Mathematically and Scientifically Precocious Youth seeks to provide challenging educational opportunities for exceptionally gifted seventh- and eighth-grade students who have been identified through large-scale testing sessions. As noted earlier, the rigorous screening process includes the College Entrance Examination Board aptitude and achievement tests and other college-level tests. A surprisingly large number of young students achieve scores on these tests equivalent to superior high school seniors (see p. 25).

Although the number of such students is significant enough to deserve special attention as a group, their percentage in the total school population is, of course, quite low. Effective educational facilitation for these students appears to require that the student move ahead of his age mates academically, either by skipping grades or by taking advanced courses. Other educational alternatives, such as special classes or "enrichment," are usually inappropriate and potentially detrimental (see p. 51).

The most frequent criticism of acceleration has been that this form of educational intervention harms the social and emotional development of the individual because it deprives him of close association with his age mates, who ostensibly comprise his social peer group. While few would argue that his age mates are his intellectual peers, others do frequently suggest that the precocious student's needs are most effectively dealt with by constant contact with his chronological peers. That is to say, it is often suggested that social needs should take priority if they conflict with intellectual needs.

[1]The authors wish to thank Julian C. Stanley and Robert Hogan for their helpful comments and encouragement.

126

Previous research addressing the emotional-development question (e.g., Pressey 1949; Oden 1968) has demonstrated that fears of adverse effects from moderate academic acceleration are groundless. Since, however, students chosen through the screening process outlined above form a more select and restricted group than those in earlier studies, and since comparatively radical intervention procedures are recommended for some of these students, it is essential that their affective (as somewhat arbitrarily distinguished from their cognitive) characteristics be investigated directly for two reasons. First, because academic achievement is not wholly a cognitive function (see, e.g., Demos and Weijola 1966), cognitive information alone is insufficient to provide all the necessary guidance material. Second, these data have an intrinsic interest owing partly to the nature of the group and partly to the nature of the data revealed by personality assessment devices (see pp. 128–29).

There were several major interests which guided our investigation. Despite Terman's (1925–1959) efforts to eliminate the prejudices against gifted children, variants of such prejudices still linger and have been noted by, among others, Syphers (1972). One of these distortions is that exceptionally gifted children are one-sided, narrow, and interpersonally ineffective. Although Terman (1925) showed that, in general, gifted children were better adjusted, had wider interests, and were more morally mature than children from the population at large, contrary attitudes and beliefs persist. Our first interest was, therefore, to determine whether this select group of mathematically precocious youth are as mature and interpersonally effective as randomly selected children of the same age; the hypothesis was that they would be more mature.

Further, if these students are to perform effectively in and benefit from challenging courses in consort and competition with older students, it is important that they not be handicapped by an inability to deal with other people in social situations (e.g., in classrooms, laboratories, workshops, and discussion groups). Taking the earlier findings of Pressey (1949) and Oden (1968) as a guide, we felt that there would be no significant deficits in interpersonal abilities when these students were compared with older student groups. Echoing these previous findings, our second question was formulated this way: Would the students selected for achievement in a special area be similar in interpersonal effectiveness to gifted students identified by more general measures?

A third hypothesis was that the mathematically precocious students, because of the special method of their selection, would be readily distinguishable from other gifted students in interpersonal style, the distinguishing personological features forming a coherent, intelligible, and predictable pattern.

The analysis presented in this paper deals with the 35 seventh- and eighth-grade boys who scored especially high on the tests of mathematics and/or general science in the general screening session and who were therefore invited back for further testing (see p. 36). Since the small number of girls retested was so small (eight), they were excluded as subjects.

## Measures

The California Psychological Inventory (CPI) (Gough 1969) was the instrument of choice for our study. It is ". . . addressed principally to personality characteristics important for social living and social interaction" (p. 5). An empirically developed assessment device, it contains 18 scales grouped into four broad clusters. The profile obtained gives a good indication of the general social functioning of the individual, as the CPI is designed to measure "folk concepts" which have broad general validity.

The inventory has been in research testing with groups of ages 12 and 13. . . . With subjects in the elementary grades and in early junior high school, some items are difficult and a few are without relevance. In spite of these problems, test results are in most cases meaningful and readily interpretable. With subjects of high school age and beyond, problems of this type are rarely encountered (Gough 1969, p. 6).

The CPI can be used with confidence, then, as a part of a selection process or research battery for students of high intellectual caliber, even though they are still in junior high school. Perhaps the best evidence for this assertion, besides the norms themselves, comes from a study by Lessinger and Martinson (1961). They used the CPI to provide an initial indication of the social and personal maturity of their gifted groups (junior and senior high school students) and thus a basis for comparing the development of these groups with that of other groups. When they analyzed their data, they did indeed find that the gifted eighth graders in their sample compared favorably with gifted high school and normal adult populations in terms of overall adjustment.

Two advantageous features of using the CPI are the many fruitful studies that have been done employing the inventory and the extensive development by Gough and others of regression equations that maximize the linear prediction of specific criteria, e.g., creativity, social maturity, and college attendance. The availability of these regression equations and the rationale behind them, coupled with extensive studies on achievement and nonachievement groups (Davids 1966; Domino 1968; Gough 1949, 1953, 1963; Lessinger and Martinson 1961) gives impressive weight to both the validity and reliability of the use of the CPI in this setting. We therefore felt confident in our choice of the CPI as the measure for the affective domain of our group.[2]

The cognitive measures that were employed have been previously described (see pp. 36–39). To maximize the chances of discovering a relationship between the affective and cognitive measures for these students, we utilized a broad range of eight cognitive tests: SAT-Mathematics, SAT-Verbal, CEEB Math I, Raven Progressive Matrices ABCDE, Raven Progressive Matrices Set II, Concept Mastery Test I, Concept Mastery Test II, STEP Science (Level I).

## Subjects and Administration of the CPI

The 35 boys who were invited back for retesting were given the CPI. This group (the mathematically gifted,[3] MG) represented the top scorers from the general testing session. One student moved from the area shortly after his inclusion in the group, and two others declined to complete or return the inventory. This reduced our sample size to 32.

While most students in the MG group took all the cognitive tests, there were five boys for whom a complete set of scores was not available. In each case, the mean score for the group was entered as the subject's score, a procedure that would not affect the mean of the group for that measure. This afforded the opportunity to use the full sample of 32 for all analyses. The mean age for this group was 12.9 years.

## Analyses and Results

The CPI protocol of each student was scored for the original 18 scales plus an additional Empathy scale developed by Hogan (1969). The comparison groups that we used for this study were those identified by Lessinger and Martinson (1961): Eighth Grade Random (EGR, N=82), Eighth Grade Gifted (EGG, N=94), and High School Gifted

---

[2]See appendix C for several case studies.
[3]Several individuals were selected solely on the science test criterion, but the designation is most appropriate for the group as a whole.

Table 7.1:  Means of the MG group compared with the means of the EGR, EGG, HSG, and HSN groups on the CPI scales

| CPI Scale | Mathematically Gifted (MG) N=32 | | Eighth Grade Random (EGR) N=82 | | Eighth Grade Gifted (EGG) N=94 | | High School Gifted (HSG) N=157 | | High School Norm (HSN) N=3,572 | |
|---|---|---|---|---|---|---|---|---|---|---|
| | $\bar{X}$ | SD | $\bar{X}$ | SD | $\bar{X}$ | SD | $\bar{X}$ | SD | $\bar{X}$ | SD |
| 1 Do (Dominance) | 25.2 | 6.0 | 19.5*** | 4.9 | 27.0 | 5.5 | 28.8** | 6.3 | 23.2 | 6.0 |
| 2 Cs (Capacity stat.) | 16.9 | 3.3 | 11.3*** | 3.5 | 17.6 | 3.7 | 20.7*** | 3.4 | 15.3* | 4.4 |
| 3 Sy (Sociability) | 20.0 | 5.6 | 20.7 | 4.2 | 24.4*** | 5.0 | 26.2*** | 4.7 | 21.5 | 5.4 |
| 4 Sp (Social pres.) | 33.4 | 7.3 | 30.6* | 6.2 | 32.9 | 5.7 | 35.6 | 6.7 | 32.7 | 5.7 |
| 5 Sa (Self-accept.) | 19.1 | 3.9 | 17.6 | 3.8 | 19.6 | 3.5 | 22.6*** | 3.8 | 18.7 | 4.1 |
| 6 Wb (Well being) | 32.2 | 4.7 | 27.2*** | 6.1 | 35.6*** | 4.8 | 35.8*** | 4.2 | 33.5 | 5.6 |
| 7 Re (Responsibility) | 28.6 | 4.9 | 21.5*** | 5.8 | 31.7*** | 4.3 | 31.1 | 5.1 | 26.7 | 5.7 |
| 8 So (Socialization) | 36.4 | 5.1 | 29.9*** | 5.3 | 40.8*** | 4.9 | 38.1 | 6.4 | 36.3 | 6.0 |
| 9 Sc (Self-control) | 25.6 | 7.6 | 18.0*** | 7.2 | 28.2 | 8.8 | 25.8 | 8.3 | 25.3 | 8.0 |
| 10 To (Tolerance) | 19.8 | 5.0 | 12.1*** | 4.8 | 22.4** | 4.4 | 23.1*** | 4.5 | 17.8* | 5.3 |
| 11 Gi (Good impress.) | 13.0 | 4.8 | 10.3** | 4.7 | 16.9*** | 6.8 | 15.8 | 6.3 | 15.1 | 6.2 |
| 12 Cm (Communality) | 23.9 | 2.5 | 23.6 | 3.5 | 26.4*** | 1.8 | 25.4*** | 2.1 | 25.2** | 2.8 |
| 13 Ac (Achiev. via conformance) | 23.9 | 3.9 | 16.4*** | 4.4 | 26.3** | 4.2 | 27.2*** | 4.6 | 22.3 | 5.3 |
| 14 Ai (Achiev. via independence) | 20.2 | 4.0 | 10.9*** | 3.5 | 18.0** | 3.9 | 20.8 | 3.5 | 14.6*** | 4.1 |
| 15 Ie (Intellectual efficiency) | 37.2 | 5.0 | 26.0*** | 5.3 | 38.7 | 4.4 | 40.5*** | 4.3 | 33.6*** | 6.3 |
| 16 Py (Psychological-mindedness) | 11.3 | 3.2 | 7.9*** | 2.7 | 11.2 | 2.7 | 12.0 | 2.6 | 9.2*** | 2.6 |
| 17 Fx (Flexibility) | 13.3 | 3.9 | 7.7*** | 2.7 | 9.4*** | 3.4 | 11.0** | 4.0 | 9.1*** | 3.4 |
| 18 Fe (Femininity) | 17.5 | 3.7 | 15.1** | 3.4 | 17.4 | 3.2 | 16.1* | 3.4 | 15.4** | 3.6 |
| 19 Em (Empathy) | 19.9 | 4.2 | — | — | — | — | — | — | — | — |

*p < .05
**p < .01
***p < .001

(HSG, N=157). These groups had also taken the CPI; means and standard deviations were available for the original 18 scales. A fourth comparison group, a norm group of high school students studied by Gough (1957) (HSN, N=3,572) was also utilized.

Means, standard deviations, and the results of significance tests among the groups for the CPI are presented in table 7.1. When the MG group was compared, in turn, with each of the four other groups, significant and interpretable differences were found. The MG group is most different from the EGR group. The greatest differences between these two groups were found on the Achievement via Independence, Intellectual Efficiency, Flexibility, and Achievement via Conformance scales of the CPI.

The MG group appears more similar to the EGG group than to the EGR group. There are, nonetheless, significant differences between these two groups. With the exception of Achievement via Independence and Flexibility, on which the MG group scored higher, the EGG group scored higher than the MG group on all scales showing significant differences. The comparisons among the profiles of the MG, EGR, and EGG groups are illustrated in figure 7.1.

When the MG group was compared with the two high school student groups, a pattern of results similar to that of the eighth-grade groups appeared. The MG group scored significantly higher than the HSN group on 10 of the 18 CPI scales. Achievement via Independence and Flexibility again showed the largest differences. When compared with the HSG group, however, the MG group scored lower on all the scales except one. Twelve of the scales showed significantly higher scores for the HSG group. Only on Flexibility did the MG group score significantly higher than the HSG group. Figure 7.2 illustrates the comparisons among the MG, HSG, and HSN group profiles. It appears, then, that the MG group, from a personological viewpoint, most closely resembles the HSN group, least resembles the EGR group, and is more closely identified with students chronologically and/or academically more advanced than with their chronological peers.

Previous research with the CPI has produced regression equations to predict creativity (Hall and MacKinnon 1969), college attendance (Gough 1968a), average scholastic achievement (Gough and Fink 1964), and social maturity (Gough 1966). All S's in the MG group were scored for these four equations, as were the four comparison groups' mean scale scores. The mean regression equation score for the MG group was also computed for each of the four equations, yielding five sets of mean scores for the four regression equations. These data provided more specific and theoretically meaningful points of comparison among the groups because of their relevance to educational endeavors.

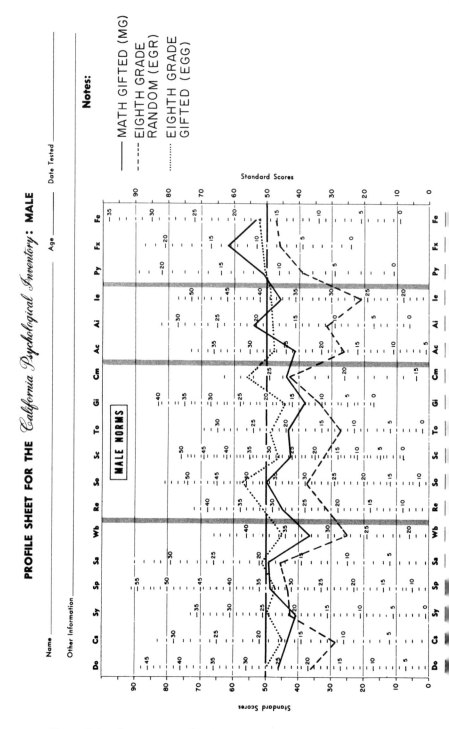

Figure 7.1:  *Comparison of MG, EGR, and EGG Groups on 18 CPI scales*

132

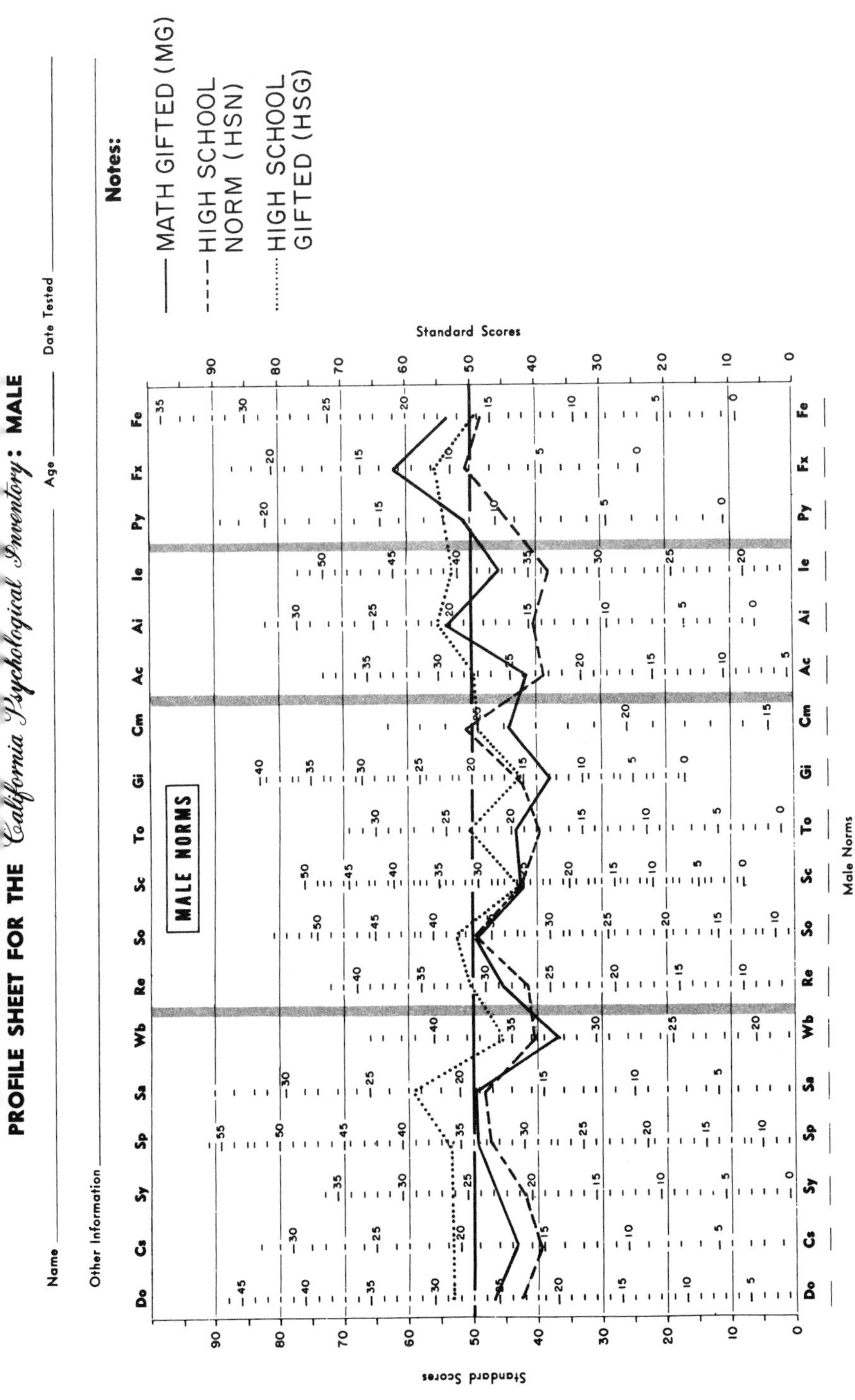

Figure 7.2: *Comparison of MG, HSG, and HSN Groups on 18 CPI scales*

133

The meaning of these regression equations should be specified before proceeding. The equation for college attendance was constructed to identify high-ability students likely to attend college. The creativity equation, derived from MacKinnon's research with creative architects at the Institute of Personality Assessment and Research (IPAR), specifies the personological correlates of rated "real world" creativity. The social maturity equation is tailored to specify the degree of responsibility, dependability, and foresight that an individual has attained. The scholastic achievement equation was developed using a sample with a large range of ability and was designed to augment predictability of scholastic achievement along a wide continuum of talent. These variables all have a direct bearing on educational facilitation for groups and individuals.

Because the MG group was the only group in which the individual CPI protocols were available, the variance of the regression scores around the mean regression score had to be estimated for each of the other four groups for all four regression equations. The procedure involved estimating the variance of the weighted composites, i.e., regression scores, by assuming that for each group the intercorrelations among the CPI scales were the same as those found in the CPI Manual, a not untenable assumption. Using this procedure, we were able to construct a unique estimate of the variance for each regression equation for the EGR, EGG, HSG, and HSN groups. These estimates are of the same order of magnitude as those that are found in previously published reports and are similar to the variances found for the MG group. We therefore felt that significance tests among some of the means for the five groups were not unconscionable, even though some of the data had been reconstructed.

Because the EGG and HSG groups did not differ from the MG group on many of the CPI scales utilized in the four regression equations, significance tests were computed only for differences between the MG and the EGR, and the MG and the HSN groups.

The results are summarized in table 7.2 and show that the MG group receives significantly larger regression scores than both the EGR and HSN groups on equations for social maturity, college attendance, and average scholastic achievement. On the creativity regression equation, however, the EGR group scored significantly higher than the MG group and there was no significant difference between the MG and the HSN groups. This finding, however, may be an artifact of our data. Because the creativity regression equation has a very large negative weight on the Achievement via Conformance scale, and because the EGR group is significantly lower on this scale than the other groups,

Table 7.2:   *MG compared with EGR and HSN on social maturity, college attendance, creativity, and scholastic achievement*

|  | Mathematically Gifted (MG) | | Eighth Grade Random (EGR) | | High School Norm (HSN) | |
|---|---|---|---|---|---|---|
|  | $\bar{X}$ | SD | $\bar{X}$ | SD | $\bar{X}$ | SD |
|  | N=32 | | N=82 | | N=3,572 | |
| Social maturity | 52.28 | 3.18 | 45.45** | 3.48 | 49.37** | 3.76 |
| College attendance | 50.26 | 5.15 | 41.0 ** | 4.94 | 47.44* | 6.00 |
| Creativity | 11.44 | 5.41 | 15.04* | 4.40 | 10.50 | 6.05 |
| Average scholastic achievement | 53.92 | 3.73 | 44.76** | 4.09 | 50.12* | 4.37 |

\*.01 $<$ p $<$ .001
\*\*p $<$ .001

the EGR group had to place highest. This means that the results may be neither interpretable nor valid when compared with the EGR group.

The picture changes somewhat when the MG group is compared with either the adult male norms or the creative architects in Hall and MacKinnon's (1969) study. Using the mean scores for the adult male norms on the appropriate scales, one obtains a creativity regression score of 7.03. This is 4.41 points below the MG group. The creative architects in the Hall and MacKinnon study had a mean regression score on the creativity equation of 11.7. This is quite close to the MG sample mean of 11.4. Caveats apply to the interpretation of these comparisons as well. The way in which the scores of the MG group will change as they grow older is unknown. But clearly any characterization of them as "uncreative" on the basis of the CPI data is unfounded.

## Discussion

The most salient and important finding to be extracted from the analyses is that the MG students as a group are not interpersonally ineffective or maladjusted. On the contrary, relative to both the EGG and the two high school groups, the students in the MG group, from a personological standpoint, are solid, competent individuals who seem to be handling their extraordinary talents in a commendable fashion. This finding should help lay to rest the notion that gifted children are by *definition* misfits and maladjusted. The refutation of this thesis carries with it important implications for educational planning and intervention.

The resemblance of the MG group to the EGG, HSG, and HSN groups and the dissimilarity of the MG group and the EGR group reinforce the observation that, in terms of personality functioning, age is not the definitive measure of maturity. Moreover, these findings demonstrate that intellectual talent, regardless of slight variations in definition and selection procedures, tends to carry with it social and interpersonal skill as well.

Although it could be held that the scores of the MG group are relatively high simply because their greater intellectual ability enables them to understand and respond to the inventory in a more mature manner, this explanation is unlikely in the light of the other findings concerning both this group and other similar groups, e.g., cognitive scores and regression equation scores. The implications of these results for educational intervention and facilitation are encouraging and favorable, if we consider only the capacity of the MG group to cope with the added responsibilities that these programs are sure to entail.

The results of the social maturity equation scores add credence to the assertion that, compared with students in general, the MG group is more mature. They are more responsible, more dependable, more perspicacious in their dealings with the rule structure of their environment, and more likely to take a firm and upright stance regarding moral matters—a finding that clearly echoes Terman's (1925) conclusion. That these qualities should be related to intellectual talent is an interesting and intelligible finding. Moreover, these data suggest two further observations. First, any educational program designed to suit the needs of such a group of students as the MG group need not be overly concerned about the social and emotional factors as impediments to accelerated progress through the educational structure. In fact, it is probably just this type of student who is able and equipped to cope with the added challenges and responsibilities of the programs that are typically discussed and advanced. Second, after Lessinger and Martinson (1961), we also suggest that the peer group of these students is not necessarily defined by age mates. On the contrary, it appears that their peer group should be defined more in terms of similarities of intellectual abilities and tastes, with an eye toward comparable levels of maturity. The comparison of the EGR profile with that of the MG profile leaves no doubt that these are highly dissimilar groups from a personological viewpoint. Thus, it is unwise to suggest that because they are age mates students will also be social peers; the concept of peer group connotes values and experiences which are probably not shared by gifted and randomly selected age mates.

### Characterization of the MG Group

The special characteristics of the MG group warrant special explication. The two most salient CPI scales associated with the MG group are Achievement via Independence and Flexibility. According to Gough (1968*b*), the flexibility scale identifies individuals who are characterized by a flexible and adaptable temperament. The Achievement via Independence scale taps innovative, independent, and self-actualizing modes of achieving. The following adjectives, culled from the descriptions of the original group of high scorers, are most strongly associated with the profile of the MG group: independent, quick, sharp-witted, foresighted, versatile, and intelligent. For students to achieve the level of competence in mathematics that these boys have requires initiative and direction far beyond that typically provided by educational institutions. If one then recalls the manner of selection of the MG group and considers the experiential history of a student in this group, the adjectival descriptions become more relevant, meaningful, and precise. Thus, the kind of personality possessed by these students seems to have facilitated their level of achievement. There may be, of course, some individuals with virtually the same personality profile who are touchy, informal, fickle, or sarcastic, but the chances of their following the same academic path are considerably slimmer. It is a blend of independent achievement and even tempered but malleable disposition that uniquely characterizes this group.

Further evidence for this assertion is found in an examination of the selection criterion, the 60-item SAT-Mathematics test, which is a power and knowledge test that requires a rapid shifting of cognitive processes. In this case, the advantage lies with a student who has the ability to use quickly many different approaches to problem solving. A kind of cognitive style embodying flexibility and foresight may characterize the MG group. Moreover, this further suggests that a rigid distinction between the cognitive and affective dimensions in human performance is tenuous at best and merely ephemeral at worst. Nonetheless, even at the extremely high end of the talent continuum, there appear to be reliable and intuitively sensible differences among talented students. Whether these differences will hold up under crossvalidation and replication procedures is an empirical question. Nonetheless, however one views the question of generalizability, there is no doubt that replication of these results and crossvalidation of these findings is essential.[4]


## Implications

One last observation is in order. Although the personality dimension of these students is important for counseling purposes, it appears that, for all but a few, radical personality adjustments are not needed. The overwhelming majority of students clearly are prepared to deal with the vicissitudes that new experimental paths will present. The reservation that their educational facilitation may be hampered by social immaturity appears to be unfounded.

That this is the case, however, does not guarantee the success of these special programs. Education, especially of precocious youth, is a two-sided affair. The students are ready, able, and willing to exercise their superior talents to the utmost. The unknown factor that may hinder efforts to provide programs for these gifted boys is the attitude of educators, teachers, other students, and the public in general to the new and innovative procedures that will be required. If the reception is cold or hostile, there is little chance that the new programs will succeed and continue. The caution that should be sounded is one that will sensitize educators to the hostility which accompanies innovation—not from the recipients of such programs but from the rest of the educational community. For example, while accelerated students are able to interact both socially and intellectually with older students, the older students may resent their presence. As much damage can result from ignorance and prejudice on the part of the uninformed as from the demands of any particular program on the students themselves.

The students are ready. What we need to determine are the attitudes of the other parties involved in the educational process. If these attitudes are negative, we need to specify approaches that will modify these potential impediments to important and progressive educational ventures. If they are positive, we need to move ahead and provide for the specific educational needs of this special group of students. In practice, attitude modification and educational facilitation will usually proceed together.

[4]Not long after the completion of this chapter, CPI results for the 1973 winners group were analyzed. Most of the major findings discussed in this chapter were replicated.

# References

Davids, A. 1966. Psychological characteristics of high school male and female potential scientists in comparison with academic underachievers. *Psychology in the Schools* 3: 79–87.

Demos, G. D., and Weijola, M. J. 1966. Achievement-personality criteria as selectors of participants and predictors of success in special programs in higher education. *California Journal of Educational Research* 17: 186–92.

Domino, G. 1968. Differential prediction of academic achievement in conforming and independent settings. *Journal of Educational Psychology* 59: 256–60.

Gough, H. G. 1966. Appraisal of social maturity by means of the CPI. *Journal of Abnormal Psychology* 71: 144–49.

———. 1968a. College attendance among high aptitude students as predicted from the California Psychological Inventory. *Journal of Counseling Psychology* 15: 269–78.

———. 1968b. An interpreter's syllabus for the California Psychological Inventory. In P. McReynolds (ed.), *Advances in Psychological Assessment*, vol. 1. Palo Alto, Calif.: Science and Behavior Books.

———. 1969. *Manual for the California Psychological Inventory*. Palo Alto, Calif.: Consulting Psychologists Press.

———, and Fink, M. B. 1964. Scholastic achievement among students of average ability, as predicted from the California Psychological Inventory. *Psychology in the Schools* 1: 375–80.

Hall, W. B., and MacKinnon, D. W. 1969. Personality inventories as predictors of creativity among architects. *Journal of Applied Psychology* 53: 322–26.

Hogan, R. 1969. Development of an empathy scale. *Journal of Consulting and Clinical Psychology* 33: 307–16.

Lessinger, L. M., and Martinson, R. A. 1961. The use of the CPI with gifted pupils. *Personnel and Guidance Journal* 39: 572–75.

Oden, M. H. 1968. The fulfillment of promise: 40-year follow-up of the Terman gifted group. *Genetic Psychology Monographs* 77(1): 3–93.

Pressey, S. L. 1949. *Educational Acceleration: Appraisal and basic problems.* Bureau of Educational Research Monographs, no. 31. Columbus: Ohio State University Press.

Syphers, D. F. 1972. *Gifted and talented children: Practical programming for teachers and principals.* Arlington, Va.: The Council for Exceptional Children.

Terman, L. M. 1925–1959. *Genetic Studies of Genius.* 5 vols. Stanford, Calif.: Stanford University Press.

# VIII · values and career interests of mathematically and scientifically precocious youth

## LYNN H. FOX and SUSANNE A. DENHAM

[Editors' Note: *Educational intervention and counseling based on cognitive test scores alone can be more harmful than helpful. In this chapter the authors examine two areas which should be of paramount concern to those who work with gifted students: career interests and values. Adding interpretable measures of these areas to the counselor's stockpile of information can increase his effectiveness.*]

Personal values and interests are important psychological indicators of a person's potential and subsequent behavior. Because of the nature of our intervention program, which provides educational counseling and facilitation to the winners and near-winners of a mathematical and scientific talent search (as described earlier by Fox in chapter 3), it was also important to learn something about the values and attitudes of these young people. We wanted to view each individual as an integrated whole by considering both affective and intellectual components. Indeed, we believe it impossible to separate these aspects in the counseling situation. It is clear that an individual's desire and ability to achieve success in a given educational setting are heavily dependent upon his personal interests and values as well as his cognitive abilities.

So little is known, however, about the relationships among interests, values, and precocious mathematical achievement for such a young group that we could not specify them with certainty. We did think it unlikely that many students would exhibit a great deal of precocious achievement in mathematics if they did not value learning for its own sake and have interests in science or mathematics as potential career areas. Nor did it seem likely that many students would enter mathematics and science competitions if they did not have some mathematical and scientific interests. Therefore, for the following two purposes it seemed desirable to collect some information about career interests and values: (1) to provide information about the student in addition to cognitive test scores which would be useful in counseling the contest winners and near-winners and their parents and (2) to learn more about the specific nature of the relationship of career interests and values to mathematical achievement and success in various programs of educational facilitation. These will guide us in refining the educational decision-making process as described by Fox in chapter 3.

This chapter presents some of the data we have collected on values and career interests of the young people who participated in our 1972 competition. We will discuss the implications of the data for understanding precocious achievement in mathematics and for planning appropriate educational programs for the highly talented.

## Vocational Interests

The first step was to collect some measures of vocational interests for the large group of students who participated in the mathematics and science competitions in the spring of 1972—396 students took the math test and 192 students took the science test, with 138 taking both. All applicants were sent a short questionnaire to complete and bring with them to the testing. It asked them to list the three careers which they considered to be most appealing at that time. The questionnaire also asked for the occupations of their parents.

On the day of the testing, the first six scales of the Vocational Preference Inventory (VPI) (Holland 1958) were administered as a one-page checklist. Six scales of the VPI were used, consisting of 14 occupations each (see figure 8.1). The six categories of occupations are realistic, investigative, enterprising, artistic, social, and conventional. The student indicates for each occupation either a liking (yes) or disliking (no) for that type of work. By tallying the "Y" checks for each of the six scales, one can rank the six occupational categories in order of preference. This rank order is expressed as a code. Thus, for example, a code of IASREC means that the student checked "Y" for the greatest number of occupations on the investigative scale, the next greatest number on the artistic scale, and so on to the least number on the conventional scale.

Underlying Holland's theory of vocational choice (1973) is the view that vocational interests are closely allied with an individual's entire personality. Holland believes that people in an occupational category tend to resemble each other on measures of interests and values. Indeed, it is this harmony which allows them to function efficiently in the same work environment. A detailed discussion of each of the personality types associated with each letter code is found in Holland (1973). The typical procedure for users of the checklist is to select three letters to form a code to characterize an occupation or personality type. All occu-

## ■ ■ OCCUPATIONS

This is an inventory of your feelings and attitudes about many kinds of work. Show the occupations that *interest* or *appeal* to you by blackening under Y for "Yes." Show the occupations that you *dislike* or find *uninteresting* by blackening under N for "No."

| | Y | N | | Y | N |
|---|---|---|---|---|---|
| Airplane Mechanic | ☐ | ☐ | Foreign Missionary | ☐ | ☐ |
| Fish and Wildlife Specialist | ☐ | ☐ | High School Teacher | ☐ | ☐ |
| Power Station Operator | ☐ | ☐ | Juvenile Delinquency Expert | ☐ | ☐ |
| Master Plumber | ☐ | ☐ | Speech Therapist | ☐ | ☐ |
| Power Shovel Operator | ☐ | ☐ | Marriage Counselor | ☐ | ☐ |
| Surveyor | ☐ | ☐ | Physical Education Teacher | ☐ | ☐ |
| Construction Inspector | ☐ | ☐ | Playground Director | ☐ | ☐ |
| Radio Operator | ☐ | ☐ | Clinical Psychologist | ☐ | ☐ |
| Filling Station Attendant | ☐ | ☐ | Social Science Teacher | ☐ | ☐ |
| Tree Surgeon | ☐ | ☐ | Director of Welfare Agency | ☐ | ☐ |
| Tool Designer | ☐ | ☐ | Asst. City School Supt. | ☐ | ☐ |
| Locomotive Engineer | ☐ | ☐ | Personal Counselor | ☐ | ☐ |
| Photoengraver | ☐ | ☐ | Psychiatric Case Worker | ☐ | ☐ |
| Electrician | ☐ | ☐ | Vocational Counselor | ☐ | ☐ |
| **Total Realistic Y's** ☐ | | | **Total Social Y's** ☐ | | |
| Meteorologist | ☐ | ☐ | Speculator | ☐ | ☐ |
| Biologist | ☐ | ☐ | Buyer | ☐ | ☐ |
| Astronomer | ☐ | ☐ | Stock & Bond Salesman | ☐ | ☐ |
| Aeronautical Design Engineer | ☐ | ☐ | Manufacturer's Representative | ☐ | ☐ |
| Anthropologist | ☐ | ☐ | Television Producer | ☐ | ☐ |
| Zoologist | ☐ | ☐ | Hotel Manager | ☐ | ☐ |
| Chemist | ☐ | ☐ | Business Executive | ☐ | ☐ |
| Independent Research Scientist | ☐ | ☐ | Restaurant Worker | ☐ | ☐ |
| Writer of Scientific Articles | ☐ | ☐ | Master of Ceremonies | ☐ | ☐ |
| Editor of a Scientific Journal | ☐ | ☐ | Traveling Salesman | ☐ | ☐ |
| Geologist | ☐ | ☐ | Real Estate Salesman | ☐ | ☐ |
| Botanist | ☐ | ☐ | Industrial Relations Consultant | ☐ | ☐ |
| Scientific Research Worker | ☐ | ☐ | Sports Promoter | ☐ | ☐ |
| Physicist | ☐ | ☐ | Political Campaign Manager | ☐ | ☐ |
| **Total Investigative Y's** ☐ | | | **Total Enterprising Y's** ☐ | | |
| Poet | ☐ | ☐ | Bookkeeper | ☐ | ☐ |
| Symphony Conductor | ☐ | ☐ | Quality Control Expert | ☐ | ☐ |
| Musician | ☐ | ☐ | Budget Reviewer | ☐ | ☐ |
| Author | ☐ | ☐ | Traffic Manager | ☐ | ☐ |
| Commercial Artist | ☐ | ☐ | Statistician | ☐ | ☐ |
| Free-Lance Writer | ☐ | ☐ | Court Stenographer | ☐ | ☐ |
| Musical Arranger | ☐ | ☐ | Bank Teller | ☐ | ☐ |
| Art Dealer | ☐ | ☐ | Tax Expert | ☐ | ☐ |
| Dramatic Coach | ☐ | ☐ | Inventory Controller | ☐ | ☐ |
| Concert Singer | ☐ | ☐ | IBM Equipment Operator | ☐ | ☐ |
| Composer | ☐ | ☐ | Financial Analyst | ☐ | ☐ |
| Stage Director | ☐ | ☐ | Cost Estimator | ☐ | ☐ |
| Playwright | ☐ | ☐ | Payroll Clerk | ☐ | ☐ |
| Cartoonist | ☐ | ☐ | Bank Examiner | ☐ | ☐ |
| **Total Artistic Y's** ☐ | | | **Total Conventional Y's** ☐ | | |

Figure 8.1: *Occupational checklist from Vocational Preference Inventory (VPI)*

pations in the Dictionary of Occupational Titles can be classified according to the Holland system (Viernstein 1972; Holland 1973).

Thus for each contestant we obtained one or more three-letter codes from the VPI scales[1] and a three-letter code for the student's first-choice occupation on the questionnaire. In addition, the occupations of the contestants' parents were assigned Holland codes. The first letter of the Holland code is the focus of interest in the following discussion.

## Vocational Preferences of the Contestants[2]

### The Occupational Checklist

The first question posed was: What are the occupational interests, as assigned by the VPI scales, of students who enter a mathematics and/or science competition? The answer was that boys and eighth- and ninth-grade girls definitely prefer investigative occupations on the checklist. Seventh-grade girls, particularly those who entered only the mathematics contest, chose artistic occupations more frequently than investigative ones. Sixty-eight percent of the girls and 70 percent of the boys checked investigative or artistic occupations most frequently. (The expected percent for chance marking would be 33.)

Table 8.1 shows the most preferred occupational code of all contestants, differentiated by grade and sex.[3] Far more boys than girls in both grade groups preferred the investigative occupations.[4] More girls than boys checked artistic and social occupations most frequently, while more boys than girls showed interest in enterprising and realistic occupations. All sex differences between seventh-grade girls and boys and eighth- and ninth-grade girls and boys were significant (p < .01) except for conventional occupation preferences such as bookkeeper, payroll clerk, or bank teller.

[1]For those students with equal numbers of first, second, or third choices in two or more categories, more than one three-digit code was obtained. For example, a first-choice tie of I and A, with S second, would result in two three-digit codes for this person: IAS and AIS. Ties on second and/or third choices would increase the number of three-digit codes accordingly.
[2]Summary data were available for 446 of 450 contestants.
[3]Students with ties were given one-half of a frequency point in each of the two tied categories, one-third of a frequency point for each of three tied categories, or one-fourth of a frequency point for each of the four tied categories. These fractional frequencies were used to determine the entries for the percentages in table 8.1.
[4]Summary information concerning age or sex categories for tables 8.1, 8.3, 8.4, 8.5, 8.6, 8.7, 8.10, and 8.11 may be found in general tables in appendix D.

mathematical talent

Table 8.1:   *Highest code on the VPI scales for all students in the math and science competition, by grade and sex*

| Grade– Sex Group | Number | Holland Category from VPI scales | | | | | |
|---|---|---|---|---|---|---|---|
| | | I | A | S | E | C | R |
| 7th grade girls | 83 | 30.5% | 40.4% | 22.3% | 2.8% | 4.0% | 0.0% |
| 7th grade boys | 103 | 59.5 | 10.6 | 4.0 | 9.2 | 4.0 | 12.8 |
| 8th and 9th grade girls | 100 | 37.8 | 26.8 | 22.8 | 6.5 | 5.5 | 0.5 |
| 8th and 9th grade boys | 160 | 57.9 | 10.6 | 3.1 | 10.3 | 9.0 | 9.1 |

I = investigative; A = artistic; S = social; E = enterprising; C = conventional; R = realistic.

Investigative, artistic, and enterprising occupational frequencies were significantly different between grades for girls only (p < .01),[5] but not for boys. Artistic, investigative, and social occupational interests were nearly equally popular among the girls, almost to the exclusion of the conventional, enterprising, and realistic categories. About 93 percent of the seventh-grade girls and 87 percent of the eighth- and ninth-grade girls preferred occupations of either investigative, artistic, or social natures. The least popular occupational category for girls was realistic, which is perhaps understandable in light of the fact that all of the occupations listed on that scale typically are considered to be very masculine.

Boys who entered the contest were most apt to be those with strong interests in the investigative occupations. In fact, no other single occupational category came close in popularity. For seventh-grade boys the realistic occupations such as surveyor, radio operator, and airplane mechanic were the second most frequently checked occupational group. Yet only 12.8 percent of this group of boys checked this category most frequently. The artistic category was the third most popular scale for seventh-grade boys, although for less than 11 percent of them. Eighth- and ninth-grade boys ranked second on the artistic occupations (10.6 percent) and third on the enterprising group (10.3 percent), but realistic and conventional occupations followed closely in popularity (9.1 and 9.0 percent, respectively). The social category was least popular with them (3.1 percent); this scale includes some occupations such as physical

[5]Chi-square tests were used to determine statistical significance; because of lack of independence in cases where the tying procedure was used, the chi-square values are somewhat low. Thus the significance that was found is truly significant, but some significant differences may have been overlooked.

education teacher, high school teacher, and assistant city school superintendent, which are not considered strictly feminine.

The majority of students entering the competition preferred occupations in either investigative, artistic, or social scales of the VPI. It should be noted that the occupations represented in these categories are typically ones requiring a college degree and often advanced degrees. Jobs listed under realistic, conventional, and enterprising categories were less often those which require bachelor's or advanced degrees. Thus, it is possible that the overwhelming preferences for the investigative, artistic, and social categories reflect the level of these students' educational aspirations and aspirations for professional careers as well as their interest in these fields for their content.

It is of course possible that students entering a mathematics and/or science contest would be more prone to list occupations on their questionnaire and check VPI occupations which were scientific in nature than students in general. Students had been told, however, that the VPI scales and questionnaire would not be used in selecting the winners.

Table 8.2 contains a further breakdown of the contestants by tests taken, occupational preference, and sex. The results are enlightening. In general, students who entered the science contest only or both the mathematics and science contests were more strongly oriented, although not significantly so, toward the investigative occupations than were those students who entered only the mathematics contest. This difference probably results from the fact that the occupations listed on the investigative scale of the VPI are all scientific and not heavily mathematical. Mathematician, engineer, and computer programmer, for example, are not listed there, although they would be considered investigative occupations under the Holland coding system.

Sex differences similar to those in table 8.1 again appear. Boys and girls who took only the mathematics tests, or both mathematics and science tests, were significantly different ($p < .001$) in their pattern of interests. Boys and girls who took the science test only did not differ significantly on interests, possibly because the few girls (13) who took only this test were generally more masculine in their interests (see chapter 4).

Students of the same sex who took different tests were not found to vary significantly in their pattern of interests, except that males who took only the mathematics tests differed ($p < .025$) from those who took both tests; they were far less investigative than the other boys (48 percent versus 71 percent and 69 percent). Overall, it is important to note that clear sex differences do again appear, except for the girls who took the science test. Even then, the girls differed from the science-only boys in the usual directions. Further, certain important differences in pref-

mathematical talent

Table 8.2:  *Percent of students preferring each occupational category, by tests taken and sex*

|  |  |  | VPI Category[a] |  |  |  |  |  |
|---|---|---|---|---|---|---|---|---|
| Tests taken | Sex | N | I | A | S | C | E | R |
| Mathematics test only | Girls | 121 | 30.0 | 32.0 | 26.2 | 6.0 | 5.8 | 0.0 |
|  | Boys | 136 | 47.4 | 11.3 | 4.6 | 9.5 | 12.8 | 14.5 |
| Mathematics and science tests | Girls | 49 | 40.8 | 36.4 | 16.0 | 3.1 | 3.7 | 0.0 |
|  | Boys | 86 | 71.1 | 10.6 | 1.4 | 3.8 | 7.9 | 5.2 |
| Science test only | Girls | 13 | 54.2 | 29.2 | 12.5 | 0.0 | 0.0 | 4.1 |
|  | Boys | 41 | 69.1 | 8.5 | 3.7 | 5.7 | 4.5 | 8.5 |

[a]See note to table 8.1 for definition of Holland categories.

erences for investigative occupations emerge between students who took different tests, particularly between males who took only the mathematics test and those who took both tests.

## First-Choice Occupations on the Questionnaire and Consistency with the VPI Scales[6]

The second question we considered was: What specific occupations did the contestants list on their questionnaire and how consistent were these with the general areas of occupational interest shown on the VPI scales? In order to answer this question we coded the occupations listed

Table 8.3:  *Percent of students whose first-choice occupation matched their highest VPI code*

| Grade– Sex Group | Total percent matched | Matching first-choice and highest code |  |  |  |  |  |
|---|---|---|---|---|---|---|---|
|  |  | I | S | A | E | R | C |
| 7th grade girls | 43.6 | 44.1 | 29.4 | 26.5 | 0.0 | 0.0 | 0.0 |
| 7th grade boys | 53.4 | 86.7 | 2.4 | 1.8 | 3.6 | 5.4 | 0.0 |
| 8th and 9th grade girls | 54.1 | 55.4 | 29.2 | 10.4 | 0.0 | 1.2 | 3.8 |
| 8th and 9th grade boys | 56.4 | 88.7 | 0.0 | 4.3 | 5.0 | 1.0 | 1.0 |

[6]In general tables corresponding to the matching of first-choice occupation with Holland code, total N does not reach 446 because of missing data.

on the questionnaire in terms of Holland's six occupational categories. (Occupational codes for almost all of the occupations listed on the checklist were found from the application of the Holland code to the Dictionary of Occupational Titles by Viernstein 1972.) One can consider the consistency between these two measures as an indication of strength of occupational interest. A comparison of the category of first-choice occupations with the preferred occupational scale on the VPI is shown in table 8.3. Fifty-four percent of all students had agreement between their first-choice occupation and most-preferred occupational scale on the VPI. The great majority of these matches were for the investigative category of occupations.

## Investigative Occupations

Occupations listed on the questionnaire were predominantly from the investigative category for both boys and girls. Careers in medicine, engineering, and science were very popular. More girls than boys specifically mentioned mathematics teacher. (Note that mathematics teacher is considered investigative, but that the general occupation of teacher is classified as social.) This was the single most frequently mentioned investigative occupation named by girls. Boys most often listed a type of scientist or the general term "scientist." The occupation of "doctor" (physician) was the second most frequently named occupation by both sexes.

Thus it seems that many of the contestants were strongly oriented toward investigative careers, some of which require a great deal of mathematical ability. Had more occupations of a specifically mathematical nature been on the checklist the agreement between the two measures might well have been greater. The agreement for the investigative category was much stronger for boys than for girls because on both measures boys indicated interests in the area of investigative occupations, particularly scientific ones, more frequently than did girls. The patterns of matches were significantly different ($p < .01$) for boys and girls in both grade groups. There were no statistically significant grade differences within the same sex on overall patterns of matches, including I.

## Social Occupations

Girls far more often than boys listed occupations of a social nature, such as teacher. The occupation of homemaker is coded as social, but, surprisingly, this career was almost never mentioned by girls or boys. This perhaps reflects the fact that the girls did not consider homemaking an occupation. Certainly, most girls, even when as young as the contestants, eventually do expect to marry. We are not sure if the girls in our contest are in some way deviant from their age-grade cohorts in terms of occupational interest. Probably they are, because they are considerably brighter and oriented strongly enough toward mathematics and/or science to enter a difficult contest. For a more detailed discussion of the relationship of vocational career interests and mathematical aptitude the reader is referred to the work of Astin (1968a, 1968b) and, particularly, chapter 4 of this volume.

Approximately 27 matches occurred on social occupations, predominantly for girls. Perhaps girls who had preferences for social occupations but who were interested enough in mathematics or science to enter a contest, see mathematics and science as instrumental in careers of a more social nature. Since women in general show strong orientations toward social values, perhaps the way to interest more girls in scientific and mathematical careers is to educate them in the ways in which science and mathematics can be applied to solve problems of a social nature. Since few women currently seek mathematical or scientific careers, this hypothesis should be studied empirically in career education programs.

### Artistic Occupations

Although the artistic occupations had been popular on the VPI scales particularly with seventh-grade girls, only a few students actually listed artistic occupations such as actress, author, or artist on their questionnaire. Seventh-grade girls listed artistic occupations more often than any other group. "Architect" occurred occasionally as a first choice for boys. This scarcity of artistic career plans seems to indicate that while many students, particularly middle-class young people, are encouraged to join choirs and theatrical groups, to take music, art, and dancing lessons, and generally to pursue artistic endeavors, few of them are expected to be talented enough to seek full-time careers in these areas.

Although the artistic scale was strongly preferred on the VPI scales (about 20 percent of all contestants checked that category most frequently), few students except seventh-grade girls (26.5 percent) matched on the two measures for that category.

### Enterprising Occupations

Enterprising occupations were not frequently listed on the questionnaire by boys or girls. When an enterprising occupation was named, it was almost always that of "lawyer." Although the number of boys who listed enterprising occupations was small, the specific occupation of lawyer was one of the four most popular specific job titles. Few boys and only one girl preferred enterprising occupations on both the questionnaire and the VPI scale.

## Realistic Occupations

Realistic occupations were not listed on the questionnaire by many girls or boys. Two seventh-grade girls were interested in the occupation of animal trainer, and a few boys listed policeman, fireman, or a job in the military. Very few contestants showed interest in realistic careers on both measures of vocational interest.

## Conventional Occupations

Occupations of a conventional nature were almost never listed on the questionnaire. Secretary was mentioned by a few eighth-grade girls, and data processor or accountant was mentioned by a few boys. Few boys or girls showed a preference for conventional occupations on either interest measure, and so matches in this category were rare.

## Occupations of Parents[7]

A third question of interest was: To what extent do the contestants come from homes where at least one parent is involved in a scientific or mathematical career? The occupations of parents were listed on the students' questionnaires and were assigned a three-letter code from the application of the Holland system to the Dictionary of Occupational Titles (Viernstein 1972). Table 8.4 shows the distribution of students by their fathers' occupational category. Although the contestants are strongly oriented toward careers in mathematics or science, few students come from homes where the parents are employed in mathematical or scientific careers.

---

[7]In general tables corresponding to parents' occupations and parent-child matching, total N's differ due to incomplete data; none reach the total of 446.

Table 8.4:   *Percent of students in each of the four grade–sex groups, by category of father's occupation*

| Grade–Sex Group | Number | Father's Occupational Category[a] | | | | | |
|---|---|---|---|---|---|---|---|
| | | E | I | R | S | C | A |
| 7th grade girls | 78 | 38 | 20 | 26 | 5 | 8 | 3 |
| 7th grade boys | 97 | 32 | 30 | 27 | 6 | 3 | 2 |
| 8th and 9th grade girls | 89 | 31 | 38 | 24 | 3 | 3 | 1 |
| 8th and 9th grade boys | 149 | 34 | 24 | 23 | 9 | 6 | 3 |

[a]See note to table 8.1 for definition of Holland categories.

## Fathers

Over a fourth of the fathers (28 percent) of contestants were employed in investigative careers. The largest proportion of fathers (34 percent) were employed in occupations which were classified as enterprising. About 25 percent of the fathers had jobs in the realistic category. Very few fathers were employed in occupations that are categorized as social, conventional, or artistic. Paternal occupational patterns were not significantly different for girls and boys or the three grade groups.

In table 8.5 we see the percent of students by sex and grade whose Holland checklist preferences were in the occupational category which corresponded to their father's occupation. Overall, more boys' than girls' career interests matched the occupational category of their fathers' occupations. By far the greatest number of matches for both boys and girls was in the investigative category of occupations.

Table 8.5:   *Percent of students whose VPI code matched their fathers' occupational code*

| Grade–Sex Group | Total percent matched | Matching Student and Father Codes[a] | | | | | |
|---|---|---|---|---|---|---|---|
| | | I | E | R | C | A | S |
| 7th grade girls | 10.8 | 82.2 | 17.8 | 0.0 | 0.0 | 0.0 | 0.0 |
| 7th grade boys | 27.5 | 70.0 | 7.0 | 23.0 | 0.0 | 0.0 | 0.0 |
| 8th and 9th grade girls | 32.5 | 72.5 | 13.2 | 3.2 | 7.9 | 0.0 | 3.2 |
| 8th and 9th grade boys | 32.4 | 49.5 | 26.7 | 13.6 | 5.7 | 4.4 | 0.0 |

[a]See note to table 8.1 for definition of Holland categories.

Table 8.6:  *Percent of students in each of the four grade–sex groups, by category of mother's occupation*

| Grade–Sex Group | Number | Mother's Occupational Category[a] | | | | | |
|---|---|---|---|---|---|---|---|
| | | S | C | E | I | R | A |
| 7th grade girls | 79 | 72 | 16 | 6 | 3 | 2 | 1 |
| 7th grade boys | 98 | 73 | 11 | 5 | 6 | 3 | 2 |
| 8th and 9th grade girls | 89 | 75 | 13 | 7 | 3 | 2 | 0 |
| 8th and 9th grade boys | 152 | 76 | 12 | 4 | 5 | 2 | 1 |

[a] See note to table 8.1 for definition of Holland categories.

## Mothers

Table 8.6 shows the distributions of contestants by grade, sex, and occupational category of mother. The mothers of the contestants were most often involved in social occupations (74 percent) such as home-maker or teacher. About 13 percent of the mothers were employed in conventional occupations such as secretary. Very few mothers were employed in enterprising, investigative, realistic, or artistic occupations. Maternal occupational patterns were not significantly different for girls and boys or the three grade groups.

In table 8.7 we see that more girls than boys showed an interest in career fields in which their mothers were employed. Girls' career interests most often matched their mothers' occupations in the social category. Boys whose career interests matched their mothers' occupations had most frequently chosen the investigative category.

Table 8.7:  *Percent of students whose VPI code matched their mothers' occupational code*

| Grade–Sex Group | Total percent matched | Matching Student's and Mother's Codes[a] | | | | | |
|---|---|---|---|---|---|---|---|
| | | S | I | C | E | R | A |
| 7th grade girls | 20.5 | 85.3 | 5.9 | 8.8 | 0.0 | 0.0 | 0.0 |
| 7th grade boys | 15.9 | 26.9 | 38.9 | 12.4 | 21.8 | 0.0 | 0.0 |
| 8th and 9th grade girls | 27.1 | 80.8 | 11.5 | 7.7 | 0.0 | 0.0 | 0.0 |
| 8th and 9th grade boys | 8.3 | 40.8 | 36.3 | 0.0 | 7.6 | 11.4 | 3.8 |

[a] See note to table 8.1 for definition of Holland categories.

Table 8.8:    *Percent of students and parents by occupational code*

| | Occupational Category | | | | | |
|---|---|---|---|---|---|---|
| | I | A | S | E | C | R |
| Girls[a] | 35 | 33 | 22 | 4 | 5 | 0 |
| Boys[a] | 61 | 11 | 3 | 9 | 7 | 10 |
| Fathers[b] of girls | 29 | 2 | 4 | 35 | 5 | 24 |
| Fathers[b] of boys | 26 | 3 | 8 | 33 | 5 | 25 |
| Mothers[b] of girls | 3 | 1 | 74 | 6 | 14 | 2 |
| Mothers[b] of boys | 6 | 2 | 75 | 4 | 12 | 3 |

[a] From VPI scales.
[b] From coding of occupations.

Table 8.8 provides a summary of distributions of students and their parents on occupational codes. It can be seen that occupational preferences of students as measured by the VPI scales were predominantly investigative. The distribution of parents by classification of occupation is quite different from the distribution of students by their interests. The patterns of employment for mothers and fathers differ. Mothers and fathers of boys have employment patterns similar to those of mothers and fathers of girls.

## Vocational Interests and Achievement

### *Mathematics*

The average score on the SAT-M for high school senior boys who take the SAT-M for college admission is about 510. In table 8.9 it can be seen that about half of the boys in the contest scored 510 or above. Of these, about half had investigative preferences on the VPI scales. Of the 117 boys in the contest (seventh and eighth grades) who scored below 510, half had investigative preferences on the checklist. In other words, there was no greater trend for boys who scored high (510 or above) on the mathematics test to be interested in investigative careers than boys who scored lower (below 510).

Table 8.9:    *Percent of high and low scoring girls and boys whose highest code on the VPI was investigative, by grade and sex*

|  |  | 7th Graders | | 8th and 9th Graders | |
|---|---|---|---|---|---|
|  |  | Number | Percent highest on I | Number | Percent highest on I |
| Girls | Scored high 460–600 | 27 | 37[a] | 55 | 35 |
|  | Scored low 210–450 | 50 | 18 | 41 | 25 |
| Boys | Scored high 510–790 | 26 | 58 | 77 | 51 |
|  | Scored low 210–500 | 64 | 50 | 53 | 55 |

[a] Of the seventh grade girls 37 percent (i.e., 27 of them) scored high on SAT-M and scored highest (of the six VPI scales) on I.

For high school senior girls who take SAT-M for college admission, the mean score is about 466. Slightly less than half of the girls in the contest scored 460 or above. Thirty-five percent of all girls (seventh and eighth grades) who scored high (460 or above) had investigative career preferences on the VPI scales, while only 20 percent of all girls who scored lower (below 460) preferred the investigative occupations. This difference was statistically significant ($p < .05$). Thus it appears that interest in investigative occupations is more closely related to the performance of girls on difficult tests of mathematical reasoning ability than to the performance of boys. A similar finding of the relationship of mathematical aptitude to professional career interests has been reported by Astin (1968*a*, 1968*b*) and in chapter 4 in this volume.

The SAT-M scores for all students in the mathematics contest in relation to grade, sex, and category of occupational interest (from the VPI scales) are shown in table 8.10. Seventh-grade boys and girls who had investigative or artistic interests had higher mean scores than other occupational interest groups of their grade and sex. Eighth- and young ninth-grade girls who were interested in conventional or investigative careers had higher average scores than girls with other interests. Eighth- and young ninth-grade boys who were interested in realistic or investigative careers had higher scores than boys with other interests. The reader is reminded that the number of students in some of the occupational interest categories is quite small, and he may wish to refer to the general table D.7 in appendix D.

mathematical talent

Table 8.10:    *Mean SAT-M score by grade, sex, and VPI code*

| Grade– Sex Group | Number | VPI Code[a] | | | | | |
|---|---|---|---|---|---|---|---|
| | | I | A | R | C | E | S |
| 7th grade girls | 76 | 440.54 | 423.35 | – | 371.37 | 389.13 | 411.94 |
| 7th grade boys | 90 | 470.29 | 468.50 | 447.46 | 427.94 | 410.89 | 406.33 |
| 8th and 9th grade girls | 95 | 470.83 | 446.78 | – | 472.73 | 442.73 | 447.40 |
| 8th and 9th grade boys | 132 | 534.59 | 519.29 | 573.25 | 512.99 | 459.94 | 483.50 |

[a]See note to table 8.1 for definition of Holland categories.

## Science

Table 8.11 shows mean science scores by grade, sex, and occupational preference. For seventh-grade girls, mean scores on the science test were highest for those who preferred investigative and artistic occupations. Seventh-grade boys' scores were highest for those who preferred realistic and investigative occupations. Eighth- and ninth-grade girls who preferred enterprising occupations had the highest mean for the girls. Eighth- and ninth-grade boys who preferred the investigative occupations had the highest mean score of all the 24 grade-sex occupational groups. Eighth- and ninth-grade boys with artistic preferences were second highest. Significant overall sex differences (p < .01) occurred in both the grade groups.

Table 8.11:    *Mean STEP Science IA and IB scores by grade, sex, and VPI code*

| Grade– Sex Group | Number | VPI Code[a] | | | | | |
|---|---|---|---|---|---|---|---|
| | | I | A | E | S | R | C |
| 7th grade girls | 24 | 72.40 | 69.95 | – | 65.00 | – | 45.00 |
| 7th grade boys | 36 | 77.99 | 73.07 | 71.00 | 64.33 | 80.71 | – |
| 8th and 9th grade girls | 37 | 75.46 | 63.17 | 78.31 | 72.43 | 55.00 | 45.00 |
| 8th and 9th grade boys | 91 | 89.74 | 84.65 | 66.63 | 69.20 | 71.04 | 77.46 |

[a]See note to table 8.1 for definition of Holland categories.

*Contest Winners and Near-Winners*

The winners and near-winners in the mathematics and science contests, like the group of contestants as a whole, favored the investigative category on the VPI scales. Sixty-five percent of the 35 boys preferred the investigative. This is higher, though not significantly so, than the 61 percent of all boys tested (see general table D.1 in appendix D). The distribution is shown in table 8.12.

College courses were offered to certain of these boys on the basis of cognitive test scores. The group of boys who were offered college courses but declined to take them showed slightly less preference for the investigative category than did both the group who took courses and those who were not offered them. Seventy-eight percent of the group that was offered courses and 78 percent of those who were not offered courses preferred the investigative occupations on the VPI scales. Sixty-seven percent of the group that declined scored highest on investigative occupations. These groups are very small; therefore this discussion is highly tentative and differences are not significant.

Only one boy who took college courses preferred the artistic category and only one preferred the realistic category. Of the group that declined, one preferred artistic, another enterprising, and a third social. Of the group not offered courses, three preferred realistic, one artistic, and one conventional.

Of the eight high scoring girls (see table 8.13), five had investigative preferences, one preferred the social category, and the other two had ties for their first preference; one of the last two tied conventional with social, and the other tied artistic with investigative. Thus, if one gives this last-mentioned girl half a point for investigative, 69 percent of the girls had investigative interests.

*Summary*

Junior high school students who elect to enter a mathematics and science competition are typically those with interests in mathematical and scientific occupations. Of the six occupational categories on the VPI, the investigative scale was preferred by nearly half of the students. Those who participated in only the science competition showed a slightly, but not significantly, greater preference for investigative occupations. Only a fourth of the fathers of contestants were employed in investigative occupations.

Boys more than girls preferred the investigative occupations on the VPI scales. However, for girls, interest in investigative occupations was

Table 8.12:  Scores of the 35 mathematics and/or science winners and near-winners (all male) on the SAT, CEEB Math Achievement I, and VPI code

| Student number | SAT-M | SAT-V | M-I | Holland | Student number | SAT-M | SAT-V | M-I | Holland |
|---|---|---|---|---|---|---|---|---|---|
| 1*   | 790 | 560 | 770 | I     | 19   | 660 | 460 | 520 | R     |
| 2**  | 780 | 620 | 720 | I     | 20** | 660 | 460 | 580 | I     |
| 3**  | 740 | 620 | 660 | I     | 21   | 660 | 420 | 530 | A     |
| 4**  | 740 | 460 | 630 | I     | 22   | 660 | 310 | 600 | R     |
| 5*   | 730 | 560 | 620 | I     | 23*  | 650 | 540 | 560 | S     |
| 6**  | 710 | 530 | 730 | I     | 24   | 640 | 580 | 610 | E/I/R |
| 7**  | 710 | 640 | 640 | A     | 25   | 640 | 400 | 510 | R     |
| 8*   | 690 | 550 | 590 | A     | 26** | 630 | 580 | 500 | I     |
| 9    | 690 | 450 | 520 | I     | 27*  | 620 | 740 | 520 | I     |
| 10*  | 680 | 670 | 720 | C     | 28   | 620 | 530 | 640 | I/R   |
| 11*  | 680 | 620 | 570 | I     | 29   | 610 | 530 | 520 | R     |
| 12   | 680 | 540 | 610 | C/I   | 30*  | 600 | 600 |     | I     |
| 13   | 680 | 450 | 500 | C     | 31   | 600 | 550 | 520 | I     |
| 14   | 680 | 500 | 510 | C/I/R | 32   | 590 | 550 |     | I     |
| 15** | 670 | 650 | 660 | I     | 33   | 560 | 620 | 540 | I     |
| 16** | 670 | 570 | 610 | I     | 34   | 530 | 550 | 470 | I     |
| 17*  | 670 | 590 | 600 | I     | 35   | 520 | 630 | 510 | I     |
| 18   | 660 | 490 | 520 | I     |      |     |     |     |       |

Mean SAT Math aptitude score:  660
Mean SAT Verbal aptitude score:  546
Mean CEEB Math I score:  585

*College course offered but declined.
**College course taken.

Table 8.13:  *Scores of the eight highest scoring girls on the SAT, CEEB Math Achievement I, and VPI code*

| Student number | SAT-M | SAT-V | M-I | Holland |
|---|---|---|---|---|
| 1* | 600 | 610 | | I |
| 2 | 600 | 560 | 450 | I |
| 3** | 600 | 490 | 520 | C/S |
| 4 | 590 | 380 | | I |
| 5 | 590 | 500 | 450 | A/I |
| 6** | 510 | 570 | 500 | I |
| 7 | 450 | 430 | | I |
| 8*** | | 470 | | S |
| Mean | 563 | 501 | 480 | |

*College course taken.
**College course offered but declined.
***Took the science test only in competition.

more strongly related to performance on the mathematics test than for boys in the total group. The lower scoring boys were as likely to prefer investigative occupations as were the higher scoring boys. More high scoring girls than low scoring girls preferred the investigative occupations. The winners and near-winners of the competition were all male, and they showed strong preferences for investigative occupations. Five of the eight highest scoring females preferred the investigative category, and for a sixth it was tied with artistic.

## Values of Precocious Youth

Another important facet of our knowledge of these students is their values. In order to intervene to facilitate their education, we should like to know the values which are most important to them. Values tend to direct actions; to the extent that they do, they are important for us to know. To date the most effective standardized measure of values for our purposes is the Allport-Vernon-Lindzey "Study of Values" (SV) (see Keating, chapter 2 in this volume). This test was primarily designed for use with college students or with adults who had attended college. It consists of two groups of questions asking for preferences in relatively familiar situations. Examinees must choose between or among two or four values on each item. The value scales so derived are ipsative, that is, reflect relative rather than absolute value levels. Two-hundred forty points are allotted to the six values; thus, the average score for any person's six values is 40.

Six value scales were formulated on the basis of Eduard Spranger's (1966) *Lebensformen*.[8] According to Spranger, the personality of a person is best known through his evaluative attitudes. Briefly, Spranger classifies his types as follows: (1) the *theoretical* man's dominant interest is the discovery of intellectual, scientific, and/or philosophical pursuits and truths; (2) the *economic* man is thoroughly practical and interested in production, consumption, and tangible wealth, (3) the *aesthetic* man values, above all, grace and symmetry and the artistic episodes of life, (4) the *social* man's highest value is his love of people, (5) the *political* man is primarily interested in power, and (6) the *religious* man is primarily mystical.

Despite some disagreement as to exactly what the six scales measure, it has been shown that certain profiles of values on the SV are tied to creativity and other traits in the real world (Hogan 1971). MacKinnon (1962), Warren and Heist (1960), and Southern and Plant (1968) asserted that bright, creative students and adults typically score high on the theoretical and aesthetic scales and low on the religious scale. Hall and MacKinnon (1969) found that similar scores on the SV correlated positively with ratings of professional creativity. Hogan (1971) cited profiles and correlations similar to these for National Merit Scholars, but cautioned that such profiles are not necessarily consistent with these gifted persons' high interest areas. Carlson and Parker (1969) stated that persons who score high on the SV aesthetic scale relative to their other values are more receptive to stimuli, more perceptive, and more intuitive.

The pairing of high scores on both theoretical and aesthetic scales is, at first consideration, paradoxical since the norming population correlations between ipsative scores on these two values are very small (–.10 for men) (see Allport, Vernon and Lindzey 1970, p. 10). The qualities observed by Carlson and Parker, coupled with the theoretical search for truth, seem advantageous for production of creative research. The aesthetic need to find an "elegant" solution to a problem appears to guide the theoretical inquisitiveness of the most creative researchers. This value also may be related to choosing "fitting" problems on which to work.

In the present study the SV was administered to the 35 highest scoring males in the 1972 Mathematics and Science competition, seven high scoring females from the same competition, and a group of their parents. In order to assess the possibility of random filling out of SV's,

---

[8]The 1966 translation of Spranger's work follows the original 1927 German version.

our results have been analyzed in comparison with random profiles generated by computer (Winer 1973). Results indicate that value scores generated by these students do in fact tend to differ significantly from chance, and thus these data show trends worthy of discussion.

### SV Results with Winners and Near-Winners

The 35 highest scoring males and seven females (all those who took the SV) were further subdivided into groups as follows: Group I, who took college courses during the summer of 1972; Group II, who were offered college courses but for various reasons declined; and Group III, who were not offered college courses.[9]

A number of trends can be discerned in these groups' SV scores. Table 8.14 lists profile codes of the three groups of males. The highest, second highest, and lowest scored values are represented by each code; subjects are arranged in descending order of theoretical score. Scores on SAT-M and Raven's Progressive Matrices, Forms ABCDE and II, are juxtaposed for comparison. The majority, 22 of 35, of these students scored highest on the *theoretical* value. Seven of nine members of Group I (78 percent) marked the theoretical value highest and 64 percent of Group II did so, while only 50 percent of Group III concurred. Thus the relative weight of the theoretical value, the seeking of knowledge for its own sake, begins at a high level in Group I and decreases over the other groups.

Mean scores for each of the six values are shown for each of the groups in table 8.15. From the table we see that all groups exceed the mean score of the standardization population of high school males for the theoretical value. Theoretical means are all significantly greater than the profile-average scores of 40 (Winer 1973). Males in Groups I and II, who were offered college courses, scored significantly higher than Group III on the theoretical value ($p < .05$). Group III's theoretical-value-score mean and their lower mean SAT-M score distinguish this group from the other two, and one might suspect that the particular educational facilitation of college courses would be less suitable for this group because of their value orientations as well as their lower cognitive test scores.

The average *economic* value for all three groups of males is close to the average for high school males. Group I's mean score is high by the high school norms, but the difference between Group I's mean and the other two groups' means did not reach significance. The economic value

[9]Groups I, II, and III basically were formed on the basis of mathematics tests scores, with some consideration being given to SV theoretical scores in border-line cases.

Table 8.14:    *"Study of Values" codes and selected value scores for three groups of mathematically talented males*

| Case number | AVL code[a] | Theoretical score | Aesthetic score | SAT-M[b] | Raven's Progressive Matrices ABCDE[c] | II[d] |
|---|---|---|---|---|---|---|
| Group I – 9 accepting offer of college courses | | | | | | |
| 1 | TE,S | 62 | 37 | 710 | 57 | 32 |
| 2 | TE,R | 57 | 40 | 740 | 59 | 33 |
| 3 | TP,R | 55 | 32 | 670 | 59 | 29 |
| 4 | TE,R | 55 | 41 | 740 | 57 | 33 |
| 5 | TE,R | 54 | 42 | 780 | 59 | 31 |
| 6 | TP,S | 53 | 38 | 670 | 55 | 33 |
| 7 | TE,S | 50 | 39 | 710 | 58 | 29 |
| 8 | EP,R | 43 | 28 | 660 | 60 | 30 |
| 9 | AE,P | 33 | 58 | 630 | 59 | 28 |
| Group II – 12 not accepting offer of college courses | | | | | | |
| 10 | TE,R | 66 | 40 | 680 | 56 | 35 |
| 11 | TP,R | 60 | 30 | 730 | 55 | 30 |
| 12 | TR,E | 60 | 38 | 620 | 58 | 31 |
| 13 | T/SA,[e]R | 56 | 47 | 650 | 56 | 30 |
| 14 | TE,R | 55 | 28 | 620 | 53 | 27 |
| 15 | TE,A | 55 | 25 | 790 | 59 | 33 |
| 16 | TS,P | 54 | 37 | 600 | 56 | 30 |
| 17 | AT,R | 50 | 57 | 670 | 54 | 33 |
| 18 | ET,R | 50 | 38 | 680 | 58 | 33 |
| 19 | TP,S | 47 | 36 | 690 | 56 | 31 |
| 20 | SP,R | 45 | 34 | 680 | 55 | 26 |
| 21 | PS/E,A | 41 | 23 | 640 | 58 | 27 |

was coded as first or second in importance by 19 of the 35 males, and the total mean was significantly greater than 40 (Winer 1973). On the observational level, wealth and entrepreneurial undertakings do seem important to these boys. They are very eager to earn spending money, as are perhaps many boys their age. Whether this value score will decrease over time, perhaps to the benefit of the aesthetic value, remains to be seen.

For the *aesthetic* value, Group I and Group II scored higher than Group III, although the difference did not reach significance. The former two groups' mean scores are higher than average for high school

Table 8.14    *(Continued)*

| Case number | AVL code[a] | Theoretical score | Aesthetic score | SAT-M[b] | Raven's Progressive Matrices ABCDE[c] | II[d] |
|---|---|---|---|---|---|---|
| Group III – 14 not offered college courses | | | | | | |
| 22 | TE,R | 55 | 36 | 610 | 59 | 34 |
| 23 | TE,R | 54 | 32 | 600 | – | – |
| 24 | TP,A | 52 | 30 | 660 | 58 | 32 |
| 25 | ST,E | 51 | 40 | 560 | 54 | 29 |
| 26 | TP,R | 50 | 33 | 590 | 57 | 31 |
| 27 | A/TE,R | 49.5 | 49.5 | 660 | – | – |
| 28 | TP,A | 49 | 36 | 520 | 51 | 28 |
| 29 | ET,A | 48 | 26 | 660 | 56 | 31 |
| 30 | TR,S | 48 | 39 | 530 | 59 | 33 |
| 31 | TP,A | 45 | 30 | 660 | 60 | 29 |
| 32 | PS,A | 43.5 | 43.5 | 680 | 56 | 32 |
| 33 | SR/P,A | 36 | 25 | 690 | 58 | 35 |
| 34 | EP,R | 36 | 39 | 680 | 51 | 25 |
| 35 | PS/E,A | 33 | 32 | 640 | 55 | 27 |

T = Theoretical; E = Economic; A = Aesthetic; S = Social; P = Political; R = Religious.

[a] Two highest, one lowest value (e.g., TE,R means that the two highest values were T and E and the lowest value was religious)
[b] Highest possible score is 800
[c] Highest possible score is 60
[d] Highest possible score is 36
[e] Slash denotes equal score on two values

boys, although their coded profiles do not indicate a high relative position for aesthetic value and their total mean is significantly lower than 40 (Winer 1973). Adult males average only 37 on this scale. In contrast, 50 percent of the males in Group III marked the aesthetic value as their lowest value.

In view of Hall and MacKinnon's (1969) analysis of creativity mentioned above, it is evident that the profiles of students in the three groups do not as yet correspond to the classic profile for creative architects and scientists. The mean score of Group I on A is fairly high compared with the mean for high school boys (39.4 versus 35.1); so it is possible that the apparently favorable TA profile will emerge for them with time. This issue will be discussed further below.

As for the *social* value, the mean for all 35 boys is also close to the mean reported for high school males. However, the mean of Group I is

Table 8.15: *Mean scores on "Study of Values" scales for three groups of mathematically talented males and a standardized population of high school males*

| | Theoretical (T) | Economic (E) | Aesthetic (A) | Social (S) | Political (P) | Religious (R) |
|---|---|---|---|---|---|---|
| Group I[a] N = 9 | 51.2 | 47.1 | 39.4 | 33.1 | 43.8 | 25.3 |
| Group II[b] N = 12 | 53.2 | 41.4 | 36.1 | 40.5 | 41.8 | 27.1 |
| Group III[c] N = 14 | 46.4 | 42.7 | 33.7 | 40.6 | 44.7 | 31.8 |
| Groups I and II[d] | 52.2 | 44.3 | 37.8 | 36.8 | 42.8 | 26.2 |
| Total | 50.3 | 43.9 | 36.2 | 38.1 | 43.4 | 28.1 |
| High school males[e] | 43.3 | 42.8 | 35.1 | 37.1 | 43.2 | 37.9 |

[a] Offered college courses and took courses
[b] Offered college courses and declined them
[c] Not offered college courses
[d] All those offered courses
[e] High school norms from the SV Manual

much less (33.1) than the means of Groups II (40.5) and Group III
(40.6). This difference between Group I's social mean score and that of
Groups II and III combined is significant (p < .05). McCurdy (1957) has
asserted that, historically, accepted geniuses have displayed a notable
lack of involvement with peers (Keating, chapter 2 in this volume). According to the SV's norms, the low social value score for Group I—our
ablest boys—would seem to lend tentative support to this finding, if
altruism and interest in peers can be said to be related.

The mean *political* value scores for all three groups are also close to
the mean for all high school males, and the three group means do not
differ much from one another. The political value was rated first or
second highest by 16 of the 35, in contrast to the 11.67 that would be
expected to occur by chance marking.

The mean *religious* value score for the boys (28.1) is what the SV
Manual calls "outstandingly low." This fits in with the general picture
of highly creative, bright persons proposed by Hall and MacKinnon
(1969). Differences among the means of the three groups did not
approach significance.

### SV Results for Seven Girls

Seven girls were included for study along with the 35 boys. Their
mean value scores are seen in table 8.16. Their average profile of values
emerges as rather different from the boys'. One must remember, however, the small sample size in generalizing these results.

First of all, the girls' mean *theoretical* score was seven points below
that of the boys. Moshin (1950) corroborates this sex difference. Even
so, probably because of the small sample size, the difference in means
was not found to be significant. It is also important to remember that
although this boy-girl gap does exist, the girls' theoretical scores are
still considered high for their sex. Three of the seven chose theoretical
as their highest value. Those who did not were lower than the high
school female mean on this value.

The girls' *economic* value score was 10 points lower than the males'
and was lower than the average for high school girls. The sex difference
here is significant (p < .05).

On the average, the girls scored fairly close to the Group I boys'
*aesthetic* scale score and even closer to the mean for high school girls.

On the *social* scale we see a dramatic difference, significant at the
.002 level, between the girls and the boys. The girls' mean social score
(47.0) is classed as high, whereas the boys' (38.1) is classed as low.
These girls are entering adolescence, and their intellectual ability not-

Table 8.16: Mean scores on "Study of Values" scales for seven mathematically talented females and a standardized population of high school females

| | Theoretical (T) | Economic (E) | Aesthetic (A) | Social (S) | Political (P) | Religious (R) |
|---|---|---|---|---|---|---|
| Group I[a] N = 1 | 48.0 | 37.0 | 40.0 | 46.0 | 45.0 | 24.0 |
| Group II[b] N = 2 | 41.2 | 28.5 | 38.8 | 50.2 | 45.2 | 36.0 |
| Group III[c] N = 4 | 41.0 | 37.5 | 39.2 | 44.8 | 44.8 | 32.8 |
| Total | 43.4 | 34.3 | 39.3 | 47.0 | 45.0 | 30.9 |
| High school females | 37.0 | 38.2 | 38.2 | 43.3 | 39.1 | 43.8 |

[a] Offered college courses and took courses
[b] Offered college courses and declined them
[c] Not offered college courses

withstanding, they are probably beginning to care quite a bit about popularity, the opposite sex, and other interpersonal relationships. This attitude, as contrasted with the boys', is seen both on the SV and in their day-to-day behavior. For these girls this social score seems to reflect gregariousness rather than altruism. The girls' topics for conversation, for example, are quite different from the boys'.

On the *political* scale the girls' mean score was somewhat higher than the boys', but not significantly so. According to the SV Manual, it is in the high score range.

Their *religious* scale was also slightly higher than the boys', but it was also their lowest mean score. The mean religious score (30.9) is classified as low by the manual.

## Results for Parents of Winners and Near-Winners

A limited group of 38 parents of members (male and female) of Groups I, II, and III were also administered the SV. Mothers' and fathers' mean scores can be seen in table 8.17.

On the *theoretical* value, both mothers and fathers were slightly lower than, but fairly close to, their offspring. Both means were high for college males or females or those having some college. The Group II parents' mean was farthest from that of their offspring. Mothers showed considerable variability on this value; those with low T or truth-seeking value scores tended to have higher philanthropic social value scores.

For both mothers and fathers, except Group II mothers, the economic scale means were also quite close to (although a little lower than) those of their children. The SV Manual classifies these means as close to the average for males and for females.

On the *aesthetic* scale, both mothers and fathers on the average exceeded their children's mean scores—by a considerable margin for mothers in Groups I and II and for fathers and mothers of children in Group III. Their means are high or nearly so by normative standards. This is consonant with part of Feldman and Newcomb's (1969) finding on the development of the aesthetic attitude. They asserted that the college experience, which most Group I parents underwent, is instrumental in increasing aesthetic scores. Our data, however, do not bear out Feldman and Newcomb's assertion that aesthetic scores decline soon after college years. Perhaps the relatively rich environment of these families negates that effect. Feldman and Newcomb's findings could also give us a possible reason why these parents' sons do not yet show the documented high TA, low R SV code for the gifted and creative; they may have not yet had the necessary experiences.

Table 8.17: *Mean scores of "Study of Values" scales for some parents of mathematically talented students*

| | Theoretical (T) | Economic (E) | Aesthetic (A) | Social (S) | Political (P) | Religious (R) |
|---|---|---|---|---|---|---|
| Group I[a] | | | | | | |
| mothers N = 9 | 45.6 | 42.7 | 43.2 | 36.0 | 41.4 | 31.1 |
| fathers N = 8 | 49.5 | 43.0 | 39.8 | 34.1 | 41.4 | 32.2 |
| Group II[b] | | | | | | |
| mothers N = 6 | 40.7 | 34.8 | 43.7 | 45.3 | 34.3 | 41.0 |
| fathers N = 5 | 44.0 | 40.0 | 37.4 | 38.4 | 38.4 | 41.8 |
| Group III[c] | | | | | | |
| mothers N = 5 | 46.5 | 39.9 | 40.5 | 36.3 | 43.5 | 33.3 |
| fathers N = 5 | 44.6 | 39.7 | 43.1 | 38.2 | 42.9 | 31.5 |

[a] Offered college courses and took courses
[b] Offered college courses and declined them
[c] Not offered college courses

The parents' means on the *social* scale were close to the boys' means (except for mothers of Group II); this is about average for the fathers, but low for the mothers. Could this low social score for most mothers reflect a less clinging type of behavior toward their offsprings' pursuits, i.e., a behavior that results in a more independent child? Such a speculation contradicts the "pushy mother of the gifted" stereotype but is highly tentative because it is based on only a small number of children and their parents.

Parents' *political* means were, in general, practically equal for both sexes and a little lower than their children's. The fathers' scores were near the mean for male adults, while Group II mothers' scores were low for adult females.

Their *religious* means, except for Group III parents, were higher than their children's, but still classified as low by the SV Manual. For the parents as well as their children, the religious score was the lowest on their mean profile. There is much variation from person to person on scores for this value. Apparently this value is uniformly low in these families, most of whom are rather well educated and relatively well off—for 19 of the 38 parents tested it was the lowest scored value.

### Relationship of Value Scores to Each Other

Table 8.18 shows, above the diagonal, intercorrelations of the scores on each SV value. Because of their very nature, these ipsative value scales correlate highly with few other scales. Most intercorrelations are negative (Gleser 1972); those scales which do not show negative correlations are usually chosen together over other scores. The negative values shown for these $r$'s indicate that scales are inversely correlated with those scales from which they "steal" points or over which they are

Table 8.18: *Intercorrelations of "Study of Values" scale scores (above the diagonal) and z-scores of these intercorrelations* [a] *(N = 35 boys)*

|  | Theoretical | Economic | Aesthetic | Social | Political | Religious |
|---|---|---|---|---|---|---|
| Theoretical |  | .06 | .04 | -.38 | -.09 | -.52 |
| Economic | .99 |  | -.15 | -.57 | .41 | -.55 |
| Aesthetic | .89 | .18 |  | -.22 | -.50 | -.26 |
| Social | -.71 | -1.44 | -0.07 |  | -.20 | .30 |
| Political | .39 | 2.32 | -1.19 | -0.03 |  | -.28 |
| Religious | -1.25 | -1.38 | -0.27 | 1.90 | -.34 |  |

[a] $z$-scores based on the $r$'s are below the diagonal. $z_r = \dfrac{r - \text{mean } r}{\text{s.d. of } r}$

chosen. Table 8.18 also shows these $r$'s in $z$-score form below the diagonal of the table, thus comparing $r$'s to their average according to the usual $z$-score formula given in the table note. The mean is $r = -.19$, while the standard deviation is .26.

For the winner population, the *theoretical* value is slightly positively correlated with the economic and aesthetic values and negatively correlated with religious, social, and political values. The $z$-score of .99 for $r_{TE} = .06$ indicates that this is a standard deviation greater than the typical intercorrelation of the SV values. The correlations are also fairly close to those for the SV norming population, as reported in the SV Manual.

The *economic* value is highly positively correlated with the political value, especially when viewed in terms of the $z$-score (2.32). The social and religious values are substantially negatively correlated with the economic value. These $r$'s differ, though not significantly, from those in the SV Manual. The relationships between economic and social values and between religious and political values are greater than those in the norming populations, while the intercorrelation of economic and aesthetic values is less negative than that in the manual.

The *aesthetic* value is particularly negatively correlated with the political value ($z = -1.19$). This correlation ($r = -.50$) is much more negative than the one in the SV Manual. If the ipsative nature of SV is taken into account, the $z$-score for $r_{TA}$ is .89, indicating that the theoretical and aesthetic values are less antithetical in this population than in an average male population.

The *social* value is correlated positively only with the religious value ($z = 1.90$). This is also the only positive correlation for the religious value.

### Relationship of Value Scores to Cognitive Test Scores

In table 8.19 we see that the *theoretical* value is positively correlated with scores on all the cognitive tests which the 35 males took, but to the greatest degree with Science (.46), SAT-V, CMT Part II (verbal analogies) and Math I. This agrees with our expectations. Of its five relationships, the *aesthetic* value correlates highest with Science (.36), SAT-V (.34), and CMT-I (.32). It correlates slightly negatively with SAT-M and Math I. As noted earlier, none of these students has shown Hall and MacKinnon's (1969) profile for creative architects. It seems probable that our students' aesthetic value is not yet developed to its maximum degree.

The *economic* value, on the other hand, is rather highly correlated (.40) with performance on the SAT-M, somewhat correlated with Math

Table 8.19: *Correlation of "Study of Values" scores with scores on six cognitive tests*

|  | Theo-retical | Economic | Aesthetic | Social | Political | Religious |
|---|---|---|---|---|---|---|
| SAT-M | .19 | .40 | -.05 | -.23 | .28 | -.42 |
| SAT-V | .41 | -.42 | .34 | .01 | -.47 | .01 |
| Math I Achievement | .26 | .18 | -.01 | -.17 | .08 | -.25 |
| Concept Mastery Test, Part I[a] | .11 | -.41 | .32 | .19 | -.51 | .14 |
| Concept Mastery Test, Part II[b] | .30 | -.12 | .17 | -.07 | -.23 | -.09 |
| STEP Science, Forms IA and IB | .46 | -.19 | .36 | -.33 | -.31 | -.06 |

[a] Synonyms-antonyms: e.g., does "big" mean approximately the same thing as "large," or approximately the opposite?
[b] Analogies (chiefly verbal) involving reasoning and information.

I (.18), but negatively correlated with SAT-V (-.42) and Part I of the Concept Mastery Test, which is composed of difficult vocabulary words (-.41).

The same general trend is seen with the *political* value; it is negatively correlated with all tests with a high verbal loading, particularly CMT I (-.51). Thus these values are highest where the boys' verbal talents are least developed; perhaps their weight will decrease as verbal abilities grow. On the ipsative SV scale, this hypothesized economic and political decrease might enable the aesthetic value to increase.

The *social* value is negatively correlated with all cognitive tests except two, especially so with STEP Science (-.33) and SAT-M (-.23). This corresponds to our observation from table 8.15 that the better male students (those taking college courses) scored rather low on the SV social (i.e., social service or altruism) scale.

The same holds true for the *religious* value, which correlates only slightly or negatively with all cognitive tests, especially SAT-M (-.42). This finding is as expected, but rather striking when the small variability of religious scores in this group is considered.

## Cautions and Research Issues

These highly talented young people are distinguished from a general population on several factors, most notably their strong theoretical value and their relatively low religious value. Intergroup comparisons and sex comparisons are also possible. However, many more questions crop up with each answer found, and a cautionary word is necessary as well. Because of the ipsative nature of the Study of Values, scores and their comparisons should be backed up with further testing and with empirical and behavioral evidence where possible. This additional information would aid in assessing each value's absolute value strength, which of course cannot be determined from the SV. For example, one person's religious score may be higher numerically than another's, but not so absolutely strong as the other's when measured on a non-ipsative scale. The ipsative scales obscure such individual differences, and more information could help us there. For these reasons, care should be exercised when generalizing about persons from ipsative data scales.

Although the nature of SV poses tricky interpretation problems, it also offers leads into certain areas of research. Our concern with the development of the aesthetic value is an example of this. Feldman and Newcomb (1969) asserted that the aesthetic value increases during college. Thus, these young people may not have had the experiences necessary for its development and cannot yet show Hall and MacKinnon's (1969) classic creative scientist "TA, R" pattern. It would also be interesting to note on particular SV items which values, if any, are consistently favored over the aesthetic value. One wonders whether the sophisticated nature of the SV aesthetic items could tap an appreciation of harmony and form in such young persons.

Other questions come up concerning the appropriateness of certain items on the SV for students this age. Some persons or terms may be unfamiliar to the students. This problem was largely alleviated in the 1973 testing through use of a definition sheet. However, more pervasive problems of appropriateness may be revealed when an item analysis of SV from the 1973 testing is done. Standardization of the SV scores of all the 1973 students will also aid in comparing our gifted group with relevant special populations.

Equally interesting but less amenable to measurement is the validity of Spranger's six dimensions as we are interpreting them for this group. Holland's six occupational codes correspond to some of Spranger's six values, and there is considerable evidence available as to the empirical utility of these dimensions (Holland 1973). In this light, a redefinition of the social scale to include gregariousness in order to account for sex differences may be inadvisable. Interpretation of value scores must be undertaken carefully. For example, the meaning of a given social score may be rather different for 12-year-old girls than for adult women.

## Summary and Conclusions

1. The majority of students who elected to enter a mathematics and/or science competition preferred the investigative occupations on the VPI scales. This trend is clearly more pronounced for boys than for girls and for those taking only the science test.

2. Most of these students were in the top 2 percent on an in-grade measure of numerical achievement such as the Iowa Test of Basic Skills. About 40 percent of these students have a strong interest in careers in mathematics or science, as evidenced by the agreement between their codes derived from the VPI scales and their first-choice occupations listed on another questionnaire.

3. The relationship of vocational interest to achievement seems complex. Although most of the winners and near-winners have strong investigative interests, those boys as a whole who scored high on SAT-M and those who scored low seemed almost equally likely to prefer the investigative occupations to the other five occupational categories. Girls who scored high, however, were more likely to have investigative interests than girls who scored low.

4. A sizable number of students interested in mathematics and science careers have already accelerated their progress in mathematical reasoning to the point that, while still in junior high school, they are able to score above the mean for entering college freshmen at highly selective universities. Rarely do these young students who are so advanced in their knowledge of mathematics and science have strong preferences for careers in nonscientific areas. The greater the degree of acceleration—as measured by scores on the SAT in the six and seven hundreds—the greater the probability that the student spends much out-of-school time working in mathematical and/or scientific endeavors for their own sake and thus sees mathematics and science as potentially very useful to his or her eventual career, and the more likely the student is to prefer the investigative occupations on the VPI scales and questionnaire. This is seen only at the extreme high level of achievement for boys, 65 percent of the winners and near-winners as compared with 58 percent of all boys, winners and nonwinners, in both contests.

5. As compared with a general population of high school students, the highest scoring boys and girls scored quite high on the theoretical (scientific truth-seeking) value and comparatively very low on the religious value.

6. For the majority of the 35 competition winners (all male) the theoretical value was the highest. Four of those who did not mark the theoretical value as their highest nevertheless had scores deemed high by the SV Manual. Students we considered accelerated enough to be

offered college courses (Groups I and II) scored higher on the theoretical value and lower on the religious value than the average of the entire 35. It is clear that these boys' highly theoretical evaluative attitudes and their interest in investigative occupations, as well as their cognitive abilities, point strongly toward possible futures for them in science or mathematics. This is of paramount importance in educational testing and creates distinct options for the students. One must be somewhat cautious, however, because abilities needed for achievement in mathematics and science tend to mature early, whereas verbal ability seems to reach its peak at a much later age (Bayley and Oden 1955; see also appendix A).

7. As a group the winners scored about average on the political and economic values. These evaluative attitudes were often second only to the theoretical value, however, and were the most frequent highest values after theoretical. It would appear that the political or economic and monetary values of these boys are also of great importance to them at this time, and this, along with their interest in realistic occupations, should be taken into consideration when educational and vocational counseling is undertaken.

8. Conclusions on the aesthetic value are difficult to make at this time. For the 35 boys as a group, the mean value score was low when compared with the aesthetic score norms for adults but was close to the mean for high school boys. For Group I, however, the value was close to that called high by the SV Manual. The intriguing part of the analysis of the aesthetic scale stems from Hall and MacKinnon's (1969) linking of the "TA, R" profile with creativity in adults. As has been remarked above, the relationship between evaluative attitudes (especially the aesthetic), interests, and future creativity is a puzzle still to be unraveled. For one thing, creativity needs to be defined for this group in particular. This matter will be pursued in the future. As of now, the aesthetic value is a promising topic for further study. Meanwhile, one may choose to assume that it is probably desirable to help theoretically oriented boys and girls develop a keen sense of form, harmony, beauty, proportion, taste, style, nicety, balance, symmetry, elegance, and fittingness in order to direct investigative energies into fruitful channels. High T with low A may produce an "all speed and no control" syndrome.

9. The social value of the boys who took college courses was low, while that of boys who did not take these courses, whether they were offered them or not, was classified as high. The differences in mean social value score between those offered college courses and those to whom they were not offered may signal a real and important motivational difference between these groups, one which should be watched for

and accounted for in the course of educational facilitation. Persons with high social value scores may be more interested in working with people than in learning for learning's sake.

10. For all groups the religious value score was below average. Other values clearly took precedence.

11. Important sex differences which have major consequences for counseling also emerged. Differences favoring the boys' level of theoretical attitudes over the girls' may suggest a reason for the girls' lower achievement. Although the girls' theoretical scores were lower than the boys', they are still considered high for their sex. Some assessment of the minimum theoretical score or rank necessary for the utilization of these girls' mathematical and scientific talents is in order here, as well as further study with a larger group of girls. Perhaps the girls' high social value score overrides their truth-seeking qualities to some extent at these ages (chiefly 12 or 13).

12. Finally, parents' responses to the SV were analyzed. Parents' occupational and value scores can also be useful during educational counseling when compared with those of their children. The parents' values—for example, the ranks of their theoretical value scores—give us clues as to how academically facilitative they may be and what their expectations may be for their children.

The implications of these findings for educational counseling are that achievement and evaluative attitudes are fairly closely interrelated. Apparently, ability without academically congruent evaluative attitudes and interests does not always lead to precocious achievement. Investigative interests may be a concomitant condition for early achievement in mathematical and scientific subject areas or, of course, may be at least partly a result of such achievement. However, the presence of high investigative interests in mathematically talented youths does not insure extremely high achievement, nor do low theoretical evaluative attitudes or low investigative interests necessarily prevent it. Other factors—cognitive, affective, and environmental—are also at work.

Many of these students have both the high ability and the interests and attitudes to enable them to go far in related academic and career pursuits. It is our goal to help them realize these potentialities through such methods of facilitation as those delineated by Fox (chapter 3 in this volume). Measures of evaluative attitudes and interests aid us in assessing the importance of the motivational component for each individual's future performance. If the theoretical value is clearly subordinate to the social value on a person's SV profile and if his or her most highly rated occupations on the Holland checklist are social, for example, there is some question whether this person would be interested and successful in some of the specific intervention programs we have devised. Of course, these measures of values and interests are always viewed hand in hand with cognitive test scores when counseling occurs. Further measures such as the Strong-Campbell Interest Inventory and the California Psychological Inventory are being used to supplement information gained from the SV and Holland occupational checklist.

Educational facilitation maintains its primary role in our study; thus our emphasis on the usefulness of value and career interest data in educational planning is of prime importance. The three instruments (SV, VPI, and talent search questionnaire) analyzed here give us important descriptive data on the first group of gifted persons with whom we are working. In the years to come, after longitudinal follow-up of this group's career choices and life plans, the worth of these predictors will be proven.

## References

Allport, G. W., Vernon, P. E. and Lindzey, G. 1970. *Manual, Study of Values: A scale for measuring the dominant interests in personality.* Boston: Houghton Mifflin Co.

Astin, H. S. 1968a. Career development of girls during the high school years. *Journal of Counseling Psychology* 15(6): 536–40.

———. 1968b. Stability and change in the career plans of ninth grade girls. *Personnel and Guidance Journal* 46(10): 961–66.

Bayley, N., and Oden, M. H. 1955. The maintenance of intellectual ability in gifted adults. *Journal of Gerontology* 10: 91–107.

Carlson, R., and Parker, J. 1969. Personality and esthetic sensitivity. *Journal of Projective Techniques and Personality Assessment* 33(6): 530–34.

Feldman, K., and Newcomb, T. M. 1969. *The impact of college on students,* vol. 1. San Francisco: Jossey-Bass.

Gleser, L. J. 1972. On bounds for the average correlation between subtest scores in ipsatively scored tests. *Educational and Psychological Measurement* 32(3): 759–66.

Hall, W. B., and MacKinnon, D. W. 1969. Personality inventory correlates of creativity among architects. *Journal of Applied Psychology* 53(4): 322–26.

Hogan, R. 1971. The Allport-Vernon-Lindzey Study of Values. In O. K. Buros (ed.), *The seventh mental measurements yearbook.* Highland Park, N.J.: Gryphon Press, p. 676.

Holland, J. L. 1958. A personality inventory employing occupational titles. *Journal of Applied Psychology* 42: 336–42.

———. 1973. *Making vocational choices: A theory of careers.* Englewood Cliffs, N.J.: Prentice-Hall, Inc.

MacKinnon, D. W. 1962. The nature and nurture of creative talent. *American Psychologist* 17(7): 484–95.

McCurdy, H. S. 1957. Childhood pattern of genius. *Journal of the Elisha Mitchell Scientific Society* 73: 448–62.

Moshin, S. M. 1950. A study of relationship of evaluative attitudes to sex differences, intellectual level, expressed occupational interest and hobbies. *Indian Journal of Psychology* 25: 59–70.

Southern, M. L., and Plant, W. T. 1968. Personality characteristics of very bright adults. *Journal of Personality and Social Psychology* 75(1): 119–26.

Spranger, E. 1966. *Types of men: The psychology and ethics of personality.* New York: Johnson Reprint. 1928.

Viernstein, M. C. 1972. The extension of Holland's occupational classifications to all occupations in the Dictionary of Occupational Titles. *Journal of Vocational Behavior* 2: 107–21.

Warren, J. R., and Heist, P. A. 1960. Personality attributes of gifted college students. *Science* 132: 330–37.

Winer, J. 1973. Random vs. non-random "Study of Values" profiles. Unpublished manuscript.

# IX · behavior of mathematically precocious boys in a college course

## DANIEL P. KEATING, STANLEY J. WIEGAND, and LYNN H. FOX

---

[Editors' Note: *If very young students are to participate in college courses, then what they do in the college classroom situation is of considerable importance. If they perform poorly there, are disruptive, or are disliked by the other students, difficult problems could arise. To get an idea of what actually goes on in such a class, the study arranged to have a participant observer in a course that several young students were taking. Chapter 9 shows the result.*]

---

In order for educational facilitation of mathematically precocious youth to be most effective, different types of "bridging" or "telescoping" mechanisms must be available. Fox (see chapter 3) has listed and examined a number of these alternatives. For some of the most mathematically advanced junior high school students, the best method is often to take college courses for credit during the summer, at night during the regular academic year, or on released time.

This method of facilitation has already been used effectively with 17 young students associated with the Study of Mathematically and Scientifically Precocious Youth at The Johns Hopkins University. The college courses were mainly computer science and mathematics (see pp. 64–65 for a list of all courses taken and grades received). Of these students, 12 were found through the first annual mathematics competition (see p. 63), and the remainder through nomination by the parent, a teacher, or in one instance, by the student himself. In no case was the student 16 years old, and most of them were 12 to 14 years old when they took the course. Their success has been remarkable, with no grade less than B and the majority receiving A's. One student completed four college courses for credit while still less than 14 years old.

The grades received by these young students for their college work indicated that they could compete well academically with the older, more experienced regular college students. These grades, however, show little more. They reveal nothing about these students' classroom behavior and interaction with the instructor. Their attitudes toward education and any changes in attitude which might evolve as a result of their experiences are also crucial. Thus the feasibility of continuing and using more extensively such forms of "radical" acceleration needed to be evaluated on bases other than grades, such as the participation of the young students in the course, the maturity and applicability of their study habits and attitudes, their attitudes about college work before and after taking the course, and the attitudes and feelings of the teacher and other "regular" students toward them. The current study was designed to provide preliminary answers to these questions and to suggest areas and methods for evaluating other programs for the gifted which involve similar bridging mechanisms. The specific goals of the study were, then: (a) to assess the study habits and attitudes of such students and to evaluate the appropriateness of such habits and attitudes for college work; (b) to observe and evaluate the classroom behavior of mathematically precocious junior high school students in a college course; (c) to discern the attitudes and feelings of the "significant others" (i.e., the instructor and other students) toward these young students; and (d) to determine the pre-course and post-course attitudes of the precocious students toward doing college work early.

## Procedure

The students selected for observation were five junior high school boys who were registered for college credit in a summer course in mathematics I (college algebra and trigonometry) at a local state college. Four of the boys had been found through the mathematics competition and had ranked 2, 3, 7½, and 10 out of 396 contestants. The fifth boy was from another area and was spending the summer in Baltimore. He had been referred to us by his family and was extensively tested. The boys' ages at the beginning of the course and their most recently completed school grades were: 13 years, 8 months, eighth grade; 12 years, 9 months, seventh grade; 13 years, 11 months, ninth grade; 13 years, 6 months, eighth grade; and 15 years, 0 months, ninth grade. Their SAT-Mathematical, Mathematics I, and Mathematics II Achievement scores are listed in table 9.1. These students were chosen because they comprised the largest group placed in one section of a college course.

Before their summer school experience, the five boys participating in the program took the Brown-Holtzman (1967) "Survey of Study Habits and Attitudes," Form H. The authors claim that this instrument is a predictor of academic success while being essentially independent of measures of scholastic aptitude. Raw scores for four subscales and combined scales are converted to percentile ranks for junior high stu-

Table 9.1:    *CEEB math scores of five junior high students taking college math*

| Student | SAT-M | M – I | M – II |
|---------|-------|-------|--------|
| 1 | 780 | 720 | 720 |
| 2 | 710 | 730 | 800 |
| 3 | 710 | 640 | 690 |
| 4 | 670 | 610 | 710 |
| 5 | – | – | 800 |

dents. The lower the student's percentile rank, the more often his answers tend to differ from those typically given by students who earn grades of A and B. The four subscales are DA (delay avoidance), WM (working methods), TA (teacher acceptance), and EA (education acceptance). The DA and WM scales are combined to give the SH scale, which is a general measure of study habits. The TA and EA scales form the SA scale, which is a general measure of study attitudes. All four subscales are combined in the SO (study orientation) scale, which gives the student's overall percentile score. It is also possible to identify certain critical responses. These critical responses are thought to indicate academic trouble spots which may be causing a student to underachieve.

In-class behavior can be evaluated properly only if it is seen and recorded. To this end an observer (the second author) was placed in the classroom without the knowledge of the students or the teacher. But an observer in the classroom, taking notes and paying little attention to the course of the lecture, might be spotted easily. Knowledge that they were being observed might affect the performances of both teacher and student. To retain the observer's anonymity and increase the possibility of obtaining a nonreactive measure (Webb, Campbell, Schwartz, and Sechrest 1966), he was formally registered as a student in the class. The observer had, in fact, just completed the junior year at Johns Hopkins. He enrolled as an auditor and was thereby exempt from tests and homework assignments. This status also tended to make his lack of class participation less noticeable.

The observational system used was based upon the method of coding developed by Bales (1970), substantially modified for simple recording of a limited number of relevant behaviors. The item coded was a verbal interchange between student and teacher. In-class verbal exchanges between students were extremely rare, occuring at a rate of less than one a day, and were therefore not analyzed. The teacher's statements were not noted unless addressed to a particular student. A single word statement or simple sentence was considered a discrete bit of information, while compound and complex sentences were treated as two or more bits, depending on the number of clauses they contained.

Each such discrete statement made by a pupil or teacher was given one of two possible code numbers based on content. One code number was given to all statements containing information of a factual, objective nature. Questions demanding information of this sort were given the same code number. An example of a question and response which would be assigned this code follows: Q: "What is today's date?" A: "February 31." The correctness or incorrectness of such a response can be objectively established, although this was not taken into account in the scoring. The second code number was applied to all statements containing opinion or suggestion. Questions requesting this type of information were also given the second code number. Thus the second code number applied to such questions as "What is the best way to approach this problem?" when several avenues of approach are available. Explanation is required, not a concise "correct" answer.

The observational system also required noting whether the verbal interchange being recorded was initiated by the student or by the teacher. The student was marked as having initiated the interaction if he raised his hand and waited for the teacher to recognize him before giving his answer or posing his question. If the student answered a question directed to another student or called out a question or an answer in class without being recognized first by the teacher, the statement and/or interchange that ensued was scored as being student-initiated. The verbal exchange was scored as being teacher-initiated only if the teacher addressed the student without the student's having raised his hand to indicate that he wished to be called upon.

For scoring purposes, the unit of consideration was the entire verbal exchange, not the discrete bit of information. A single exchange began when the teacher first addressed a particular student or when the student first addressed the teacher. The interaction was considered to be terminated when the teacher addressed a second student or resumed the lecture. Each verbal interaction defined in this manner was scored in one of three categories based on content. An exchange was scored under the *fact* category if all bits of information in that exchange involved questions and answers pertaining to objective, factual information. An exchange was scored under the *opinion* category if all questions and statements recorded in that exchange consisted of opinions, explanations, and suggestions. If the exchange contained both facts and opinions it was scored in the *both* category. All verbal interactions were further subdivided as student- or teacher-initiated.

During the first few days of class, five of the six male students taking the course but not in our program were chosen to form a control group. The responses of the remaining male and six female students were also recorded and added together. Absences from class of all individuals were taken into account in analysis of the data.

Before and after the summer school course, the five students participating in the program completed interview questionnaires. Several regular college students (four of the five male controls and two female students) and the teacher of the class were also interviewed personally by the observer following completion of the course.

## Results

### Classroom Interaction

The results of the observation of classroom interaction are summarized in table 9.2. In the classroom situation, there is virtually no difference between control and experimental groups with respect to teacher-initiated interaction. In the case of student-initiated interaction the experimental group tended to be more active, averaging 3.07 student-initiated interactions per day per student, while the control group averaged only 2.13. This difference, however, is not statistically significant. The remaining students in the class showed even less initiative, averaging only 2.06 student-initiated exchanges per day per student. In short, the observations indicated that there were no substantial differences in classroom behavior (by this method of measurement) between the regular college students and the five junior high school students associated with the project.

The quality of the remarks made in class by these young students demonstrated their keen insight into the subject matter. For example, the teacher at one point asked the class if any two infinite sets could be put into a one-to-one correspondence. A student in the control group answered in the affirmative, saying that for every element in set A there would be an element in set B, since the number of elements in each set was inexhaustible. Two of the younger students disagreed, saying that one infinite set could be a proper subset of another infinite set and that by definition these could not be put into a one-to-one correspondence.

### Grades Received

The competence of these young students is further attested to by the fact that they all earned a grade of A in the course. One student, who

Table 9.2: *Classroom interaction of five precocious boys, five male controls, and other noncontrol students by initiator and type of exchange*

| Student | Student Days | Student-initiated interaction | | | Subtotal | | Teacher-initiated interaction | | | Subtotal | | Total | |
|---|---|---|---|---|---|---|---|---|---|---|---|---|---|
| | | Fact | Opinion | Both | Raw Score | Per Day | Fact | Opinion | Both | Raw Score | Per Day | Raw Score | Per Day |
| Group I Experimental 1 | 18 | 14 | 2 | 6 | 22 | 1.22 | 20 | 0 | 3 | 23 | 1.28 | 45 | 2.5 |
| 2 | 18 | 96 | 24 | 8 | 128 | 7.11 | 18 | 2 | 0 | 20 | 1.10 | 148 | 8.2 |
| 3 | 13 | 14 | 0 | 0 | 14 | 1.08 | 5 | 0 | 3 | 8 | .62 | 22 | 1.7 |
| 4 | 19 | 18 | 5 | 0 | 23 | 1.21 | 28 | 0 | 0 | 28 | 1.47 | 51 | 2.6 |
| 5 | 15 | 47 | 12 | 9 | 68 | 4.53 | 18 | 0 | 2 | 20 | 1.35 | 88 | 5.9 |
| Group I Subtotal | 83 | 189 | 43 | 23 | 255 | 3.07 | 89 | 2 | 8 | 99 | 1.19 | 354 | 4.26 |
| Group II Control 1 | 16 | 8 | 1 | 3 | 12 | .75 | 17 | 0 | 0 | 17 | 1.06 | 29 | 1.8 |
| 2 | 15 | 3 | 3 | 1 | 7 | .47 | 12 | 2 | 3 | 17 | 1.13 | 24 | 1.6 |
| 3 | 16 | 56 | 13 | 22 | 91 | 5.69 | 20 | 4 | 1 | 25 | 1.56 | 116 | 7.2 |
| 4 | 19 | 24 | 7 | 5 | 36 | 1.90 | 25 | 0 | 0 | 25 | 1.32 | 61 | 3.2 |
| 5 | 16 | 21 | 5 | 3 | 29 | 1.81 | 13 | 1 | 2 | 16 | 1.00 | 45 | 2.8 |
| Group II Subtotal | 82 | 112 | 29 | 34 | 175 | 2.13 | 87 | 7 | 6 | 100 | 1.22 | 275 | 3.35 |
| Group III n=7 (Others) | 130 | 201 | 31 | 36 | 268 | 2.06 | 164 | 9 | 12 | 185 | 1.42 | 453 | 3.48 |
| Total | 295 | 502 | 103 | 93 | 698 | 2.37 | 340 | 18 | 26 | 384 | 1.30 | 1082 | 3.67 |

Table 9.3:   *Final grades of all students in the class*

| Accelerated junior high students | Control students | Other students |
|:---:|:---:|:---:|
| A | A | A |
| A | A | B– |
| A | A– | C |
| A | F | D |
| A | C | D |
|   |   | D |
|   |   | F |

had just completed the seventh grade, also earned a grade of A in math II (mainly analytic geometry), which he took concurrently with math I at the suggestion of the instructor. Another earned a grade of A in a computer science course taken concurrently. In the control group there were two A's, one A–, a C, and an F. The A– was earned by a graduate student, and one of the A's was earned by a high school student not associated with the project who had just completed the eleventh grade. He was also taking the course for college credit to be held in escrow. There was one other A earned by a girl in the class. All grades are listed in table 9.3.

### Impressions of Teacher and Other Students

Interviews with the teacher and other students in the class after the course ended were both interesting and informative. During the course of the interview, the teacher was asked whether she thought any one in her class was not a regular college student but was participating in a college-in-escrow program. She replied in the affirmative but named only two of the five students in the project. In her opinion, they stood out only in appearance and were otherwise well assimilated into the class. Earlier in the interview the instructor was asked to identify the students in her class who, in her opinion, had the greatest mathematical aptitude. Of the five people she named, four were precocious students associated with the project, including the two that she later stated were probably not of college age. The teacher also expressed the opinion that the class as a whole was more able than usual, causing a disproportionate number of A's to be given. That this was largely due to the presence of the five talented youths and the other high school student can hardly be doubted. At this point it should be noted that though there was a very great variation in classroom participation within both control and experimental groups there was no relationship between final grade and number of verbal exchanges.

In interviews with six of the college students enrolled in the course, it was discovered that they themselves were able to identify only two or three of their classmates as being unusually young. Sometimes students named by those interviewed as being young were not associated with the project but were instead regular college students. All persons interviewed stated that the junior high school students were well assimilated into the class.

## Survey of Study Habits and Attitudes

The data gathered from the administration of the Brown-Holtzman (1967) SSHA were quite surprising at first. The mean percentile on the SO scale for these especially able junior high school students was only 46. In studying the validity of their test, Brown and Holtzman (1967) found that 70 percent of junior high A–B pupils make 10 or less critical responses and 77 percent of D–E pupils make more than 10 critical responses. These five very able students were all A–B students; yet they averaged almost 23 critical responses each, or more than twice the number indicative of the typical high achiever. In every way their SSHA profiles would indicate poor achievement. Their SSHA percentiles are listed in table 9.4. Yet we have seen compelling evidence of their capacity for superior achievement even at the college level in the area of their special competence.

Table 9.4:    *Percentile scores of five precocious students on the Survey of Study Habits and Attitudes*

| Student | Brown-Holtzman scales | | | | | | | Number of critical responses |
|---|---|---|---|---|---|---|---|---|
|  | DA | WM | SH | TA | EA | SA | SO |  |
| 1 | 90 | 80 | 90 | 60 | 30 | 45 | 75 | 22 |
| 2 | 5 | 35 | 13 | 40 | 40 | 35 | 25 | 23 |
| 3 | 55 | 75 | 65 | 5 | 15 | 10 | 30 | 23 |
| 4 | 15 | 75 | 40 | 85 | 50 | 70 | 55 | 19 |
| 5 | 15 | 90 | 55 | 35 | 40 | 35 | 45 | 27 |

*KEY*
DA:  delay avoidance            SH:  study habits
WM:  working methods            SA:  study attitudes
TA:  teacher acceptance         SO:  study orientation
EA:  education acceptance

Some insight into this apparent anomaly can be afforded by studying the subscales of the SSHA. Of the two secondary subscales (i.e., SA and SH) the mean score earned by these students on the study attitude scale is lower than their mean score on the study habits scale (in the 39th and 53rd percentiles, respectively). Of the two primary subscales subsumed under the study attitudes scale (i.e., TA and EA), the lower mean score is evidenced in the educational acceptance scale. It seems, then, that it is their attitude toward their past educational experiences and toward traditional educational processes and requirements which contributes most importantly to their unexpectedly low scores. This disaffection can be seen more clearly when the students' critical responses are examined. All five stated either that, in general, their teachers did not make their subjects interesting and meaningful or that they would study harder if given more freedom to choose subjects that they liked. They all indicated that their grades did not show what they could really do, even though their grades were typically quite good.

### Effect on the Precocious Students

These students were anxious to accelerate their education. Even before attending the summer school course, four of the five indicated that they would like to take college-level courses during the upcoming school year. The one student who previously had indicated no desire to continue studying math at the college level during the regular school year had changed his mind when interviewed after his completion of the course. The other four continued to desire more advanced work. It seems clear that the summer school had proved to be rewarding from the students' perspectives.

Indeed, four of the five students also took math II the same summer, thus completing two semesters of precalculus mathematics. The fifth returned to his home in another state. The instructor recommended to student 2 in table 9.1 (p. 178) that he take math II concurrently with math I, since the latter alone was too elementary for him. Student 2 earned an A in both math I and II. Three of the other four took math II in the second summer session, earning two A's and a B.

### Conclusions

In many ways, enabling an exceptionally gifted youngster to take college-level courses on released time during the regular school year or during the summer as a nondormitory student is an appropriate and usually successful solution to his particular educational problems, as noted by Fox in chapter 3. His education can be selectively accelerated in his area of exceptional ability. He is not completely removed from the high school milieu and remains in a situation where he can interact with both his social and intellectual peers, although the composition of the former group is uncertain (see p. 136). College mathematics courses are likely to be much more intellectually stimulating for mathematically highly able students than their regular junior or senior high school course would be. Moreover, they can provide a quickly traveled bridge to more advanced courses such as eleventh- or twelfth-grade mathematics. For example, the three boys in the group who had been eighth graders the previous year enrolled the next fall in high school calculus courses, in effect bypassing several years of high school mathematics. Two of them skipped the ninth grade in order to enroll in courses on an appropriate level, including chemistry.

Analysis of the SSHA indicated a deep dissatisfaction with educational opportunities available to these students in their high school. They all wished more freedom in choosing courses of greater personal interest, relevance, and challenge. This study indicates that such young and gifted students are able to exercise this freedom well and profit by it.

## References

Bales, R. F. 1970. *Personality and interpersonal behavior*. New York: Holt, Rinehart, and Winston.

Brown, W. F., and Holtzman, W. H. 1967. *Survey of study habits and attitudes*. New York: The Psychological Corporation.

Webb, E. J.; Campbell, D. T.; Schwartz, R. D.; and Sechrest, L. 1966. *Unobtrusive measures: Nonreactive research in the social sciences*. Chicago: Rand McNally & Co.

# epilogue

## THE EDITORS

The nine papers of this volume examine and discuss many aspects of the Study of Mathematically and Scientifically Precocious Youth at The Johns Hopkins University. Chapters 1 through 4 report on the background, philosophy, goals, and major findings of the study after its first full year. In chapter 5, Anastasi has provided the reader an excellent synthesis and critique of those four papers and thus they need not be reviewed again.

If there is a "unifying theme" for the second half of the volume (chapters 6 through 9), it could best be characterized as "second thoughts." This is not to say that these chapters are of secondary importance, but rather that they are attempts to answer the questions which inevitably arise after one has digested somewhat the findings of this research project. The order in which these "second thoughts" occurred and are addressed here is as follows:

1) Can this type of precocious mathematical achievement be fostered? Is it something which can occur only "naturally," or can it be brought about educationally with a bright but not necessarily mathematically precocious group? If such precocity is "educable," at what pace can it be accomplished?

2) What about the "social and emotional development" of such students? Might they be harmed by even moderate separation from their chronological peer group? Are they mature enough personally to handle such radical educational change?

3) Are all of these students really mathematically and scientifically oriented? Are they perhaps precocious achievers in mathematics but more interested in other things? What is the pattern of their interests? What things do they think are most important; what do they value highly?

4) How do these students actually act in a college classroom? How does the teacher react to them? Perhaps more important, how do the other students react to them? How do these precocious students react to their college experiences?

As the reader will note, these concerns are the concerns of chapters 6, 7, 8, and 9 respectively. In general, we found that the potential problem areas which are suggested by these questions are not actual problem areas when investigated directly. The findings reported in these chapters give us little reason to withdraw or moderate the strong suggestions made in the earlier chapters. In fact, in many instances they lead us to desire even more rapid change. In chapter 6, for example, the remarkable success in teaching mathematics at four times the normal pace to a bright and motivated group—selected only on information gained from a typical in-grade standardized test—suggests that interesting and challenging subjects can be tackled by young students who wish to do so.

The findings in chapter 7 contradict the idea that the precocious students' social and emotional development is harmed by separation from their peer group by posing the question, "Who comprises the social peer group of these students?" These precocious students are more socially mature and interpersonally effective than unselected students of the same age, and they resemble gifted high school students. May we not be harming their social and emotional development when we *keep* them with their age mates, if indeed their age mates are not their social peers?

Although most of the students with whom we have been working are mathematically and scientifically oriented in interests and values as well as in abilities, some are not, as we learn in chapter 8. The importance of these factors, together with the personality factors discussed in chapter 7, cannot be overemphasized when counseling and guiding gifted students. In the process of removing academic roadblocks for them it is crucial that other equally dangerous obstacles not be placed in their path. This can happen all too easily if one fails to consider the interests and values which the individual expresses.

In chapter 9, the authors return to pick up a line of reasoning suggested in chapter 3. If these students are to take college courses while still of junior high school age, then the classroom atmosphere will be extremely important. Again we wish to avoid a situation in which the cure is worse than the disease. As has happened frequently in the study, fears proved to be unfounded. The accelerated students participate freely, are not disliked by the other students (and frequently are not even recognized by them as being younger), and regard the college experience as an enjoyable one. This is confirmed by some unanalyzed impressions not reported in chapter 9 that many of the students continue to take college courses, often year-round.

As is often the case, and justly so, ideas gain a momentum all their own. We frequently find ourselves being urged to move even more quickly by the students and parents whom we serve. The optimism which we hope this volume communicates will undoubtedly be dented by future setbacks as we encounter and investigate other potential problem areas. But through careful and thorough investigation we hope to generate a realistic optimism which will have an excellent chance of resulting in concrete changes for the better. We invite your comments, criticisms, and suggestions to help us further that endeavor.

# APPENDIX A

## 1973 Testing

In January and February of 1973, a second talent search was held for seventh, eighth, and accelerated ninth graders in the state of Maryland. The second search was different from the first in several ways:

1) The Scholastic Aptitude Test-Verbal replaced the STEP science test. As mentioned above (on p. 36), the science test had proven itself to be an ineffective screening instrument for this population. In addition, the Study of Verbally Gifted Youth, directed by Robert Hogan, Catherine Garvey, and Roger Webb at Johns Hopkins was getting under way, and it was hoped that a verbally talented sample would be found through the use of the SAT-Verbal.

2) Those students primarily interested in the mathematics competition were urged to come in January 1973, and those most interested in the verbal competition to come in February 1973. Although there was some overlap, most students came on the appropriate test date. Two different forms of the SAT were used in January and February.

3) The suburban counties of Washington, D.C., especially Montgomery County in Maryland, were encouraged to participate by means of a greater publicity effort in those areas. Many students also came from the District of Columbia area, and they did extremely well in the competition.

4) The Allport-Vernon-Lindzey Study of Values replaced the VPI.

The data from this most recent talent search have not been completely analyzed, but some preliminary results can be reported. Table A.1 shows the mean scores on SAT-Math and Verbal by sex, grade, and date of test taken. (This last is preferable to characterization of the January and February groups as "math-oriented" and "verbal-oriented," respectively, since the degree of overlap between the two groups cannot be exactly specified.) The number of students taking the tests increased dramatically over 1972. A total of 451 students participated the first year, and 953 the second year.

In the mathematics competition, the distribution of scores was approximately the same in the second year, with a proportionate increase in the *number* of very high scorers. The scores and frequencies of those scores on SAT-Math from 660 (which is the percentile of male high school seniors) up are 660,9; 670,5; 680,3; 690,2; 700,2; 710,2; 720,2; 730,2; 740,1; 750,3; 760,2; 770,1; and 800,2. One of the two students scoring 800 was 13 years, 0 months, and a ninth grader, and the other was 12 years, 2 months, and a *seventh* grader. (The seventh grader subsequently scored 800 on the CEEB Mathematics I Achievement Test, and also 800 on the Mathematics II Achievement Test.)

The sex difference which is reported in chapter 4 was replicated in the second testing. The highest score obtained by a girl was 650; 42 boys, or 4.4 percent of the total number of boys, earned scores that were high or higher. In appendix B, Fox discusses a new program to discover and hopefully ameliorate some of the social factors which may be contributing to this difference.

Table A.1: *Mean scores of 953 students by sex and grade on Scholastic Aptitude Test of second annual talent search*

| | 7th Grade | | | | 8th and 9th Grade | | | |
| | Boys | | Girls | | Boys | | Girls | |
| Group/Score | Verbal | Math | Verbal | Math | Verbal | Math | Verbal | Math |
| --- | --- | --- | --- | --- | --- | --- | --- | --- |
| **January 1973** | | | | | | | | |
| N | 135 | 135 | 88 | 88 | 285 | 285 | 158 | 158 |
| Mean | 395 | 495 | 384 | 440 | 431 | 551 | 442 | 510 |
| S.D. | 71.4 | 85.2 | 73.6 | 66.3 | 89.9 | 85.2 | 82.9 | 62.6 |
| **February 1973** | | | | | | | | |
| N | 52 | 52 | 67 | 67 | 65 | 65 | 103 | 103 |
| Mean | 410 | 434 | 393 | 396 | 476 | 490 | 476 | 446 |
| S.D. | 76.9 | 90.4 | 86.3 | 79.6 | 90.2 | 90.6 | 90.3 | 78.1 |
| **Combined January and February** | | | | | | | | |
| N | 187 | 187 | 155 | 155 | 350 | 350 | 261 | 261 |
| Mean | 392 | 478 | 382 | 421 | 439 | 540 | 455 | 485 |
| S.D. | 73.7 | 90.7 | 79.7 | 75.3 | 91.6 | 89.4 | 87.3 | 76.0 |

The relative precocity in the mathematics and verbal areas, which we speculated might be somewhat different (see above, p. 39), did favor mathematics. For example, 37 boys scored above the 88.4th percentile of male high school seniors in mathematics; there were only 19 boys above the comparable percentile (a converted score of 610) in the verbal test.

# APPENDIX B

## New Programs

Our success with the first summer program has led us to offer another accelerated summer mathematics class. In the summer of 1973, 84 seventh- or eighth-grade students (50 boys and 34 girls) who scored at least 500 on SAT mathematics aptitude and at least 400 on SAT verbal aptitude in our 1973 contest were invited to take an algebra I test to qualify for a special program of algebra II.[1] (One sixth-grade boy who did not participate in the contest was also invited.)

Of the 85 students invited, 41 came for the testing (29 boys and 12 girls); all but one of these (an eighth-grade boy who had not studied algebra I *per se*) were deemed to have qualified for the class. Of the 40 eligibles, 31 (22 boys and 9 girls) enrolled. The classes were held two days a week for 1½ hours each day for eight weeks. Students who were successful in this program were invited to continue during the school year to study more advanced mathematics. The ability level of this group is high, and we have great expectations for their success. Many of them should be ready for the twelfth-grade calculus course by the time they enter the tenth grade.

In our initial program we felt that we had more success with the boys than with most of the girls. Of the group of 22 students, nine of the 13 boys successfully completed algebra II and seven went on to more accelerated courses. Of the nine girls in the program, six completed algebra II, but only three managed to go beyond that. All the girls expressed some dissatisfaction with the program. The nature of the complaints indicated that the girls found the competitive nature of the class somewhat distressing. (In chapter 4, Astin discusses sex differences in mathematical precocity.) So, since girls usually score higher on social values, we decided to plan a program just for girls which might be more appealing to them *socially*. This would mean an all-girl class with women teachers.

Thirty-four seventh-grade girls were invited to participate in the special algebra workshop from May through July of 1973. Twenty-six girls enrolled for the program, 18 of whom completed the program successfully. Most of these girls were allowed to take algebra II in the eighth grade. The success of this all-girl program is currently being evaluated.

---

[1]A few students who qualified on the basis of contest scores were not invited because they were already included in other aspects of the project.

# APPENDIX C

## Case Studies

The following seven representative profiles are presented to demonstrate both the accuracy and utility of the CPI for counseling purposes with gifted seventh and eighth graders. The case studies allow the comparison of CPI evaluations with evaluations based on a broader range of behavior, including cognitive test scores, questionnaires, and observations of the individual and his family. Richard Haier, who did not know the students personally, wrote the first section of each case study using only the CPI protocol. Daniel Keating, who has worked closely with these students, wrote the second part of each case study from all available material minus, of course, the CPI protocols. The match is good under the circumstances, and provides some compelling nonstatistical evidence for the validity of the CPI with this group. (For names of the CPI scales and their abbreviations, see table 7.1, p. 130.)

### Case 1

Compared with other eighth graders, this person is less socially skillful and somewhat less mature. The relatively high scores on achievement via independence and flexibility indicate that he is independent, insightful, and capable of achieving academically, although the low score on dominance and intellectual efficiency indicate a possible lack of motivation. Because of a lack of interpersonal effectiveness and maturity, it is doubtful that this person is ready for an advancement program.

\* \* \*

This boy possesses one of the more variable cognitive "profiles" in the sample, with high mathematical aptitude but only slightly above average verbal ability. His family background is decidedly "middle-middle-class," with no apparent major input intellectually from either parent. His chances for rapid advancement would seem to be hindered by the combination of his relative unfamiliarity with intellectual pursuits and his unremarkable verbal ability.

### Case 2

Compared with those of other eighth-grade boys, this profile has generally high scores and indicates a mature, interpersonally effective, and academically advanced person. While the particularly high scores on So and Fe may indicate

# PROFILE SHEET FOR THE *California Psychological Inventory*: MALE

Name _____ 8th Grade Random Profile (N=82)                Age _____          Date Tested _____

Other Information _____ from Lessinger and Martinson (1961)

**Notes:**

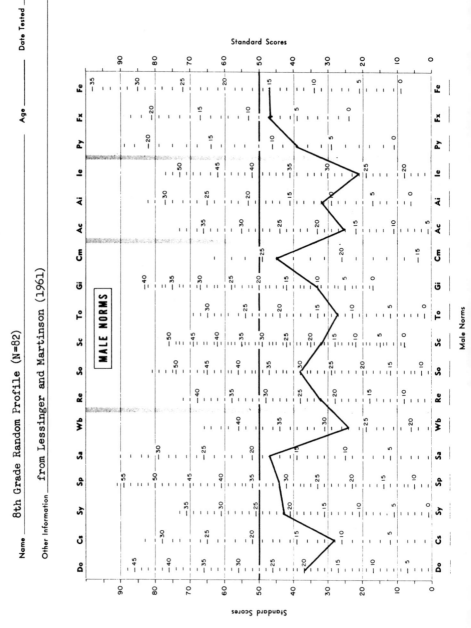

192

## PROFILE SHEET FOR THE *California Psychological Inventory*: MALE

Name _____ Case 1

Age _____ 14 _____ Date Tested _____

Other Information _____

Notes:

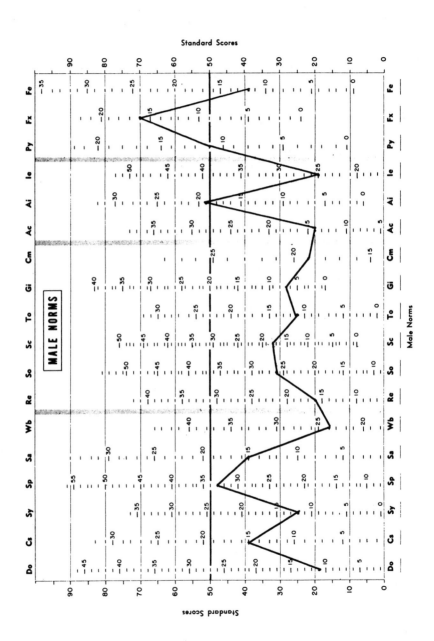

MALE NORMS

193

# PROFILE SHEET FOR THE California Psychological Inventory: MALE

Name _____ Case 2 _____ Age __12__ Date Tested _____

Other Information _____

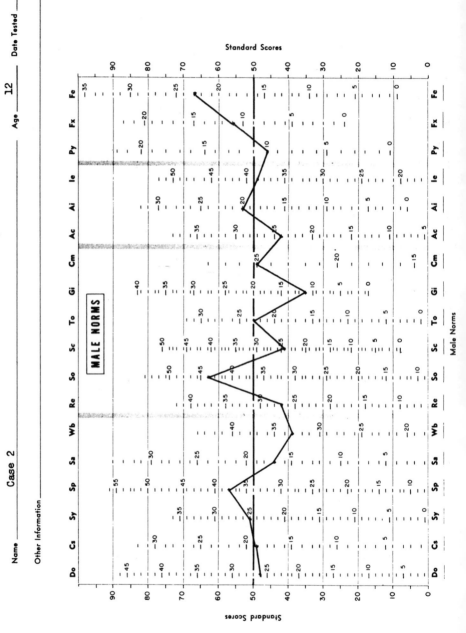

Notes:

overly conventional and possibly nervous behavior, these scores in conjunction with the high Ac, Ai, and Ie scores present a picture of an individual who is serious, industrious, helpful, gentle, and self-reliant. This combination suggests that he does well academically and socially although he may be a somewhat rigid rule-follower.

\* \* \*

This student is cognitively one of the most able we have worked with in SMSPY. He is strong in almost all areas, but especially in reasoning type tests. The home background is markedly professional and intellectual. This boy's motivation is excellent, as has been demonstrated by his successful performance in a difficult college course. It seems likely that he will be one of the most rapidly accelerated of the sample. The probability of eventual success seems at this point among the highest in this group.

### Case 3

This profile shows more maturity and academic orientation than those of most eighth graders although this individual's interpersonal effectiveness is average for this age group. The high scores on socialization and flexibility indicate an industrious but informal and insightful disposition. The low communality score indicates some degree of disorderliness. Nothing on the profile indicates a reason to believe or not to believe that this person possesses special qualities for effective interaction with older groups.

\* \* \*

In the mathematics and science fields, this student is perhaps the most knowledgeable of the group. His deep interest and ability in these fields reflect his father's concern and extensive facilitation. Although not as verbally able as some of the other students in the sample, his industry and increasing mathematical sophistication make it probable that he will move ahead quickly and successfully. The range of areas in which he could be eventually successful, however, are somewhat limited by his early specialization.

### Case 4

Overall the level of effectiveness of this profile is higher than that of other eighth graders. The distinctive features are low scores on well-being and self-control, which indicate self-defensiveness, unhappiness, and impulsivity in action. High scores on dominance, self-acceptance, psychological-mindedness, flexibility, and empathy indicate a talkative, informal, and perceptive disposi-

# PROFILE SHEET FOR THE California Psychological Inventory: MALE

Name _____ Case 3

Other Information _____

Age _____ 12 _____ Date Tested _____

Notes:

Standard Scores

MALE NORMS

Do Cs Sy Sp Sa Wb Re So Sc To Gi Cm Ac Ai Ie Py Fx Fe

Standard Scores

196

Name _____ Case 4 _____ Age _____ 13 _____ Date Tested _____

Other Information _____

Standard Scores

MALE NORMS

| Do | Cs | Sy | Sp | Sa | Wb | Re | So | Sc | To | Gi | Cm | Ac | Ai | Ie | Py | Fx | Fe |

Male Norms

Standard Scores

197

# PROFILE SHEET FOR THE *California Psychological Inventory*: MALE

Name _____ Case 5

Age ___ 13 ___ Date Tested _____

Other Information _____

**Notes:**

Standard Scores

MALE NORMS

Male Norms

tion. The social skills this person possesses probably allow him adequate interpersonal effectiveness, but his impulsivity may be the cause of some friction or unhappiness. School acceleration should be considered very carefully.

\* \* \*

Although this student has high scores even within this group on most measures, there are several disconcerting discrepancies, especially on spatial and reasoning tests. He comes from a nonprofessional, middle-class background, and this is perhaps reflected in his attitudes toward advanced work; he is not nearly as eager as most of the other students of his ability level to participate. These factors would seem to attenuate significantly the possibilities of rapid advancement and weaken an otherwise strong prediction of eventual success.

### Case 5

A high degree of academic and intellectual advancement characterizes this profile when it is compared with either eighth-grade or adult norms. The overall profile is generally effective and high scores on achievement via independence, flexibility, and dominance create a picture of a person who is confident, independent, spontaneous, and quite possibly creative. The low score on communality indicates some degree of disorderliness or, perhaps, daring. His interpersonal skills are average for an eighth grader, but may be enhanced by his high degree of flexibility and confidence.

\* \* \*

This student scores consistently near the top of the group on mathematics and reasoning tests and does quite well on verbal tests as well. He has taken several college courses while in junior high and high school and done well but seems not to have as effective an approach or as positive an attitude to challenging work as some of the other students. Although he appears to be capable of extremely rapid academic acceleration, the amount of acceleration should be tempered by these other considerations—especially his somewhat immature approach to college courses.

### Case 6

This person appears more socially mature and more academically advanced than other eighth graders, although his interpersonal effectiveness is typical of the eighth-grade norm. The very high score on femininity suggests a confused sex-role identification and a degree of nervousness. The high scores on socialization and self-control indicate conventional and controlled behavior. This

PROFILE SHEET FOR THE *California Psychological Inventory*: MALE

Name _____ Case 6 _____ Age _____ 13 _____ Date Tested _____

Other Information _____

Notes:

# PROFILE SHEET FOR THE *California Psychological Inventory:* MALE

Name __Case 7__  Age __12__  Date Tested _____

Other Information _____

Notes:

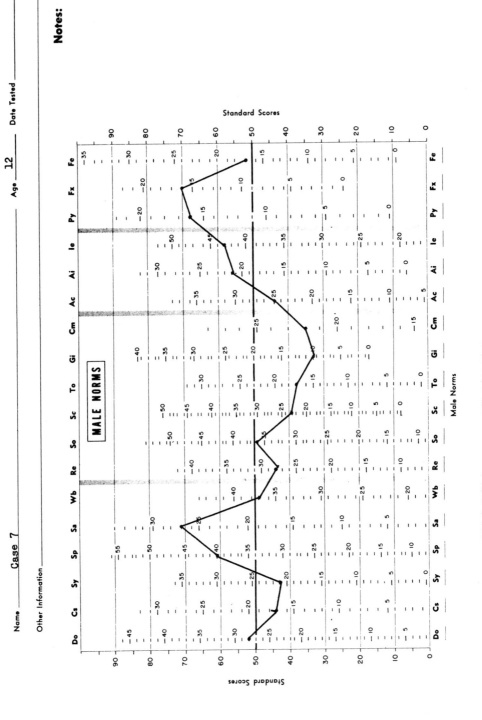

201

person may be described as "high-strung." Since his interpersonal skills are not as advanced as his academic interests and abilities, the relatively low score on well-being appears to indicate some degree of unhappiness. This person may have trouble adjusting to an accelerated school program.

\* \* \*

This student's main strength is in mathematical aptitude, in which he ranks at about the middle of this select group. His other scores are good but not especially impressive in comparison with the rest of the sample. The home background of this boy tends toward the lower range of middle-class. He has not shown a great deal of interest in academic pursuits and opportunities. These indications, when taken together, suggest little possibility of exceptional achievement, although he may eventually have a relatively successful college career.

## Case 7

This profile depicts a person more mature and more socially and academically advanced than most other eighth graders. The high scores on social presence and self-acceptance indicate poised, sharp-witted, and enthusiastic interpersonal effectiveness. High scores on the academic and intellectual scales and high scores on psychological-mindedness and flexibility indicate intelligent, spontaneous, informal, and quite possibly, creative behavior. None of the scores falls below the eighth-grade norm profile. In all likelihood, this person can be expected to interact very effectively across a variety of situations.

\* \* \*

This student stands out from the group in several important respects. His abilities are probably the most far-ranging in the group, and he is more socially skilled and mature than most individuals several years older. His diverse interests and abilities and his eagerness and industry mark him as "most likely to succeed" in many possible endeavors.

# APPENDIX D

## Appendix to Chapter 8

## General Tables

Table D.1: *Number and percent of students by highest code on the VPI by grade and sex*[a]

| | Total | I | | A | | S | | E | | R | | C | |
|---|---|---|---|---|---|---|---|---|---|---|---|---|---|
| | No. | No. | % | No. | % | No. | % | No. | % | No. | % | No. | % |
| 7th grade girls | 83.0 | 25.3 | 30.5 | 33.5 | 40.4 | 18.5 | 22.3 | 2.3 | 2.8 | 0.0 | 0.0 | 3.3 | 4.0 |
| 7th grade boys | 103.0 | 61.2 | 59.5 | 10.9 | 10.6 | 4.1 | 4.0 | 9.5 | 9.2 | 13.2 | 12.8 | 4.1 | 4.0 |
| All 7th grade | 186.0 | 86.6 | 46.5 | 44.4 | 23.9 | 22.6 | 12.1 | 11.8 | 6.4 | 13.2 | 7.1 | 7.4 | 4.0 |
| 8th & 9th grade girls | 100.0 | 37.8 | 37.8 | 26.8 | 26.8 | 22.8 | 22.8 | 6.5 | 6.5 | 0.5 | 0.5 | 5.5 | 5.5 |
| 8th & 9th grade boys | 160.0 | 92.7 | 57.9 | 17.0 | 10.6 | 4.9 | 3.1 | 16.5 | 10.3 | 14.5 | 9.1 | 14.4 | 9.0 |
| All 8th & 9th grade | 260.0 | 130.5 | 50.2 | 43.8 | 16.8 | 27.8 | 10.7 | 23.0 | 8.8 | 15.0 | 5.8 | 19.9 | 7.6 |
| All girls | 183.0 | 63.2 | 34.5 | 60.3 | 33.0 | 41.3 | 22.6 | 8.8 | 4.8 | 0.5 | 0.3 | 8.8 | 4.8 |
| All boys | 263.0 | 153.9 | 58.5 | 27.9 | 10.6 | 9.0 | 3.4 | 26.0 | 9.9 | 27.7 | 10.5 | 18.5 | 7.0 |
| All students | 446.0 | 217.1 | 48.7 | 88.2 | 19.8 | 50.3 | 11.3 | 34.8 | 7.8 | 28.2 | 6.3 | 27.3 | 6.1 |

[a]Fractional numbers in code columns occur because of fractional tying method described in the text.

Table D.2:  Number and percent of students for whom the code of their first-choice occupation matched[a] their VPI code

| | Total No. | Total Matched No. | Total Matched % | I No. | I % | S No. | S % | A No. | A % | E No. | E % | R No. | R % | C No. | C % |
|---|---|---|---|---|---|---|---|---|---|---|---|---|---|---|---|
| 7th grade girls | 74.0 | 34.0 | 45.9 | 15.0 | 44.1 | 10.0 | 29.4 | 9.0 | 26.5 | 0.0 | 0.0 | 0.0 | 0.0 | 0.0 | 0.0 |
| 7th grade boys | 94.0 | 55.0 | 58.5 | 47.7 | 86.7 | 1.3 | 2.3 | 1.0 | 1.8 | 2.0 | 3.6 | 3.0 | 5.4 | 0.0 | 0.0 |
| All 7th grade | 168.0 | 89.0 | 52.9 | 62.7 | 70.4 | 11.3 | 12.7 | 10.0 | 11.2 | 2.0 | 2.2 | 3.0 | 3.4 | 0.0 | 0.0 |
| 8th & 9th grade girls | 88.0 | 53.0 | 60.0 | 29.3 | 55.4 | 15.5 | 29.2 | 5.5 | 10.4 | 0.0 | 0.0 | 0.7 | 1.2 | 2.0 | 3.8 |
| 8th & 9th grade boys | 149.0 | 96.5 | 64.8 | 85.3 | 88.4 | 0.0 | 0.0 | 4.2 | 4.4 | 5.0 | 5.2 | 1.0 | 1.0 | 1.0 | 1.0 |
| All 8th & 9th grade | 237.0 | 149.5 | 63.1 | 114.6 | 76.7 | 15.5 | 10.4 | 9.8 | 6.6 | 5.0 | 3.3 | 1.7 | 1.1 | 3.0 | 2.0 |
| All girls | 162.0 | 87.0 | 53.7 | 44.3 | 51.0 | 25.5 | 29.3 | 14.5 | 16.7 | 0.0 | 0.0 | 0.7 | 0.8 | 2.0 | 2.3 |
| All boys | 243.0 | 151.5 | 62.3 | 133.0 | 87.7 | 1.3 | 0.9 | 5.2 | 3.6 | 7.0 | 4.6 | 4.0 | 2.6 | 1.0 | 0.6 |
| All students | 405.0 | 238.5 | 53.7 | 177.3 | 74.3 | 26.8 | 11.2 | 19.8 | 8.3 | 7.0 | 2.9 | 4.7 | 1.9 | 3.0 | 1.2 |

[a]Fractional totals in matched column are due to persons with tied Holland Codes, only one of which matched the code of their first-choice occupation; e.g., a person tied on I and A with a first-choice occupation coded I would receive 0.5 tally point for matching.

206

Table D.3:   *Number and percent of students by category of father's occupation, by grade, and sex*

| | Total No. | E No. | E % | I No. | I % | R No. | R % | S No. | S % | C No. | C % | A No. | A % |
|---|---|---|---|---|---|---|---|---|---|---|---|---|---|
| 7th Grade Girls | 78 | 30 | 38 | 16 | 20 | 20 | 26 | 4 | 5 | 6 | 8 | 2 | 3 |
| 7th Grade Boys | 97 | 31 | 32 | 29 | 30 | 26 | 27 | 6 | 6 | 3 | 3 | 2 | 2 |
| All 7th Grade | 175 | 61 | 35 | 45 | 26 | 46 | 26 | 10 | 6 | 9 | 5 | 4 | 2 |
| 8th & 9th Grade Girls | 89 | 28 | 31 | 33 | 37 | 21 | 24 | 3 | 3 | 3 | 3 | 1 | 1 |
| 8th & 9th Grade Boys | 149 | 51 | 34 | 36 | 24 | 35 | 23 | 13 | 9 | 9 | 6 | 5 | 3 |
| All 8th & 9th Grade | 238 | 79 | 33 | 69 | 29 | 56 | 23 | 16 | 7 | 12 | 5 | 6 | 2 |
| All Girls | 167 | 58 | 35 | 49 | 29 | 41 | 24 | 7 | 4 | 9 | 5 | 3 | 2 |
| All Boys | 246 | 82 | 33 | 65 | 26 | 61 | 25 | 19 | 8 | 12 | 5 | 7 | 3 |
| All Students | 413 | 140 | 34 | 114 | 28 | 102 | 25 | 26 | 6 | 21 | 5 | 10 | 2 |

Table D.4:   *Number and percent of students by category of mother's occupation, by grade, and sex*

| | Total No. | S No. | S % | C No. | C % | E No. | E % | I No. | I % | R No. | R % | A No. | A % |
|---|---|---|---|---|---|---|---|---|---|---|---|---|---|
| 7th Grade Girls | 79 | 57 | 72 | 12 | 15 | 5 | 6 | 2 | 2 | 2 | 2 | 1 | 1 |
| 7th Grade Boys | 98 | 71 | 73 | 11 | 11 | 5 | 5 | 6 | 6 | 3 | 3 | 2 | 2 |
| All 7th Grade | 177 | 128 | 72 | 23 | 13 | 10 | 6 | 8 | 5 | 5 | 3 | 3 | 1 |
| 8th & 9th Grade Girls | 89 | 67 | 75 | 12 | 13 | 5 | 7 | 3 | 3 | 2 | 2 | 0 | 0 |
| 8th & 9th Grade Boys | 152 | 115 | 76 | 18 | 12 | 6 | 4 | 8 | 5 | 3 | 2 | 2 | 1 |
| All 8th & 9th Grade | 241 | 182 | 76 | 30 | 12 | 11 | 5 | 11 | 5 | 5 | 3 | 2 | 1 |
| All Girls | 168 | 124 | 74 | 24 | 14 | 10 | 6 | 5 | 3 | 4 | 2 | 1 | 1 |
| All Boys | 250 | 186 | 75 | 29 | 12 | 11 | 4 | 14 | 6 | 6 | 2 | 4 | 1 |
| All Students | 418 | 311 | 74 | 53 | 13 | 21 | 5 | 19 | 4 | 12 | 3 | 5 | 1 |

Table D.5: Number and percent of students whose VPI code matched their father's occupational code, by code, grade and sex[a]

| | Total | Total Matched | | I | | E | | R | | C | | A | | S | |
|---|---|---|---|---|---|---|---|---|---|---|---|---|---|---|---|
| | No. | No. | % | No. | % | No. | % | No. | % | No. | % | No. | % | No. | % |
| 7th Grade Girls | 79.0 | 7.3 | 10.8 | 6.0 | 82.2 | 1.3 | 17.8 | 0.0 | 0.0 | 0.0 | 0.0 | 0.0 | 0.0 | 0.0 | 0.0 |
| 7th Grade Boys | 100.0 | 27.5 | 27.5 | 19.0 | 70.0 | 2.0 | 8.0 | 6.5 | 23.0 | 0.0 | 0.0 | 0.0 | 0.0 | 0.0 | 0.0 |
| All 7th Grade | 179.0 | 34.8 | 19.4 | 25.0 | 71.8 | 3.3 | 9.5 | 6.5 | 18.7 | 0.0 | 0.0 | 0.0 | 0.0 | 0.0 | 0.0 |
| 8th & 9th Grade Girls | 97.0 | 31.5 | 32.5 | 22.8 | 72.5 | 4.2 | 13.2 | 1.0 | 3.2 | 2.5 | 7.9 | 0.0 | 0.0 | 1.0 | 3.2 |
| 8th & 9th Grade Boys | 164.0 | 53.1 | 32.4 | 26.3 | 49.5 | 14.2 | 26.7 | 7.2 | 13.6 | 3.0 | 5.7 | 2.3 | 4.4 | 0.0 | 0.0 |
| All 8th & 9th Grade | 261.0 | 84.6 | 32.4 | 49.1 | 58.0 | 18.4 | 21.3 | 8.2 | 9.7 | 5.5 | 6.5 | 2.3 | 2.7 | 1.0 | 1.2 |
| All Girls | 176.0 | 38.8 | 23.4 | 28.8 | 74.2 | 5.5 | 14.2 | 1.0 | 2.6 | 2.5 | 6.4 | 0.0 | 0.0 | 1.0 | 2.6 |
| All Boys | 264.0 | 80.6 | 31.2 | 54.3 | 56.2 | 16.2 | 16.2 | 13.7 | 17.0 | 3.0 | 3.8 | 2.3 | 2.8 | 0.0 | 0.0 |
| All Students | 440.0 | 119.4 | 28.0 | 74.1 | 62.1 | 21.7 | 18.1 | 14.7 | 12.3 | 5.5 | 4.6 | 2.3 | 2.0 | 1.0 | 0.8 |

[a]Fractional totals are due to persons with tied Holland codes, only one of which matched their parents code; see table D.2.

Table D.6: *Number and percent of students whose VPI code matched their mother's occupational code, by code, grade, and sex*

| | Total No. | Total Matched No. | Total Matched % | S No. | S % | I No. | I % | C No. | C % | E No. | E % | R No. | R % | A No. | A % |
|---|---|---|---|---|---|---|---|---|---|---|---|---|---|---|---|
| 7th Grade Girls | 83.0 | 17.0 | 20.5 | 14.5 | 85.3 | 1.0 | 5.7 | 1.5 | 8.8 | 0.0 | 0.0 | 0.0 | 0.0 | 0.0 | 0.0 |
| 7th Grade Boys | 101.0 | 16.1 | 15.9 | 4.3 | 26.9 | 6.2 | 38.9 | 2.0 | 12.4 | 3.5 | 21.8 | 0.0 | 0.0 | 0.0 | 0.0 |
| All 7th Grade | 184.0 | 33.1 | 18.2 | 18.8 | 56.9 | 7.2 | 21.9 | 3.5 | 10.6 | 3.5 | 10.6 | 0.0 | 0.0 | 0.0 | 0.0 |
| 8th & 9th Grade Girls | 96.0 | 26.0 | 27.1 | 21.0 | 80.8 | 3.0 | 11.5 | 2.0 | 7.7 | 0.0 | 0.0 | 0.0 | 0.0 | 0.0 | 0.0 |
| 8th & 9th Grade Boys | 161.0 | 13.1 | 8.3 | 5.3 | 40.8 | 4.8 | 36.3 | 0.0 | 0.0 | 1.0 | 7.6 | 1.5 | 11.4 | 0.5 | 3.8 |
| All 8th & 9th Grade | 257.0 | 39.1 | 17.4 | 26.3 | 67.4 | 7.8 | 19.8 | 2.0 | 5.1 | 1.0 | 2.6 | 1.5 | 3.8 | 0.5 | 1.3 |
| All Girls | 179.0 | 43.0 | 24.0 | 35.5 | 82.6 | 4.0 | 9.3 | 3.5 | 8.1 | 0.0 | 0.0 | 0.0 | 0.0 | 0.0 | 0.0 |
| All Boys | 262.0 | 29.2 | 11.4 | 9.7 | 33.1 | 11.0 | 37.7 | 2.0 | 6.9 | 4.5 | 15.4 | 1.5 | 5.1 | 0.5 | 1.7 |
| All Students | 441.0 | 72.0 | 16.4 | 45.2 | 62.6 | 15.0 | 20.8 | 5.5 | 7.6 | 4.5 | 6.2 | 1.5 | 2.1 | 0.5 | 0.7 |

Table D.7: Percent and mean SAT-M scores for all mathematics contestants by VPI code, grade, and sex

| | Total Number | I % | I Mean SAT | R % | R Mean SAT | A % | A Mean SAT | E % | E Mean SAT | C % | C Mean SAT | A % | A Mean SAT |
|---|---|---|---|---|---|---|---|---|---|---|---|---|---|
| 7th Grade Girls | 76.0 | 28.3 | 440.54 | 0.0 | 0.00 | 40.8 | 423.35 | 3.1 | 389.13 | 4.4 | 371.37 | 23.7 | 411.94 |
| 7th Grade Boys | 90.0 | 56.0 | 470.29 | 14.4 | 447.46 | 12.2 | 468.50 | 10.0 | 410.89 | 4.5 | 427.94 | 2.9 | 406.33 |
| All 7th Grade | 166.0 | 43.2 | 455.42 | 7.8 | 447.46 | 25.3 | 445.92 | 6.8 | 400.01 | 4.5 | 399.66 | 12.4 | 409.14 |
| 8th & 9th Grade Girls | 95.0 | 37.2 | 470.80 | 0.0 | 0.00 | 27.2 | 446.78 | 6.8 | 442.72 | 5.8 | 472.73 | 23.0 | 447.40 |
| 8th & 9th Grade Boys | 132.0 | 57.1 | 534.59 | 8.3 | 573.25 | 10.2 | 519.29 | 11.5 | 459.94 | 9.2 | 512.99 | 3.7 | 483.50 |
| All 8th & 9th Grade | 227.0 | 48.8 | 502.70 | 4.8 | 573.24 | 17.3 | 483.04 | 9.5 | 451.34 | 7.7 | 492.86 | 11.8 | 465.45 |
| All Girls | 171.0 | 33.1 | 455.88 | 0.0 | 0.00 | 33.2 | 435.06 | 5.2 | 415.92 | 5.2 | 422.05 | 23.3 | 429.67 |
| All Boys | 222.0 | 56.6 | 502.44 | 10.8 | 510.36 | 11.0 | 493.89 | 10.9 | 435.42 | 7.3 | 470.46 | 3.4 | 444.92 |
| All Students | 393.0 | 46.4 | 479.16 | 6.1 | 510.36 | 20.7 | 464.48 | 8.4 | 425.67 | 6.4 | 446.26 | 12.1 | 437.30 |

Table D.8: Percent and mean STEP science scores (Forms 1A and 1B combined) for all science contestants by VPI code, grade, and sex

| | Total Number | I | | E | | A | | S | | R | | C | |
|---|---|---|---|---|---|---|---|---|---|---|---|---|---|
| | | % | Mean STEP | % | Mean STEP | % | Mean STEP | % | Mean STEP | % | Mean STEP | % | Mean STEP |
| 7th Grade Girls | 24.0 | 52.1 | 72.40 | 0.0 | 0.00 | 39.6 | 69.50 | 6.2 | 65.00 | 0.0 | 0.00 | 2.1 | 45.00 |
| 7th Grade Boys | 36.0 | 80.1 | 77.93 | 2.8 | 71.00 | 9.2 | 73.07 | 4.2 | 64.33 | 3.7 | 80.71 | 0.0 | 0.00 |
| All 7th Grade | 60.0 | 68.8 | 75.16 | 1.7 | 71.00 | 21.3 | 71.51 | 5.0 | 64.66 | 2.2 | 80.71 | 0.8 | 45.00 |
| 8th & 9th Grade Girls | 37.0 | 37.4 | 75.46 | 4.8 | 78.31 | 31.6 | 63.17 | 22.2 | 72.43 | 1.3 | 55.00 | 2.7 | 45.00 |
| 8th & 9th Grade Boys | 91.0 | 66.7 | 89.74 | 8.4 | 66.63 | 10.2 | 84.65 | 1.4 | 69.20 | 7.2 | 71.04 | 6.1 | 77.46 |
| All 8th & 9th Grade | 128.0 | 58.2 | 82.60 | 7.4 | 72.47 | 16.4 | 73.91 | 7.4 | 70.82 | 5.5 | 63.02 | 5.1 | 61.23 |
| All Girls | 61.0 | 43.2 | 73.93 | 2.9 | 78.31 | 34.7 | 66.56 | 16.0 | 68.72 | 0.8 | 55.00 | 2.4 | 45.00 |
| All Boys | 127.0 | 70.5 | 83.84 | 6.8 | 68.82 | 9.8 | 78.86 | 2.1 | 66.76 | 6.2 | 75.88 | 4.4 | 77.46 |
| All Students | 188.0 | 61.6 | 78.88 | 5.6 | 73.56 | 17.9 | 72.71 | 6.6 | 67.74 | 4.5 | 65.44 | 3.8 | 61.23 |

# APPENDIX E

## Supplementary References for SMSPY

Denham, S. A. 1973. Personality characteristics of the mathematically precocious. Paper presented at annual meeting of American Psychological Association, Montreal, Canada.

Fox, L. H. 1973. Values and career interests of mathematically precocious youth. Paper presented at annual meeting of American Psychological Association, Montreal, Canada.

———. In progress. Facilitating the development of mathematical talent in young women. Doctoral dissertation in psychology.

———, and Stanley, J. C. 1973. Educational facilitation for mathematically and scientifically precocious youth. Paper presented at annual meeting of the American Educational Research Association, New Orleans.

Gleser, L. J. 1972. On bounds for the average correlation between subtest scores in ipsatively scored tests. *Educational and Psychological Measurement* 32(3): 759–66.

Jenkins, E. 1973. Express route to learning fashioned for precocious. *New York Times*, February 28, pp. 35, 66.

Keating, D. P. 1973. Creative potential of mathematically precocious youth. Paper presented at annual meeting of the American Psychological Association, Montreal, Canada.

———. 1973. Discovering quantitative precocity. Unpublished paper.

———. 1973. Precocious cognitive development at the level of formal operations. Ph.D. dissertation, Department of Psychology, The Johns Hopkins University, Baltimore, Maryland.

———. In press. Possible sampling bias in *Genetic Studies of Genius. Educational and Psychological Measurement*, vol. 35, no. 3.

———. 1972. Extreme measures for the exceptionally gifted in mathematics and science. *Educational Researcher* 1(9): 3–7.

———, and Stanley, J. C. 1972. From eighth grade to selective college in one jump: Two case studies in radical acceleration. Paper presented at the annual meeting of the American Educational Research Association, Chicago.

———. 1973. Discovering quantitative precocity. Paper presented at annual meeting of the American Educational Research Association, New Orleans.

Stanley, J. C. 1973. Using tests to discover talent. Division 5 Presidential Address at annual meeting of the American Psychological Association, Montreal, Canada.

———. 1973. Accelerating the educational progress of intellectually gifted youths. *Educational Psychologist* 10(3): 133–46.

———; Keating, D. P.; and Fox, L. H. 1972. *Annual report to the Spencer Foundation on its five-year grant to The Johns Hopkins University covering the first year of the grant, 1 September 1971 through 31 August 1972,* "Study of mathematically and scientifically precocious youth (SMSPY)." Baltimore, Maryland 21218: The authors, Department of Psychology.

————; Denham, S. A.; and Kanter, L. R. 1973. *Annual report to the Spencer Foundation on its five-year grant to The Johns Hopkins University covering the second year of the grant, 1 September 1972 through 31 August 1973,* "Study of mathematically and scientifically precocious youth (SMSPY)." Baltimore, Maryland 21218: The authors, Department of Psychology.

Trombley, W. 1973. University project seeks out and assists gifted youngsters. *Los Angeles Times,* June 4, pp. 3, 20.

Winer, J. A. 1973. Profiles of bright young students on an ipsatively scored values inventory compared with randomly generated profiles. Unpublished paper.

# index of names

(Pages in italics denote articles in this volume.)

THE JOHNS HOPKINS UNIVERSITY PRESS

This book was composed in Times Roman text and display by Jones Composition Company, Inc. from a design by Victoria Dudley. It was printed on 60-lb. Warren's 1854, regular, by Universal Lithographers, Inc. The cloth edition was bound in Columbia Llamique.

**Library of Congress Cataloging in Publication Data**

Hyman Blumberg Symposium on Research in Early Child-
    hood Education, 3d, Johns Hopkins University, 1973.
    Mathematical talent.

    "Expanded version of a symposium of the American
Association for the Advancement of Science entitled
'Discovering and nurturing precocious talent in
mathematics and physical science.' "
    Includes bibliographies.
    1. Mathematics—Study and teaching (Secondary)
—Congresses. 2. Gifted children—Education—
Mathematics—Congresses. 3. Science—Study and
teaching (Secondary)—Congresses. 4. Gifted
children—Education—Science—Congresses. I. Stanley,
Julian C., ed. II. Keating, Daniel P., 1949–
ed. III. Fox, Lynn H., 1944–     ed.
IV. American Association for the Advancement of
Science. Discovering and nurturing precocious talent
in mathematics and physical science. V. Title.
QA11.A1H95        1973        371.9'5        73-19342
ISBN 0-8018-1585-1
ISBN 0-8010-1592-4 (pbk.)

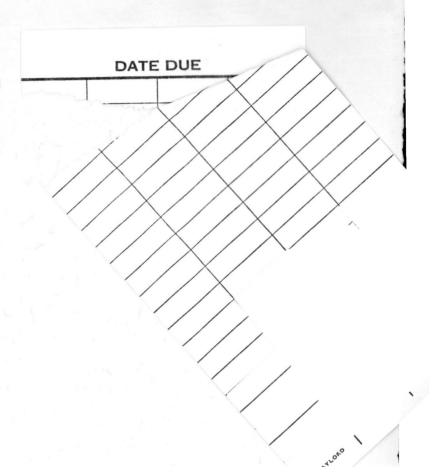

**DATE DUE**

GAYLORD